Born Round

ALSO BY FRANK BRUNI

Ambling into History:
The Unlikely Odyssey of George W. Bush

A Gospel of Shame:
Children, Sexual Abuse, and the Catholic Church
WITH *ELINOR BURKETT*

Born Round

The Secret History

of a

Full-Time Eater

FRANK BRUNI

THE PENGUIN PRESS

NEW YORK

2009

THE PENGUIN PRESS
Published by the Penguin Group
Penguin Group (USA) Inc., 375 Hudson Street, New York, New York 10014, U.S.A. •
Penguin Group (Canada), 90 Eglinton Avenue East, Suite 700, Toronto, Ontario, Canada M4P 2Y3
(a division of Pearson Penguin Canada Inc.) • Penguin Books Ltd, 80 Strand, London WC2R 0RL, England •
Penguin Ireland, 25 St Stephen's Green, Dublin 2, Ireland (a division of Penguin Books Ltd) •
Penguin Books Australia Ltd, 250 Camberwell Road, Camberwell, Victoria 3124, Australia (a division
of Pearson Australia Group Pty Ltd) • Penguin Books India Pvt Ltd, 11 Community Centre,
Panchsheel Park, New Delhi – 110 017, India • Penguin Group (NZ), 67 Apollo Drive,
Rosedale, North Shore 0632, New Zealand (a division of Pearson New Zealand Ltd) •
Penguin Books (South Africa) (Pty) Ltd, 24 Sturdee Avenue,
Rosebank, Johannesburg 2196, South Africa

Penguin Books Ltd, Registered Offices:
80 Strand, London WC2R 0RL, England

First published in 2009 by The Penguin Press,
a member of Penguin Group (USA) Inc.

1 3 5 7 9 10 8 6 4 2

Copyright © Frank Bruni, 2009
All rights reserved

Grateful acknowledgment is made for permission to reprint excerpts from the following articles by Frank
Bruni published in the *The New York Times:* "Life in the Fast-Food Lane," issue of May 24, 2006; "Giving Luxury the Thrill
of Danger," February 7, 2007; "Where Only the Salad Is Properly Dressed," February 28, 2007; and "A Plea for Respect for a
Familiar Fish," August 1, 2007. Used by permission of *The New York Times.*

Photograph credits: Page 228: The White House; 287: Davina Zagury; 313 and 331: Soo-Jeong Kang;
346: Katharine Q. Seelye; Other photographs courtesy of the author

Library of Congress Cataloging-in-Publication Data

Bruni, Frank.
Born round : the secret history of a full-time eater / Frank Bruni.
p.   cm.
ISBN 978-1-59420-231-5
1. Bruni, Frank.   2. Bruni, Frank—Childhood and youth.   3. Overweight men—United States—Biography.
4. Compulsive eating—United States—Case Studies.   5. Reducing diets—United States—Case studies.
6. Food writers—United States—Biography.   7. New York Times Company—Biography.
8. Italian Americans—Biography.   I. Title.
RC552.C65B78 2009
362.196'85260092—dc22
[B]
2009009532

Printed in the United States of America

Designed by Claire Naylon Vaccaro

To my brothers
Mark and Harry
and my sister, Adelle.
You three are the luckiest hand I ever drew.

And to my nieces
Christina and Annabella,
because you missed out the last time around.

· CONTENTS ·

Author's Note

The names and certain identifying details of a few people in this book have been changed out of respect for their privacy. And while none of the people, events or conversations in this book were invented, some conversational details lay beyond the reach of memory, so dialogue has been reconstructed through interviews and other reporting, and fashioned in line with what I know and remember of how the people, including me, spoke. I can't vouch for its pinpoint accuracy in all cases, but I can vouch for its truth.

Born Round

Introduction

got the phone call in early January 2004, as I looked out over the
uncertain expanse of a new year.

I was in my office in Rome, and I was probably drinking an
espresso. I was almost always drinking an espresso. The newspaper's
Rome bureau, like any self-respecting Italian workplace, had a proper
espresso machine, and my assistant, Paola, like any self-respecting Italian, knew how to make a proper espresso. So whenever she said, "*Ti serve
un espresso?*" I said, "*Sì! Sì!*" even if she'd last served me one just forty-five
minutes earlier. An espresso allowed me to consume *something* without
consuming anything of caloric consequence, to finagle a pleasure along
the lines of eating without actually eating. And the acids and caffeine in
it revved up my metabolism. I had read that somewhere. Or maybe I had
simply made it up and then, as with so many of the greater and lesser
food lies I'd told myself, made the executive decision to believe it.

On the other end of the line was an editor in charge of a depart-
ment of the newspaper different from mine. I worked for the Foreign
News desk, keeping one eye on a sinking Venice, the other on a flagging
Pope. She supervised several "soft" sections: the Style pages, the Home

pages and—the reason for her call—the Dining pages. I assessed prime ministers; she, prime beef.

But she had a thought about that. She had an idea.

"Restaurant critic," she said.

I wasn't sure I'd heard her right.

"Restaurant critic," she repeated, in the middle of a sentence explaining that the job was open, that there were people at the newspaper who thought I might be right for it, and that she happened to be one of them.

She wanted my reaction. She wanted to know: How did I feel about eating for a living?

Eating for a living?

Without meaning to, I laughed.

She didn't appreciate the robust absurdity of what she was asking, the big, fat irony of whom she was asking.

Because she had stayed put in New York while I'd moved frequently and traveled widely for the newspaper, she hadn't laid eyes on me for the better part of a decade. She wasn't clued in to what had happened to me during that time: the way I'd given in to my crazy hungers and crazier habits; how large I'd grown; how long I'd been trapped at that size, in that sadness; how determinedly I'd slogged my way back to a leaner, better place.

The Rome assignment had presented itself toward the end of that slog, in mid-2002, when I was living in Washington, D.C., and part of what it promised and then delivered was a clean break, a new beginning. In Rome I made friends who hadn't known me at either my fattest or my fittest, hadn't watched me ricochet between the two, back and forth, up and down, never at rest, never at peace. They saw me afresh: a fairly average guy in his late thirties, maybe fifteen to eighteen pounds over the strict medical ideal for someone just under five feet, eleven inches tall, certainly chunkier than the Italian norm, but broad-shouldered and attractive nonetheless. Nothing unusual. Nothing humiliating.

In Rome I ate relatively ordinary meals and I ran or went to the gym at least three times a week and I wore jeans again—I finally wore jeans again, not worrying about how much more snugly than chinos they fit. I had a serious romantic relationship, my first in more than seven almost entirely celibate years. At the beach I took my T-shirt off. Not right when I got there, and not all the time. But some of the time: if there weren't too many narrower people around; if I was standing up or stretched out; if I'd done a decent run or workout that morning or the night before; if I was feeling light and good.

Was this how I'd be from now on? Was I finally safe?

I couldn't know.

But some sort of confidence—maybe even courage—had apparently taken hold.

I didn't cut the editor's call short. With welling interest I listened as she made a case that I was a quick enough learner, a self-assured enough thinker and a nimble enough writer to set off in an unanticipated direction and try my hand at something wildly different.

And then I told her I'd consider it.

It wasn't likely to go anywhere, anyway. In my nine years at the newspaper, I'd written about politics, religion, crime, immigration, movies, books and the Miss America pageant. I'd never written about food, not unless you counted stray paragraphs about George W. Bush's fondness for peanut butter and Cheez Doodles, not unless you factored in a feature story about Las Vegas residents larding themselves at all-you-can-eat buffets. (That was one from the heart.)

I knew more about papal encyclicals than about Peking duck, and had little more reason to believe I'd get this restaurant-critic job than to believe I'd be anointed the next Pope. But why not revel in the compliment of being thought capable of such a stretch? Why not let the idea bounce around my head, imagine the miter on *my* head? It was a harmless fantasy.

And then it wasn't.

Just weeks after that first call from the editor in New York came another: the job was mine if I wanted it.

Did I?

Saying yes would mean leaving Rome about midway through what was typically a four-year stint, and that gave me pause. While I had made my way to Sicily for stories on three occasions and had managed four trips to Florence, I was still trying to find a justification for Capri and Positano, and in time I was sure I would. And my Italian had finally progressed from deducible to out-and-out discernible. Serviceable was right around the bend.

Saying yes would also mean putting myself in the path of sometimes withering scrutiny in New York, where the newspaper's restaurant critic had a significant effect on the fortunes of chefs and restaurateurs, who sporadically (and understandably) fought back. I didn't long for that.

But there was, of course, an even more compelling reason not to say yes, and it came up during one more call, this one from an editor higher up the newspaper's chain of command, an editor who *had* seen me over the past decade.

She wanted some reassurance, but not about my confidence in tackling this new subject matter or my comfort in switching from correspondent to critic. And not about whether I had made peace with leaving Italy, when living there had been a lifelong dream.

Speaking as a friend more than a boss, she pressed me on a different issue altogether: whether an agenda of eight to ten major meals a week in serious restaurants—a mandatory program of night after night of ambitious and sometimes excellent food—was a risk I really wanted to take. Something I could really handle.

"Are you sure," she asked me, "that you're willing to sacrifice the good shape you've gotten into?"

I was sure I wasn't. And for reasons I was still working out in my head, I'd come to believe I wouldn't have to. I told her that, and we agreed that I would set off on this strange adventure, in spite of a past in which appetite and circumstance had combined to such neurotic and sometimes pitiable effect.

Maybe, I thought, *this decision is insane.* But it was also irresistible, even poetic, the kind of ultimate dare or dead reckoning that a good narrative called for.

My life-defining relationship, after all, wasn't with a parent, a sibling, a teacher, a mate. It was with my stomach. And among all the doubts, insecurities and second-guessing that had so often shadowed me, there was one certainty, one constant. I could eat.

Me in early 2001 (left) and more than four years later, after becoming a restaurant critic, with my sister, Adelle.

· ONE ·

I'm Eating as Fast as I Can

One

have neither a therapist's diagnosis nor any scientific literature to
support the following claim, and I can't back it up with more than a
cursory level of detail. So you're just going to have to go with me on
this: I was a baby bulimic.

Maybe not baby—toddler bulimic is more like it, though I
didn't so much toddle as wobble, given the roundness of my expanding
form. I had been a plump infant and was on my way to becoming an
even plumper child, a ravenous machine determined to devour anything
in its sights. My parents would later tell me, my friends and anyone else
willing to listen that they'd never seen a kid eat the way I ate or react the
way I reacted whenever I was denied more food. What I did in those circumstances was throw up.

I have no independent memory of this. But according to my mother,
it began when I was about eighteen months old. It went on for no more
than a year. And I'd congratulate myself here for stopping such an
evidently compulsive behavior without the benefit of an intervention or
the ability to read a self-help book except that I wasn't so much stopping
as pausing. But I'm getting ahead of the story.

A hamburger dinner sounded the first alarm. My mother had cooked and served me one big burger, which would be enough for most carnivores still in diapers. I polished it off and pleaded for a second. So she cooked and served me another big burger, confident that I'd never get through it. It was the last time she underestimated my appetite.

The way Mom told the tale, I plowed through that second burger as quickly as I had the first. Then I looked up from my high chair with lips covered in hamburger juice, a chin flecked with hamburger bun and hamburger ecstasy in my wide brown eyes. I started banging my balled little fists on the high chair's tray.

I wanted a third.

Mom thought about giving it to me. She was tempted. For her it was a point of pride to cook and serve more food than anybody could eat, and the normal course of things was to shove food at people, not to withhold it.

But she looked at me then, with my balloon cheeks and ham-hock legs, and thought: *Enough.* No way. He can't fit in another six ounces of ground chuck. He *shouldn't* fit in another six ounces of ground chuck. A third burger isn't good mothering. A third burger is child abuse.

I cried. I cried so hard that my face turned the color of a vine-ripened tomato and my breathing grew labored and a pitiful strangled noise escaped my lips, along with something else. Up came the remnants of Burger No. 2, and up came the remnants of Burger No. 1. Mom figured she had witnessed an unusually histrionic tantrum with an unusually messy aftermath. But I've always wondered, in retrospect and not entirely in jest, if what she had witnessed was the beginning of a cunning strategy, an intuitive design for gluttonous living. Maybe I was making room for more burger. *Look, Ma, empty stomach!*

It became a pattern. No fourth cookie? I threw up. No midafternoon meal between lunch and dinner? Same deal. I had a bizarre facility for it, and Mom had a sponge or paper towels at hand whenever she was about to disappoint me.

As I grew older and developed more dexterity, stealth and say, I could and did work around Mom, opening a cupboard or pantry door

Mark (left) *and me.*

when neither she nor anyone else was looking, or furtively shuttling some of the contents of a sibling's trick-or-treat bag into my own, which always emptied out more quickly.

I wasn't merely fond of candy bars. I was fascinated by them and determined to catalog them in my head, where I kept an ever-shifting, continually updated list of the best of them, ranked in order of preference. Snickers always beat out 3 Musketeers, which didn't have the benefit of nuts. Baby Ruth beat out Snickers, because it had even more nuts.

But nuts weren't crucial: one of my greatest joys was the KitKat bar, and I couldn't imagine any geometry more perfect than the parallel lines of its chocolate-covered sections. I couldn't imagine any color more beautiful than the iridescent orange of the wrapping for a Reese's Peanut Butter Cup.

Me, on a plump trajectory.

And the sweetest sound in the world? The most gorgeous music?

The bells of a Good Humor truck.

Every summer evening, just before sundown, one of these trucks would come tinkling down Oak Avenue, a narrow road near the shoreline in Madison, Connecticut, just north of New Haven, where my father's parents owned an extremely modest summer house. Mom and Dad would frequently bring my older brother, Mark, my younger brother, Harry, and me to visit Grandma and Grandpa there, and they would later bring my sister, Adelle, the youngest of the brood by more than four years, too. We would splash in the water, slaloming between the jellyfish, and dig in the sand. And after a dinner too big to leave room for anything more, we would run from the house to the street at the first, faintest whisper of those bells.

I knew the options by heart. There was the Strawberry Shortcake bar, coated with sweet nibs and striped with pink and white. There was the cone with vanilla ice cream and a semihard hood of nut-flecked chocolate over that, and an argument in its favor was the way the eating of it had discrete chapters: hood first, ice cream second, lower half of the cone after that.

And then there was the Candy Center Crunch bar, which was vanilla ice cream in a crackling chocolate shell, with an additional, concealed element, a bit of buried treasure. When you got to the middle of the bar, you bumped up against a hard slab of nearly frozen dark chocolate, clumped around the wooden stick. You had to chisel away at it in focused bites, so that chunks didn't tumble to the ground—lost, wasted. The eating of the Candy Center Crunch bar lasted longest of all. Almost without fail, that's the bar I got.

I remember almost everything about my childhood in terms of food. In terms of *favorite* foods, to be more accurate, or even favorite parts of favorite foods.

Age six: homemade chocolate sauce over Breyers vanilla ice cream. Mom used squares of semisweet chocolate, along with butter and milk, and as the chocolate melted in a saucepan in the galley kitchen, it perfumed the entire first floor of our Cape Cod on Manitou Trail in northern White Plains, a forty-five-minute train ride from Manhattan, where Dad worked. Mom made chocolate sauce every Sunday night, as a special weekend treat, and Mark and Harry and I got to eat our bowls of ice cream (three scoops each) and chocolate sauce in front of the TV set while watching *Mutual of Omaha's Wild Kingdom*. Sundays were for sundaes and lion kills in the Serengeti. I always volunteered to carry the empty bowls back into the kitchen, because Mark's and Harry's were never entirely empty. There was always some neglected sauce hardening—like fudge!—at the bottom. I would sweep it up with a finger en route to the dishwasher.

Age seven: I discovered quiche. Quiche *Lorraine*. Mom baked it in the upper of the double ovens on the south wall of the eat-in kitchen in our Tudor on Soundview Avenue in a section of White Plains that made believe it was part of ritzier Scarsdale, which it bordered. The quiche needed to cool for about forty-five minutes before it could be eaten; I knew because I'd often kept count. The crust annoyed me. This pastry didn't have the opulence or lusciousness of the custardy, cheesy quiche itself. Whenever Mom made her quiche, I rooted for her to cut the round pie in a crosshatched fashion, so that there would be square pieces from the center that didn't have any pastry rim—that had almost no crust, just a thin sheet of it on the bottom. I took only those pieces, and I reached for them before anybody else could.

Age eight: lamb chops. Musky, gamy lamb chops. Mom served them to us for dinner at the table in the Soundview kitchen about once every three weeks. I ate not just the meat but also the marrow inside the sectioned bone in some chops and—best of all—the curls and strips of fat at the edges of the meat. Mark and Harry winced when I did that and merely picked at their own chops, wishing aloud that it were steak night or hamburger night or pork chop night. We were a meaty family, the chops, strips, patties and roasts filling a separate freezer in the garage. Wherever we lived, we had a separate freezer in the garage. Mom was puzzled by, and censorious of, families who didn't. How could they be sure to have enough kinds and cuts of meat on hand, enough varieties of ice cream to choose from? Was that really any way to live?

She got that thinking from Dad, the firstborn son of Italian immigrants who arrived in the United States just before the Depression, struggled to make ends meet, and when they'd finally attained some success, held on to a sense of wonder at how far they'd traveled from the sun-scorched olive and almond groves of their southern Italian homeland. Dad grew up in a cramped apartment in a gritty section of White Plains, and the language in which he communicated with his parents was different from the one his schoolmates spoke.

Those schoolmates had nicer homes, nicer clothes. But they didn't eat any better than he did. The Brunis never skimped on food. A well-stocked icebox and a table whose surface all but disappeared under contiguous or overlapping platters of meat, fish, pasta and vegetables gave them their sense of security in the world. The bigger the feasts, the better the times.

Even decades later, with no real cause, that thinking lived in Dad. For him a house brimming with tubs of Breyers and boxes of his beloved Mallomars was as reassuring as his diploma from Dartmouth College, which he'd attended on a full scholarship, or his master's degree from Tuck, the business school there, which he'd paid for with ROTC money and a brief service in the Navy. It meant as much as his rapid promotions within the large accounting firm for which he worked. It was the best and clearest sign that he'd made it.

Although Mom, like Dad, had grown up in White Plains, she'd belonged to the leafier, quieter, paler part of the city: Cheever territory. Her father, Harry Wendell Frier, worked as an advertising executive on Madison Avenue; her mother, Kathryn Chapman Owen Frier, dropped him off at the White Plains train station every morning and picked him up every night. The couple would shoo their two children, Leslie Jane and Bruce, upstairs during cocktail hour, so that they could have their martinis in peace. The dinners that followed were prim, contained affairs. Harry would get eight ounces of steak. Everyone else would get four to five ounces apiece. And everyone would chew it slowly, with firmly closed mouths.

There were no such limits and no such calm at Dad's family dinners, which were more like gastronomic rugby matches, dishes colliding, tomato sauce splattering, cutlets flying. As soon as Mom made contact with this violent, thrilling sport, she took it up, her WASP reserve crumbling in the face of Grandma Bruni's spicy, fatty Italian sausages—fried with slivers of green pepper that soon shimmered with sausage grease—and Grandma's fervent belief that you had to make and

serve enough of every dish to guarantee plenty of untouched, extra food on the table at the end of an endless dinner. If there wasn't some of every kind of food you'd served left over, it meant that you had perhaps run out of something before someone had gotten his or her fill of it. There was no shame greater than that.

Mom was incessantly feeding people: friends who'd dropped by for a hello, not a ham and cheese omelet; whole second-grade classes, to which she'd deliver four or five batches of brownies she had made, on a whim, the midnight before; people she'd hired to do work around the house. She'd carry broad trays of tuna and egg salad sandwiches, along with deep pitchers of lemonade and iced tea, to men raking leaves in the Soundview yard. She'd insist that the cleaning woman who came once a week stop what she was doing around lunchtime and sit down to a bowl of homemade clam chowder, a plate of homemade chocolate chip cookies and, if the timing worked out just right, an episode of *All My Children*. Food was how she showed people the amount of time she was willing to spare for them, the sorts of sacrifices she was willing to make for them.

But while it was part courtesy, it was also part boast. She wanted to demonstrate what she could pull off. She'd chosen full-time motherhood over a formal profession, so she channeled all of the ambitions, vanities and competitive impulses that might have been satisfied by a career into the way she raised us and ran the house. Cooking was at the center of it all.

She cooked with a ferocity that belied her gentle appearance—lightly freckled skin, hair that was an age-darkened echo of her strawberry blond youth—and with an ethnic bent that also contradicted it. Apart from that once-monthly quiche Lorraine, the occasional *coquilles St. Jacques* and a twice-yearly beef Wellington, she focused on Italian food, and pumped

My parents on their wedding day.

it out in a volume that would have done any Mario Batali restaurant proud. She could make lasagna for eighty as easily as for eight—and, in fact, preferred the grander gesture. She put together mammoth pasta dishes for neighborhood Fourth of July parties, massive pasta dishes for PTA meetings, monumental pasta dishes for events at the YMCA. The planning and execution required many hours over many days, but they were redeemed, at the end, by the second helpings people took, the moaning they did about being too full, the sauce stains on their shirts: Mom's version of applause.

All of us could eat, but Dad and I could eat the most. I took after him that way.

I'm told that in high school and college he was trim, and I can see that in pictures. But I remember him always carrying around extra weight. The amount varied—sometimes it was as little as ten pounds, sometimes as much as thirty, which wasn't insignificant on a man just under five feet, nine inches tall. He'd grouse about it. From time to time he'd even diet. But he loved his lasagna and relished his Mallomars, especially after a twelve-hour day at the office. He worked many twelve- and fourteen- and even sixteen-hour days. And food was how he rewarded himself.

Before he left for work in the morning, he'd ask Mom what she planned to cook for dinner that night. He wanted to start thinking about it and to be sure that whatever he had for lunch wouldn't make it redundant—wouldn't spoil his appetite for it or dim his enjoyment of it. If Mom didn't have the answer just then, he'd call her midday for an update. And if she promised meat loaf and he came home to beef Stroganoff, his whole face collapsed. Then he grumbled through the meal and maybe even skipped seconds. But that only meant he snacked more later.

At nine p.m. or so I'd often see him trudge into the kitchen or into the garage in his pajamas, on the hunt for ice cream bars or ice cream sandwiches. He'd reach into the freezer, grab two Eskimo Pies or two Flying Saucers and then, sometimes, after a moment's hesitation, grab a third. I once went to talk to him in his and my mother's bedroom, where he had an enormous leather recliner situated just opposite the television set, and spotted four Eskimo Pies stacked up on the table next to the chair. He had settled in for a long Yankees game, and didn't want to take any chances that he'd need to rouse himself for another trip to the freezer.

During the Soundview years, he frequently took Mark, Harry and me into the city to watch the Yankees play baseball, the Knicks play basketball or the Rangers play hockey. Mark and Harry loved those games. I loved the peanuts, pretzels, hot dogs and ice cream bars with which vendors roamed the aisles, looking for takers.

"You're getting another hot dog?" Dad would ask when he saw me waving down one of these vendors. He wouldn't be opposed—just surprised. Mark and Harry would still be on their first hot dogs. Dad, too. The game seemed to distract them.

I was only a year and a half in age behind Mark. Harry trailed me by just two and a half years. And as in so many families with children of the same sex clustered so closely together, the three of us defined ourselves—and were defined by Mom and Dad—in relation to one another. We competed fiercely against one another, each of us looking for distinction.

Mark was the charismatic and confident one, most at ease with his peers, able to waltz into a new classroom and instantly find himself at the epicenter of the in crowd. Had there been fraternities in elementary school, he would have pledged the most desirable one, and might well have ended up its president. There were many years—in elementary school, middle school and, to a lesser extent, high school—when my social life was an auxiliary of his, dependent on his and his friends' good graces. More often than not he put up with that. I loved him for it, and sometimes hated him for it, too.

He was also the agile one, adept at just about any sport Dad foisted upon us. Little League baseball? Mark could play the infield positions that required swift movements and a slingshot arm: shortstop, second base. Beginners' football? He could play not only running back but also linebacker, less hampered by his size—he lagged a good three to four inches in height behind most of his peers, and always would—than he should have been. He swung a tennis racket with authority, even grace. And he hit a golf ball on the first try, not whiffing repeatedly, the way a certain envious younger brother did.

As for food, he didn't share my curiosity about it. He ate steadily but boringly: plain bagels with butter, cheeseburgers with ketchup but no other adornments, slices of cheese pizza instead of the pizza with sausage, peppers and onion that Mom and Dad preferred. I ate both kinds of pizza and I ate Big Macs and I ate pumpernickel bagels with cream cheese. And for every bagel Mark ate, I ate a bagel and a half.

Harry was the "space cadet," a phrase I first heard in relation to him. I thought Dad and Mom had coined it just to describe him. It spoke, correctly, to the way he often zoned out from the interactions and physical circumstances immediately around him, deaf to Mom's exhortations that he turn off the TV in the family room or to Dad's bellowing that he come out of his bedroom and take a seat at the breakfast table.

But it also carried the erroneous suggestion that Harry was floating, adrift. Hardly. What he had was an extraordinary ability to focus on one task or thought to the exclusion of all others. He could spend whole days putting together the most intricate models, whole weekends building the most ambitious backyard forts.

That ability, coupled with an innate physical coordination that rivaled Mark's, aided him in certain athletic pursuits. Not the team sports that Mark was good at—they didn't hold the same appeal for him. But he was the smoothest and most acrobatic of any of us on a skateboard and, later on, the fastest and most agile on skis. Golf, too, came naturally to him. He seldom got mired for three or four strokes in a sand trap, the way a certain envious older brother did.

As an eater, too, he fixated on a single object of interest and lost sight of much else. For a while his fixation was French fries, and if Dad was working late and Mom took us to Howard Johnson's or Friendly's, he would get two orders of fries for dinner, then a third for dessert. He'd still be eating fries while I'd be eating the most rococo sundae or banana split on the menu. During another phase his fixation was bacon. In a restaurant at breakfast time he'd order an extra side of bacon to go with his bacon and eggs, and he'd leave the eggs untouched.

But if none of his special foods were around, he merely picked at what was in front of him, not so much disappointed as disinterested, never complaining of hunger or, as best as I could tell, experiencing it. If the meal Mom served wasn't to his liking, he just left three-quarters of it on his plate, even as she idly threatened to put the peas he had passed over in a sandwich for lunch the next day. If the meal Mom served wasn't to my liking—a rare event—I ate all of it anyway. Food that was only marginally appealing beat no food at all.

I was the most avid reader of the bunch, intent at one point on working my way through every children's novel that had recently won the Newbery Medal: *Island of the Blue Dolphins, Sounder, Mrs. Frisby and the Rats of NIMH.* I had more vanity about schoolwork and grades, lording my report cards over Mark and Harry, even though theirs were nearly as good. I was also the skeptical one, first to question the tooth fairy, God and the rest of it, in a manner Mom and Dad always recalled as equal parts endearing and obnoxious.

"Is there really a Santa Claus?" I supposedly asked Mom at the dinner table one night when I was six.

"Frankie," she responded, not wanting to lie but not wanting to upset Mark and Harry, who had definitely perked up, "I would like to believe there is."

"I didn't ask what you'd like to believe," I corrected her. "I asked whether there is or isn't."

Above all I was the physically lazy one. Mom and Dad would later remind me of this, too, citing the first time Dad had recruited Mark, Harry and me to help him rake autumn leaves in the yard. This was on Manitou Trail, before we had gardeners, before Dad had climbed higher up the corporate ladder. He figured it was time that we boys started learning to pitch in a little, even though we were still too young to be much real help.

"Here's our plan," Dad said, outlining what lay ahead and trying to ease us into it. "Every hour we'll rake for forty minutes, and we'll rest for twenty minutes. OK?"

We nodded.

"So if someone needs to go to the bathroom or if someone needs a drink, there's a twenty-minute break for that," he said. "Twenty minutes out of every hour. Forty minutes on and twenty minutes off."

We nodded again. It was all very clear.

"Any questions?" Dad asked.

I had one.

"What is it, Frankie?" he asked.

"Can I begin," I asked, "with the twenty-minute break?"

On my Little League team, I was always given the positions that required the least running: third base, maybe, or right field. Tennis balls whizzed past me as I swung hard but spastically at the air. Golf—well, I've covered that. If forced onto the fairway, I begged to drive the electric cart and just watch Dad, Mark and Harry. Steering was easier than putting, and much less humiliating.

Harry (left), Mark (center) and me. Mark's older, but I'm bigger.

Although I liked the idea of skateboarding, my initial attempts left me with a broken foot, incurred just days before a family trip to Disney World. I hobbled around the amusement park on crutches, slowing everyone down. Although I liked the stomach-tingling rush of barreling down a steep slope on a sled, I lacked proper control of my Flexible Flyer. It slammed straight into a tree, and I ended up in the emergency room with a gash below my chin that required a half dozen stitches. I never even bothered to try skiing. The widely held belief in our family was that if I did, I'd likely wind up in a full body cast.

I was the "klutz," a word Mom and Dad tossed my way about as often as they hurled "space cadet" at Harry.

"How's my big klutz?" Mom would say—tenderly—as she mussed my hair and investigated a bruise on my cheek that I had gotten from losing my balance on the way up the stairs and falling face forward onto the steps.

"Watch it, klutz!" she would yell—testily—when I plopped an empty plate on the counter in a way that made a plate already there plummet to the floor and shatter. "How can you be so klutzy?"

I didn't know, but I suspected it had something to do with my weight. That was the most obvious physical difference between Mark and me, between me and Harry. By the time I was six, I was bigger than Mark: not just taller, but heavier, by a good ten to twelve pounds, only a few of them attributable to the then-slight discrepancy in our heights. I wore pants with a waist size two to three inches bigger than his, and I sometimes had to be taken to the husky section of boys' departments to find them. Husky: I knew that wasn't a good thing, a flattering thing. Other kids made sure of that.

Me (left), *Harry and Mark.*

They joked that my initials, F.B., stood for Fat Boy. Mom told me to ignore it, but there were moments when she herself reminded me that I was larger than I should be. Frustrated by my failure to fend off an older girl at school who regularly taunted and shoved me until I gave her my lunch money, Mom said: "Next time, why don't you just *sit* on her?" Mom had never seen her, but made the safe assumption that I outweighed her.

Whenever I went to the doctor for a routine checkup I hurried off the scale, trying my best not to hear him tell Mom, yet again, that I was more than a few pounds above the recommended weight for a child of my size. I could see, in the Christmas card pictures that Mom took every year, how much fuller my cheeks were than Mark's or Harry's, how much broader my waist was, and I knew that in one of these pictures, I was holding Adelle—had *volunteered* to hold Adelle—because it was a way of obscuring the whole middle stretch of my body.

I wasn't obese. I didn't prompt stares or gasps. I was just chubby, and sometimes quite chubby, with a hunger that threatened to make matters worse and a gnawing self-consciousness about how bad things already were. And I couldn't understand why my body just wouldn't behave, whether I was using it to swat at a baseball or willing it not to clamor so loudly for more ice cream—willing it to shrink, even just a little, and look more like Mark's or Harry's or most of my schoolmates'.

Encouraging more exercise, Mom might suggest that I join a game of neighborhood tag, but I'd resist: I was slower than other kids, and didn't want them to say anything about that. She might suggest that I skip a second helping of rice, and I'd know that was a good idea, but I'd eat it anyway, her gentle protest trailing off in the face of my blunt enthusiasm. I just *liked* it so much, the taste of the rice (lavishly buttered and salted, of course), the chewing of it, the way it filled my mouth, the way it filled my stomach. In the moment it made me happy, and I got lost in the moment.

She wanted to help me but couldn't figure out how. Then, shortly after I turned eight, a new possibility emerged.

Mom was a sucker for fad diets. Like Dad she was always heavier than she wanted to be, though her range was smaller—she'd be, at any given moment, between five and fifteen pounds over her goal weight—and her resolve to do something about it was more frequently renewed. She started many weeks and many months determined to be lighter by the end of them. She succeeded; she failed; the results lasted the better part of a year; the results didn't last a nanosecond. It was an endless cycle, punctuated with the Scarsdale Diet and the Beverly Hills Diet and any other diet with a fancy zip code and the connotation of a gilded, svelte life.

She did some diet that required the consumption of a half grapefruit at a half dozen intervals during the day—it didn't work, as I recall, but it certainly kept her safe from scurvy. There was a popcorn diet of some kind, and for a while the sounds that most frequently escaped the kitchen were the vacuum-like whirring of an air popper and the *crack-ping-crack* of the kernels.

In time there would be prepackaged meals from the Diet Center, which ceded their territory years after that to prepackaged meals from Jenny Craig. There was a period when she swore by Wasa bread—those hard, flat rectangles that could pass for wood chips and made sheets of matzo seem pillowy and buttery—and there was a period when she swore by artificially sweetened Jell-O. My mother believed that somewhere out there was a holy grail of weight loss, and she'd be damned if she wasn't going to find it.

But the diet I remember best, because I joined her on it, was Dr. Atkins's low-carbohydrate diet. People who became wise to it only in the 1990s tend to forget that it made its initial splash back in the early 1970s, which was when Mom and I first gave it a whirl. Here was Dr. Atkins, saying that someone with an appetite that wouldn't be tamed—an appetite like mine—didn't have to tame it. He or she just had to channel it in the right direction, away from carbohydrates.

Of course I had never heard the word "carbohydrate" before, but I was thrilled by all the consonants and syllables in it. To me they meant that something terribly scientific—something nutritionally profound— was at hand. I interrupted whatever latest Hardy Boys mystery I was plowing through to crack open *Dr. Atkins' Diet Revolution*, which Mom had bought in hardcover, anxious to get her hands on it, convinced it was a keeper. I read about blood sugar levels and these chemicals called "ketones" and this charmed metabolic state in which you began to generate them or expel them or swirl in them or something along those lines. I didn't exactly understand it but knew that my goal was to achieve this state, called "ketosis." Ketosis was my preadolescent nirvana. It was what I wished for: ketosis, along with a new five-speed bicycle.

The Atkins diet prohibited certain things I loved, like pretzels and ice cream, but it let me have as much as I wanted of other things I also loved, like Cheddar cheese omelets with pork sausage at breakfast or hamburger patties—three of them if that was my desire, so long as I dispensed with the bun and the ketchup—at dinner. It allowed snacks like hunks of Cheddar and roll-ups of turkey breast and Swiss cheese. I could even dip the roll-ups in mayonnaise and not be undermining the Atkins formula. According to Atkins, it was important to stay sated, because any empty crevasse of stomach was nothing but a welcome mat for a Reese's Peanut Butter Cup. So I left no crevasse unfilled. And I felt relieved—liberated. Silencing taunts and getting into smaller pants wouldn't mean going hungry.

For lunch on most days I had tuna salad. Mom tried to make it seem more special and eventful by presenting it in geometrically interesting and colorful ways. She used the largest round dinner plate she could find. She covered the plate with several overlapping leaves of iceberg lettuce. She molded the tuna salad—always Bumble Bee solid white tuna, never chunk light, never Chicken of the Sea—into three large scoops, which she put over the lettuce, within a ring of cherry tomatoes. Three scoops looked prettier than one or two. Besides, there wasn't any doubt I'd be able to finish that many.

"Aren't you going to have some?" I'd ask.

"Maybe later," she'd say, and then I'd hear the *crunch-woosh* of the metal peel coming off another bright pink can of Tab, the worst diet cola ever made, the diet cola Mom never betrayed, *her* diet cola, its distance from sweetness and its metallic taste a way of patting herself on the back. When it came to beverages, was anyone more virtuous and penitential than she? Tab was her rosary, and she said it as many as eight times a day.

Mom often skipped lunch, even on Atkins. When she did deprivation, she did deprivation all the way. Dinner, in any case, was her preferred meal. Until dinnertime Tab alone could sometimes get her through the day. Years later, Tab would become harder to find and she would turn to Diet Rite, assiduously steering clear of Diet Coke and refusing to entertain the notion of Diet Pepsi. Some people assert their independence and individuality through what they wear. Mom asserted hers through the artificially sweetened canned drink she favored.

I drank Tab on Atkins. I drank Fresca, too, and sugar-free iced tea of various kinds. I was concerned less with my choice and range of beverages than with the little paper strips in the medicine cabinet of the bathroom off my parents' bedroom. The strips went along with the Atkins diet, and they were clustered in a tiny cylindrical container, the way toothpicks might be.

In the morning, in the late afternoon and just before bedtime, I'd slide or shimmy one of the strips from the jar, hold it in my left hand and get ready to pee. Then I'd pass the strip through the stream of urine and wait to see if it changed color. If it changed color, Mom had told me, the diet was working. If it changed color, I was in ketosis and I was melting the fat away.

It didn't change color on the second day. Or the third. But on the fourth, it did, going from white to a pinkish purple. And after just a few more days, I noticed a loosening in my pants. A tightening in my stomach. I was shrinking every second!

And now that I'd crossed into ketosis, I could expand my carbohydrate intake somewhat, add more kinds of food to my regimen. I could have celery stalks slathered with peanut butter. Mom could fry instead of broiling my chicken, so long as its coating was only a subtle dusting of flour. I toted up and reveled in the possibilities. Less than a week and a half into this new state of sacrifice, I was already anxious for ways to mitigate it, already keeping a tally of indulgences deferred and rewards around the corner.

I stayed on Atkins for close to three weeks. I lost something like seven pounds: enough to land me on the slender side of stocky. Then . . . well, Mom hadn't really worked that out. The idea, I suppose, was that I'd be so encouraged by the change in my weight that I'd safeguard it with less gluttonous behavior, and I'd revisit Atkins for a tune-up from time to time.

But Atkins hadn't been so easy to pull off, not with so many others at the dinner table eating different, less monochromatic meals. Not with the occasional naysayer outside the family questioning the wisdom of such a restrictive fad diet for an eight-year-old and saying I'd just grow out of my weight. And not with Grandma Bruni around.

At one point during the diet we went to see her. Except for the summer months, she and Grandpa lived in White Plains, just a ten-minute drive from us. Mom ushered me, Mark, Harry and Adelle, just a baby then, into Grandma's kitchen, where Grandma had a platter stacked high with hunks of fried dough—*frits*, she called them. The word, rhyming with "treats," was an abbreviation of *fritti*, which in Italian meant "fried things." Grandma served *frits* with nearby piles of sugar, which you dragged them through. They weren't Atkins-approved, so I didn't reach for one.

It took Grandma all of two seconds to notice.

"What's the matter for you?" she asked in her thickly accented, preposition-challenged English.

"It's fine, Ma," said Mom, who addressed Grandma as if Grandma were her own mother. Grandma wouldn't have it any other way.

"He's not eating!" Grandma protested. That was a shock in and of itself, on top of which it was offensive. Not lunging for and mooning over whatever fried, baked, boiled or broiled offering Grandma put before you was a violation of the unspoken covenant between her and anyone she cared about.

Mom and I held our ground, neither of us eating *frits*. Grandma glared at us and banged pots and dishes and utensils loudly on the counter and complimented Mark and Harry more than usual on their own consumption.

"You love Grandma's *frits*?" she checked with them.

They nodded.

"Then you love your Grandma!" she said, throwing another big glare at Mom, and then a small one at me, whom she blamed only partly.

To her thinking, Mom and I had done the equivalent of turning our faces away when she went to kiss us. We'd resisted the most heartfelt gesture she could make. We'd denied her the form of expression at which she was most fluent.

Two

To understand why food meant so much in the Bruni family, you have to understand why it meant so much to Grandma. For her, food was a currency and communicator like no other, trumpeting pride, establishing wealth, proving love. It gave her what bearings she had in the world. In fact, she'd come to the United States to cook.

It was 1929, and she was seventeen. The voyage from Italy was a great adventure to her, a privilege for which her father, Vincenzo Mazzone, had singled her out. Her sisters were to remain in Ruvo di Puglia, a rural town outside the southeastern port city of Bari where the Mazzone family tended its olive and almond groves. Only she among the Mazzone girls would accompany her father and two of her brothers, Agostino and Giacinto, to America. Only she, Adelina, would experience this rich, magical country.

Vincenzo had been to America before, to ascertain that there was more money to be made here than in southern Italy. He wanted to set his sons up in America as gardeners; although they didn't have much education, they knew about soil and sunlight and how to make things grow. But they were young—Giacinto was eighteen and Agostino just shy of fifteen—and it would be a while before they were ready to marry. In the meantime they'd need someone to make their meals and clean up after them, and so would Vincenzo, for the few months he would stay in America to help his children get settled. That's where Adelina came in. That was her America: an instant transition from daughter and sister to, really, wife and mother; an instant promotion, if it could be called that, from coddled teenager to take-charge, overwhelmed, premature matriarch.

They lived in a two-bedroom cold-water flat in a four-family home in White Plains, where the poorer neighborhoods, like theirs, had concentrations of both African Americans and recent Italian immigrants like them. And they struggled. Just three months after they arrived, the stock market crashed and the stage was set for the Great Depression. But still they had to send money back to Italy—that was a big part of why they'd left, a central part of the plan. In addition to her responsibilities at home, Adelina worked as a seamstress, doing piecework.

Not too long after she arrived she met Mauro Bruni. He had also come from the area of southern Italy around Bari and had also landed in White Plains. But while her route had been a fairly direct one, his hadn't. After saving up as much money as he could from his work as a stonemason in the Italian coastal town of Bisceglie, he had traveled to Yugoslavia and then France and then across the Atlantic, all in the hope of getting to America. He entered the country from Canada, using forged papers. It would be many years before he finally became a legal citizen, in the late 1930s, and he initially lied to my grandmother and her father about his status, so that he wouldn't be branded an undesirable suitor.

They married in 1933 and moved into the cold-water flat, which by then was home only to Adelina, Giacinto and Agostino. She and Mauro took one bedroom; her brothers stayed together in the other. My father, whom they named Frank, was born in 1935, and he slept in his crib in their bedroom until Giacinto married and moved into a home of his

My grandparents Mauro and Adelina on their wedding day.

own two years later. Then my father took Giacinto's place in the room with Agostino until Agostino married and moved out another three years after that.

Giacinto, who became known as Jack, and Agostino, who went by the Americanized name of Gus, both married women of Italian descent, and that set up a friendly, and sometimes not so friendly, rivalry between the three sisters-in-law, Adelina (who went by Adele), Fiorina (Florence) and Liliana (Lillian).

This rivalry played itself out in many ways. Florence prided herself on keeping the most immaculate home, and it was pretty much impossible for Adele or Lillian to challenge her on this front. Every day Florence swept the floor or vacuumed the carpet of every room, and every week she carried a broom outside and swept the *curb* in front of her house. She did the windows twice a week.

Adele prided herself on her three boys: my father; his younger brother, Jim; and the youngest, Mario. Their hair was always cut short and slicked back with Dippity-do. During summer they got a fresh set of clean clothes after dinner, so that anyone who saw them walking through the neighborhood at eight p.m., when it was still light out, beheld perfect children. They did unusually well in school, and Adele made sure Florence and Lillian knew about that. Her bragging was ruthless.

And Lillian, the only one who grew up in America, prided herself on being the least hidebound, the most flexible, the one whose home you could enter without any sense of ceremony, the one who would greet you in a housedress with the readiest, widest smile. When Adele and Mauro broke down and got their boys a cocker spaniel, it was confined to certain rooms, and it moved cautiously through them, alert to its lesser place in the household and aware that any misstep could trigger their wrath. The dogs owned by Lillian and Gus went wherever they pleased, squirming around the legs of guests even on special holidays and sometimes nipping at people's ankles.

Of course the rivalry played itself out in the kitchen, especially between Florence and Adele. Each had dishes she was known for, dishes that, everyone in the extended family agreed, she did better than anyone else. This agreement wasn't acknowledged when the women were around, but it was made clear to them by how much of something family members ate, by how often family members mentioned it and pined for it when they knew it was scheduled to be served on an upcoming night or holiday.

Florence's frittata, an audaciously dense omelet with green and red peppers and locatelli Romano cheese, was mentioned very often, to Adele's obvious consternation.

"I could make a frittata like that," she would sniff, "if I used *four dozen* eggs."

Florence was also famous in the family for her breaded, fried veal cutlets, which had to be drained on, and pressed between, brown paper grocery bags, not paper towels, because paper towels weren't to her mind as effective. She was famous, too, for her homemade ravioli, filled with ricotta and herbs. They were gorgeous, perfect: each one the same size, because she used the rim of a glass to cut the circles of dough from a long sheet. Each one also had the same cinching around the edges, the same pattern of dimples, made in a meticulous fashion with the tines of a fork.

Lillian made ravioli, too, but she didn't have Florence's patience. So she improvised with the implements she used to trace and cut each raviolo. She traded the kind of glass Florence used for a small bowl, then the small bowl for a bigger bowl, these changes lessening the number of ravioli she needed to make. Over time her ravioli grew so big that one per person was nearly enough, and the filling would seep or poke through the envelope of pasta, because a raviolo this sprawling was a raviolo on borrowed time.

Adele's specialty was what most Italian food lovers know as *orecchiette*, which means "little ears." Her name for them, *strascinat*, pronounced something like strah-zshi-NOT, came from her southern Italian dialect. It alluded to the Italian verbs for "to trail" and "to drag" (*strascicare* and *trascinare*), because to make this pasta, you'd drag a knife along a sheet of dough, repeatedly pressing down and pinching off just enough of the dough to make an ear-shaped nub of pasta. The method was even more tedious than Florence's process for ravioli.

Adele used her thumb as the mold for each *strascinat*. She would sit at a sizable table, an enormous rectangle of dough before her, and pinch and mold and then flick, the concave nubs landing in a nearby heap. She'd sit for hours, because there was no reliable machine for this endeavor, no dried pasta from a box that could emulate the density and pliancy of her *strascinat*, no alternative to doing the work, no matter how numbing it was. And even if there had been an alternative, she wouldn't have taken advantage of it. Dried pasta from a box didn't advertise how long and hard you had labored. Dried pasta from a box didn't say love. When you ate a bowl of Grandma's *strascinat*, covered in the thick red sauce that she and most other Italians simply called "gravy," you knew that every piece of pasta had the imprint of her flesh, that the curve of each nub matched the curve of her thumb.

Another of her signature dishes was a sort of casserole made with many alternating layers of *mezzani*, a noodle similar to penne, and thin slices of fried eggplant. The eggplant was the tough part, the messy part, because the dish required scores of slices, especially if you were making enough for a dozen or more people, and Adele was always making that much. Each slice had to be a particular weight: too thin and it might get mushy and fall apart; too thick and it wouldn't cook to a silky enough state in the center. Each slice had to be dredged in flour and given its own discrete space in scorching oil, so she had to deploy several stovetop pans at once or a big electric fryer, the kind that plugged into an outlet and sat on the counter.

Some cooks recall landscape artists at their easels, pausing to ruminate as they apply dabs of paint to a brilliant canvas. Grandma recalled a mechanic under the hood of a car, clanging and huffing and covered in gunk. Cooking was steamy, sweaty drudgery for which she didn't just roll up her sleeves. She wore something ratty and sleeveless—the fewer obstructions to movement, the better—along with comfortable slippers or flip-flops, even though she preferred heels in all other circumstances. She stood just four feet, eleven inches tall, not counting her hair, which got her all the way up to five foot three if she'd just come from the beauty parlor.

She did as much of this cooking as possible outside of view, in a space where she didn't have to worry about the mess. By the time my father turned sixteen, she had a whole second kitchen, in a two-family house that she and Mauro bought on Fifth Street in the Battle Hill neighborhood of White Plains. They rented out the second floor and lived on the first floor and in the basement, where Grandma churned out her fried eggplant and *strascinat*. She never had to sully the nicer kitchen on the ground level, and she could bask in the wonderment visitors expressed at its sparkling cleanness, which seemed to contradict the freshly made banquet she was laying out for them on the table in the center of the room. Where had all that food come from? Why weren't there any telltale signs of its production?

Although she and Grandpa didn't have all that much money, they had food to share and made sure that anyone entering their home knew it. They had it in part because they sold it, in a tiny store in White Plains that was a cross between a delicatessen and a bodega. Mauro opened it to supplement his erratic work and undependable income as a stonemason. It succeeded in part because its hours were longer than those of larger grocery stores, many of which shut their doors early in those days. Because of those long hours, Frank, who was five and a half years older than Jim and eleven years older than Mario, often had to head straight from school to the store to relieve his father.

Certain nights of the week were devoted to certain meals, and that schedule rarely varied. Sunday afternoon was the big weekly feast, antipasti followed by a pasta course followed by meat. Monday was soup night: something light, like minestrone, a retrenchment from Sunday's excess. Tuesday was a dish of peas and pasta, or what the Brunis pronounced *peas-an'-pas'*, mashing three words together in a hurried exhalation. Chicken had its designated night; so did steak.

Holiday meals were also set in stone. Grandma always hosted her brothers and their wives and children for Christmas Eve, when she hewed without exception to the tradition of seven fishes. She put canned tuna on an antipasti platter; mixed clams into a sauce for spaghetti; folded anchovies into a calzone; boiled octopus; and fried salt cod, squid and scallops. Sometimes she expanded the meal to include more than seven fishes, but she never contracted it to include fewer. There were things in this world a person should be able to depend on. Eating the right meals on the right occasions was foremost among them.

She told her children that they should never, ever leave anyone with the impression that they wanted for food, drilling into them that when someone offered them something to eat, they should refuse it. Period. If the offer was repeated, they might consider accepting it, but it was probably best to wait for a third or even fourth offer. Otherwise, she said, "the people" might get the wrong idea.

She spoke of "the people" constantly, usually in the form of a question that was basically her life's refrain: "What will the people think?" She asked her children this whenever one of them was about to head out in a shirt that was torn or pants with the barest of stains. She asked Grandpa this whenever he dawdled in attending to some home repair whose necessity might be apparent to a neighbor or passerby. Her children—and, later, their wives and the rest of us—liked to tease her by asking, "Who are *the people*? Do they have names?" But we knew. They were anyone and everyone who might get a glimpse of, and draw a conclusion about, you. They were the jury, seen and unseen, before whom you maintained a *"bella figura,"* a bedrock Italian expression that literally translates into "beautiful figure" but really means "good impression" and refers to your image and standing in the world.

The house on Fifth Street wasn't fancy, but Adele made sure it had fancy flourishes. In a magazine she once saw garage doors painted in the manner of a black-and-white chessboard, and realized that her garage doors, formed by a grid of squares, could yield to a similar decorative treatment. So she and Jim, her middle son, went to work, improvising somewhat by replacing the black paint with turquoise, which matched the metal patio furniture. The results thrilled her, in no small part because they were visible to the neighbors, who had boring garage doors, monochromatic garage doors, garage doors that looked like, well, garage doors. Hers looked like a mosaic.

Before long, Domenica's did as well. Domenica owned the house next door, and seemed always to be sitting at the window with the best view of the goings-on at the Brunis, her unblinking eyes staring out. She watched the garage makeover, then decided to mimic it. She painted her own chessboard, only in *pink* and white, and it was fewer than twenty feet away from Adele's. To Adele this was an outrage. Had the phrase "copyright infringement" been in her vocabulary, she would have muttered it, or muttered whatever words in her southern Italian dialect came closest, along with references to plagiarism and theft of intellectual property. She wasn't about to sit still for this. She and Jim plotted, and then made a stencil, and then went back to painting, at the end of which the grid on her garage doors comprised turquoise squares with inscribed white circles: a sort of chessboard with plump polka dots. Game, set, match.

She wanted to feel rich, and to her thinking a rich person would speak on a gold telephone. When she couldn't find one in a store, she applied glittering gold paint to the glossy black surface of a normal phone. But the surface wasn't right for paint, which didn't fully dry on it, not after several hours, not even after several weeks. To place or answer a call at Adele's house was to risk a wet, sticky hand and a wet, sticky cheek. And if the telephone conversation was a long one, you might wind up looking like you'd been mauled by Midas.

As each of her sons married, the house on Fifth Street became a sort of culinary school for their wives, none of whom were Italian but all of whom were expected—and in fact eager—to master the essential dishes: the eggplant macaroni; the cutlets; the frittata; the *pizza dolce*, a fluffy cheesecake made with ricotta; manicotti stuffed with ricotta; lasagna. Many of these dishes involved gravy, and my uncle Jim's wife, Vicki, visited the basement kitchen to see how Adele made hers. So did my uncle Mario's wife, Carolyn, who cooked with her as often as once a week. My aunts observed which meats she put into her gravy and how much of them, which sorts of tomatoes and seasonings she used. They knew that watching the way Adele worked was their best hope of replicating it, because they'd heard the story of my mother's first attempt to make gravy for my father.

It was 1957; they had just been married, and were living in San Diego, where my father, then a junior officer in the Navy, was stationed. The first time he shipped out for several months, my mother decided she wanted to surprise him when he got home by making pasta with his mother's style of gravy. So she wrote Adele and asked her for the recipe.

But Adele didn't have recipes. She had only memories, routines and loose guidelines. If, for example, she was telling you how to make lentils, she'd say that you needed two fingers of water in the bottom of the pot. Then she'd press an index and middle finger together and hold them sideways, illustrating that the water should rise as high as the combined widths of those fingers. She never considered that different people might use pots of different sizes.

When she got my mother's letter, she turned to her son Jim for help. How could she give my mother a recipe that didn't exist? Jim said that she should talk him through the gravy process, and he would write it down, and then there would be a recipe, and into the mail it would go. He fetched a piece of paper and a pen.

Adele began. "You get a nice piece of pork," she said, setting a tone for the specificity of the instructions. "You put it in a pot of olive oil and brown it nice-nice."

Whatever document she and Jim produced no longer exists, but its limited utility is easy to imagine, as is my mother's befuddlement when she received it. She apparently believed that with a little extra coaching and coaxing, she could pry something more concrete out of her mother-in-law, so she wrote back, asking: "How many cubic inches is a nice piece of pork?"

Jim read the letter to his mother, and fielded her questions.

"What does she mean," Adele asked him, "by 'cubic'?"

My mother confronted complications beyond the nonexistent recipe. She couldn't find the right ingredients in San Diego, which didn't have the Italian population or ethnic groceries that White Plains did. So Adele rounded them up and sent them along: cans of imported plum tomatoes, bottles of acceptable olive oil, packages of dried pasta, and, wrapped in several layers of aluminum foil, an enormous hunk of pecorino Romano.

In those days it took a fair amount of time for a package of this size to travel from coast to coast, and when it arrived it was kept in the post office until my mother could be notified to come and get it. She stepped into the post office and was stopped short by a horrible smell. She wondered what could be causing it and why the post office hadn't done something about it. She presented the slip for her package, noticed the curious expression on the face of the worker who looked at it and, as the package was carried to her, realized that the smell was getting stronger and stronger. Aluminum foil could do many things, but preventing unrefrigerated cheese from spoiling wasn't among them.

The summer house on Oak Avenue, which had its own spit of private beach on Long Island Sound, came later, after Mom and Dad had been married for many years. It was painted white, at Grandma's

Grandpa and Grandma Bruni in a fancy mood.

insistence, with sky blue shutters and sky blue flower boxes under each of the front windows. And it had a white stone fountain along the bend of a crescent-shaped gravel driveway. To Grandma a fountain was the very definition of elegance.

Mark, Harry and I would spend long July and August afternoons on the beach. With a dragnet we'd walk back and forth through the shallow water to see what we could catch for Grandma. Mostly we caught silver shiners, each no bigger than a pinkie. We would bunch them into a corner of the net and bring the net to Grandma, who sat waiting in a beach chair, ready to perform for us and for the neighborhood kids who'd heard about and learned to enjoy this particular show. She'd pinch a shiner between two fingers and, while it still wriggled, drop it in her mouth and eat it. Sometimes she pinched it hard enough at one end to lop the head off, sometimes not. Either way, those of us watching her would wince, speechless, then carry the net back into the shallows for another sweep through the water.

Long Island Sound wasn't considered a source of exceptional seafood; most of her neighbors on Oak Avenue didn't use what the waters yielded. So they brought the bluefish and the clams and the mussels to Grandma's back door. She could be counted on to turn them into meals, especially the mussels, which she steamed in enormous pots. Years later I'd learn to love mussels, along with squid and octopus, but back then I wouldn't even try them. I couldn't get around the way they looked, those squiggles of peachy orange flesh, and their briny aroma unnerved me.

The treat I associated most with the summer house were Grandma's *frits*. She seemed to make these even more often in Madison than in White Plains, although I suppose she was sometimes serving *frits* she had in fact transported to the summer house up Interstate 95, in a gold-colored Oldsmobile sedan whose cargo of food rivaled any 18-wheeler's.

She made *frits* two ways. In addition to the plain *frits*—the ones to be eaten with sugar—there were *frits* stuffed with mozzarella and tomato sauce. Stuffed *frits* were like miniature thick-crust pizzas turned inside out, or rather outside in, only better, so much better, than any pizza could be. A pizza wore its soul on the surface, baring all. It didn't harbor any surprises. The cheese and sauce in Grandma's stuffed *frits* were secrets you had to eat your way into, and the dough around them was different from a pizza crust, denser and richer and glistening with all of the oil it had sopped up during the frying.

While Mark and Harry preferred plain *frits*, I favored the stuffed ones, and prided myself on my own version of X-ray vision, which allowed me to look at a platter of mixed *frits* from a few feet away and tell which were which, spotting a telltale pinprick of red tomato sauce on the otherwise tawny surface of a stuffed *frit* or recognizing a plain *frit* by its less swollen form. I'd count how many stuffed *frits* were on the platter—there were always fewer, because they were less popular. If there were twenty *frits* in all and only four were stuffed, I'd keep a close eye on my siblings, willing them not to stray from the plain ones.

Apart from my experiment with Atkins, I didn't try to restrain myself around Grandma's cooking, on the grounds that it would be selfish, even churlish, to do so. Enjoying her food was a kind of altruistic gluttony, and I embraced it as a rare escape—increasingly rare as I grew older—from watching and fretting over and berating myself for what I ate.

Away from her, I had to question and try to control my appetite, at least if I wanted to avoid the "fat boy" catcalls and the husky section. Away from her, I had to work on this weird psychic muscle Mom kept chattering about, this thing called willpower.

Until, somewhat miraculously, I didn't. Something other than Atkins came along. Something more effective.

Three

om and Dad signed up Mark, Harry and me for swimming lessons because it was the responsible, safe thing to do, given all the time we spent on the shore in Madison. In between our Little League games and our tennis lessons, Mom ferried us to the pool at the White Plains YMCA, where we graduated rapidly from beginner to intermediate to advanced classes, the ascending levels named for ever-bigger fish: guppy, then minnow, then shark. It didn't take us long to become sharks. We were naturals, all three of us. Even me.

So we joined the YMCA team and started regularly attending practices, at first just a few times a week, then every day. Before long, swimming elbowed out all the other sports in our lives.

"If you're going to do something, you should do it well," Mom always said to us, by which she meant we should be the absolute best at it, at least if there was any possibility of that. When it came to her children, she seldom thought there wasn't the possibility of that.

Besides, she wanted a family of winners, wanted to stand on the pool deck and bask in the compliments from other parents, in the envy she was certain they felt.

"Mrs. Turner couldn't even look at me after you beat Johnny in the freestyle," she'd say to me, her expression and voice gleeful. "Next time, you have to beat him in the butterfly, too."

"You *can*," she'd continue, less as show of support than as admonition. "You were only a half second behind today, and that's only because you got off the blocks so slowly. You were klutzy off the blocks. You need to work on your start."

I was good in the freestyle and the butterfly and even the backstroke. To the astonishment of everyone in the family—and to my astonishment most of all—I was good at more events than Mark or Harry, and I got better all the time. By eleven I had so many trophies and medals that Mom boxed the oldest and smallest of them and toted them up to the attic. Water, it turned out, was my element. All my fumbling, flailing and sluggishness vanished when I entered it.

Dad would have been as happy to have Mark, Harry and me spending our athletic hours on a basketball court or in a hockey ring: those were the sports he watched on TV and knew well. Those were guys' sports.

But Mom was partial to swimming. It didn't make her nervous the way some other sports did; there wasn't any way for us to get scratched, bruised or knocked down. It was easy to follow, each competitor given a lane of his or her own, the goal no more complicated than getting to the wall at the end of the last lap before anyone else did.

Most of all, it didn't leave me out. She'd found something that Mark, Harry and I could all participate in with some success. She'd found an arena in which I had cause to feel confident among other kids my age, in which I could mingle with them from a position of strength. Good grades in school had never won their respect the way first-place finishes in the pool did.

On top of which, I was getting exercise. I was slimming down. Not as much as I should have been, because I was eating more than I had before all the swimming—I was even hungrier. But the extra exercise outpaced the extra eating; the balance worked in my favor. Mom, I could tell, was relieved.

To me, though, it didn't feel like an out-and-out victory or even like clear-cut progress. It felt in some ways like a mean little joke: I'd lost some of my flab only to put what remained on more prominent display, in a bathing suit. I wished I'd tripped across a talent for fencing—and been able to tent my body in one of those beekeeper-style suits. But instead I had to squeeze into those tiny, tight Speedos, which pinched my waist so that the extra flesh there protruded all the more conspicuously.

At a swim meet, standing behind the starting blocks, I'd glance at the narrow waist of the boy in Lane 3, to my left, and at the even narrower waist of the boy in Lane 5, to my right. Then I'd look down at my own waist and notice that the distance from the farthest point of one love handle to the farthest point of the other rivaled the distance between my shoulders. My torso wasn't a V, the way I knew the body of a fit athlete was supposed to be. It wasn't a straight line, the way the bodies of so many young boys were. It was more of an hourglass—womanly, really.

When I climbed the starting block, my thoughts were less prone to turn to the laps ahead than to the spectators who now had an even better view of me and to what they might be noticing and thinking. I'd fiddle with my bathing suit and then fiddle some more, tying the strings tighter, loosening them, yanking the suit higher, sliding it lower. Did my belly and my love handles bulge less when the suit was like *this*? Or should I wear it like *that*?

Suck in your gut. That was the mantra that went through my head. *Suck in your gut.* The starter's gun was a mercy, because it got me into the water and out of view. And at the end of the race, I'd hurry to the towel I'd left behind the starting block and immediately put on the baggy T-shirt I'd left next to it. At a swim meet or a swim practice, other kids would romp around the pool deck in nothing but their Speedos, visibly happy to be free of clothing, to feel the air on their skin. I'd have on my baggy T-shirt, which went halfway down my thighs, and over my shoulders I'd sometimes drape a big red beach towel, which would billow behind me like a cape. I'd look like some burlesque of a superhero.

First-place finishes were an answer to that self-consciousness, a protection against the old teasing. By the seventh grade no one was calling me "fat boy" anymore. That taunt wouldn't fly and wouldn't stick, not to someone who usually built up a lead of four body lengths by the final lap of the 200-yard freestyle and hadn't been beaten in the individual medley all season. Sure, I carried around more weight than the other boys—I'd overhear their parents express surprise to Mom and Dad that I didn't have the "typically lean build" of a champion swimmer—but it didn't stop me from winning.

I liked winning. I liked the reel of memories that it put in my head, a movie I could turn to whenever I was away from the pool and filled with doubts, or embarrassed: about my uselessness in an impromptu game of soccer; about my latest failed attempt to hit a golf ball from the tee to the fairway.

"Frank's a swimmer!" Dad would tell any amused, chuckling onlooker as I swung the golf club in vain. "Aren't you, Frankie?" As Dad beamingly ticked off the events I'd won at the last meet I'd been to and the county or state records I held for my age group, I'd feel redeemed. But something about how relieved he sounded—and how quick he was to crow—made me resentful, too. What if there hadn't been any swim meets, or if I hadn't won anything at them? Would he still find some way to rise to my defense on the golf course? Or would he just stand a few paces farther away from me?

I still glommed on to Mark's friends, but now many of them were fellow swimmers, so I wasn't as much of an interloper. I was the best

Mark (far left) *and me* (second from right) *with swimming teammates.*

swimmer in the group, after all. I kept watching, nervously, for some sign that Mark was bothered by that. But he cheered as hard as Mom, Dad or anyone else when I was in a close race. He seemed to think it was cool to be my brother. And I felt that I'd finally done something to deserve to be his.

Mom and Dad moved us from the YMCA team to a private swim club with a more serious training program. It was the sort of operation that prepared future college superstars and maybe even Olympic contenders, or tried to. Mom talked about that all the time—the notion that I might be good enough to be an Olympian. When I was twelve, I was clocking some of the fastest times in the country—in the 500-yard freestyle, in the 200-yard individual medley—among swimmers my age. And our family was taking weekend trips to Montreal, Cincinnati and Washington, D.C., to attend regional swim meets with suitably stiff competition.

In addition to two-hour or two-and-a-half-hour swimming practices after school every day, Mark and I would do ninety-minute workouts *before* school, from five thirty to seven a.m., usually three mornings a week. It was our job—my job, actually—to set the alarm for four forty-five, pad into my parents' room and poke quietly at Mom, our driver, who would try to get out of bed noiselessly enough not to wake Dad. A few pokes and she'd be sitting upright; a few seconds more and she'd be clear-minded enough to remember that she had set an unopened Tab on the nightstand before she'd gone to bed. She'd reach for it. The *crunch-woosh* of that metal peel coming off the top of the can was the loudest sound she'd make.

Sometimes, though, my alarm would buzz and I'd look at the glowing digits—4:45—and then register how pitch black it was outside the windows of the bedroom Mark and I shared. I'd think about the desolate feel of the roads between our house and the pool at this hour, about how silent and depressing the drive was. I'd imagine the cold slap of the pool water on a body not really fully awake. And instead of hitting the snooze on the alarm clock, I'd just turn the alarm off. About forty-five minutes later, I'd sense a disturbance in the room, crack open an eye and glimpse Mom standing above my bed, arms crossed, shaking her head.

"What happened?" she'd ask, though there wasn't much mystery about it.

I'd grunt weakly and mumble incoherently, as if too exhausted to comprehend or respond to what she was saying.

"Someone," Mom would observe, "didn't get up."

I'd roll over so that I faced away from her, and I'd maybe even put my spare pillow over my head.

"Fine," she'd say testily. "But if I'd been so fortunate as to have a God-given talent like yours, I wouldn't have wasted it." Mom wasn't particularly religious, but when laying on a guilt trip, she liked to bring along backup, and she figured God was the only disapproving authority as fearsome as she.

Over time the pressure—to be as dedicated as she expected me to be, to keep my national rankings high—wore me down. I worried that I was always on the verge of disappointing everyone: not God (I wasn't so sure about Him in the first place, and couldn't imagine that He'd be particularly invested in the 100-yard backstroke), but definitely Mom, Dad, Mark, my coaches. I also couldn't stand the tedium of so many hours in the water, of 200 to 350 pool lengths every practice and at least ten practices a week (counting Saturdays and Sundays) for at least forty-eight weeks of the year.

And then, when I was about to turn thirteen, I got a way out. Dad's firm decided to transfer him from its Manhattan office to Hartford, Connecticut, where there weren't swim teams of the caliber we were used to, the caliber I needed if I was going to remain among the fastest swimmers nationally for my age.

Mom asked me if I wanted to do what some talented young swimmers did and go to live with a family in Mission Viejo, California, home to one of the country's most famous swim clubs, but I recoiled from the idea, and she didn't press it. As attached as she was to the dream of me with an Olympic medal around my neck, she was more attached to me.

In the Hartford area, over the course of my teenage years, I would gradually scale back: fewer morning practices; fewer hours in the pool all in all; less traveling; no more talk about the Olympics; none of the runaway nervousness I had felt whenever that talk had come up; no more fear that by setting the bar that high I'd fail all the more spectacularly to reach it. I wouldn't quit swimming altogether, because I depended on it for a social life and for a measure of self-esteem, and because swimming was supposed to help me get into a good college, or so Mom and Dad always said, going on and on about the importance of showing colleges how versatile you were.

Mom in particular went on about this, her obsession with college admissions manifest in her attention to the college stickers that many other parents displayed on the rear windows of their cars, advertising where their children were studying.

"Stanford, Duke, Brown," Mom would say, ticking off the stickers on a family station wagon just ahead of ours. "They did well."

She'd spot another set of stickers on another car and read them aloud, too: "Harvard, Oberlin . . . *Fairfield Community College*." She'd pause before the last school, which she'd mention in a lower, sad voice. "Ouch," she'd add. "Somebody didn't come through."

I continued to swim so that I'd come through. And I continued because I knew it helped with my weight, which wasn't where I wanted it to be but wasn't nearly as bad as I knew it could be.

When Mom and Dad told Grandma that we were leaving White Plains, she cried. No, wait—scratch that description, a disservice to the operatic scale of her emotions and their display. She *wailed*, brushing off all attempts to console her, saying, "I'll be fine here. All alone. *Like a dog*." That was one of her favorite expressions, a reliable bid for pity that she'd come to use with particular frequency since Grandpa's death a few years earlier. Another bid was subtler, to the extent that anything Grandma said or did had any subtlety at all. Whenever one of her three sons or three daughters-in-law visited or called her, no matter how recent the previous visit or call, her greeting was the same.

"Hello, *stranger!*" she'd trill, and it was the most pointed, acerbic trill you'd ever heard.

Whenever one of them let what she considered to be too much time elapse between calls or visits, she muttered, "Better to raise pigs. At least you eat at Easter." She made the case that mothers were more important than wives—and that her sons should never lose sight of that—with a little lesson in phonetics and in the way a person's mouth made the letter M. "*Moglie*," she'd tell her sons, referring to the Italian word for wife, "sticks on your lips once. 'Mamma' sticks there twice."

And if her sons suggested that she might get more time with them and with her grandchildren if she were willing to buck her homebound nature, leave her house on Fifth Street more frequently, and maybe even stay for a few days in a guest bedroom at one of her sons' places, she trotted out what was perhaps her most beloved maxim, an assertion that people couldn't change the most fundamental aspects of their natures.

"Born round, you don't die square," Grandma said.

She had more upbeat maxims, too, and these came out in the middle of a visit, once she was done with the accusations of neglect upon her visitors' arrivals and before she had proceeded to the *predictions* of neglect upon her visitors' departures. During a card game, she'd urge other players not to be too cautious by saying, "Take a chance. Columbus did." She'd tell my brothers and me that it was important, when dating, not to "stop at the first church."

Grandma had such a hard time accepting Dad's move because she'd been so spoiled for so long. From the time Dad had finished graduate school, he and Mom—already married by then—had always lived within about a fifteen-minute drive of her. Uncle Mario had seldom lived more than forty-five minutes away, and Uncle Jim never more than an hour. The ninety-minute drive between White Plains and Avon, Connecticut, the suburb of Hartford where we settled, was utterly new territory, a chilling precedent. Mom and Dad called her at least twice a week in the beginning to ease her shock and pain, and tried not to laugh when she inquired about the weather "all the way up there," or when she asked, in mid-September, if it had snowed yet.

That first year and for many years after, we drove down to White Plains and back on Christmas Eve, because Christmas Eve was Grandma's big night, in terms not only of cooking—the seven fishes, *strascinat*, Italian cakes, Italian cookies—but also of certain rituals, especially the one in which she played midwife to millennia of religious drama.

She had this unusual crèche. It wasn't one of those tabletop assemblages of Lilliputian camels and wise men paying bent-head homage to a Lilliputian new family. Her crèche took up a significant patch of the front lawn on Fifth Street, and its centerpiece was a tall, broad wood shack, the pieces of which were hauled every year from a shed attached to the garage and hammered together so that Mary and Joseph would have somewhere dry to hang out from the end of November until the Big Day. They and their plaster-of-Paris entourage were more than half life size. It was as if Grandma had invited a large party of anachronistically dressed dwarfs to camp out in the yard for the holiday season.

But something was missing: baby Jesus, who was perhaps three-quarters life size. He would stay missing—metaphorically in utero, though technically in a bottom drawer of Grandma's bedroom dresser—until just before the midnight moment when Christmas Eve became Christmas Day. Grandma held to this pinpoint schedule as if indisputable historical accuracy were at stake and White Plains were in the same time zone as ancient Bethlehem. At 11:58 p.m. on December twenty-fourth—two minutes before the Christ child's birth—she would dim the lights. She would put on a record of Dean Martin or someone like him singing "Silent Night." And she would fetch baby Jesus from that dresser drawer, where he lay swaddled in the finest white linens Grandma owned. She'd cradle him in her arms, carry him out to the shack on the front lawn, and put him in his manger, nestled between Mary and Joseph. And she would cry, because it was an emotional moment and because, well, she hadn't been feeling so well lately. This Christmas, it always pained her to say, would most likely be her last.

Holiday celebrations—which were when the Brunis' talent for excess really came out—got divvied up so that everybody in the family could host one. Until she grew too old to pull it off, Grandma had Christmas Eve. Uncle Jim and Aunt Vicki had Easter. Uncle Mario and Aunt Carolyn had the Fourth of July or Labor Day or some other holiday that took on more importance than it normally would, so that they, too, would have their rightful chance to put together a feast. Mom and Dad had Thanksgiving, and held on to it even after the move to Avon.

Whoever was hosting a given holiday treated it as an opportunity—no, a challenge—to lay out more food than anyone else had at their holiday. If there were two kinds of pie at Easter, there might be three kinds of pie at the following Thanksgiving. If there were three choices of ice cream to go with the pies at one event, there might be four choices, plus hot fudge, at the next. There'd be a cake in addition to the pies, in honor of the family members whose birthdays fell in the vicinity of the holiday. There'd be cookies, and probably cannoli, because someone might want something sweet to nibble on after pie, ice cream and cake.

But the dessert spread usually paled next to all that preceded it: the six, seven or eight kinds of appetizers passed around before the main meal; the main meal itself, which always included a pasta dish on top of a gigantic turkey or an enormous ham, unless the pasta dish supplemented a gigantic turkey *and* an enormous ham. And the amount of each kind of food was plotted with this rule of thumb in mind: If every guest decided to eat nothing but mashed potatoes, or nothing but turkey and only white meat at that, would there still be enough mashed potatoes or white-meat turkey to go around?

The holiday pasta dishes varied from host to host. While Grandma favored her thumb-molded *strascinat*, Mom liked to serve manicotti, which were like oversize, thin-shelled, sleeve-shaped ravioli stuffed with ricotta and herbs. Sometimes, though, she served eggplant macaroni. Aunt Vicki and Aunt Carolyn liked to serve ricotta-stuffed shells, which were thicker and smaller than manicotti.

Over the years, on the many occasions in addition to holidays when the extended family got together, and even on occasions when Grandma cooked just for my siblings and me, I noticed that she stopped making the dishes that Mom, Aunt Vicki and Aunt Carolyn made so well. One by one they fell away, although it might be more accurate to say they were

Some members of the extended Bruni clan, from left: Uncle Mario, Aunt Carolyn (holding their son Mauro), Dad, Aunt Vicki, my sister, Adelle (with my cousin Adele just beneath her), Mom, Grandma (with me standing over her), my brother Mark, my brother Harry (with my cousin Marc beneath him) and Uncle Jim.

forfeited: manicotti and lasagna to Mom; stuffed shells and *pizza dolce* to Aunt Vicki; chicken cutlets and a range of Italian cookies to Aunt Carolyn. I think that after so many years of competing with her sisters-in-law, Grandma didn't have the heart to compete anew with her daughters-in-law. But I think she was also validating them—letting them know they'd arrived. In some ancient public ceremonies, a torch was passed. In the extended Bruni family, the responsibility for eggplant macaroni was.

A holiday feast required days and days of planning and preparation. Mom's Thanksgivings in Avon, for example, tended to go like this:

T MINUS SIX DAYS—Sit down at the kitchen table with a ruled steno notebook and, over the course of three to four hours, make, revise, refine and double-check a series of lists. On the first two pages list every dish you plan to make. Use a third page if necessary. On yet another page list every dish that, in contradiction to your controlling nature, and in a moment of rare and laudable flexibility, you have permitted Vicki or Carolyn to bring. On yet another page list every item of ready-made food you plan to put on a platter, and on several pages after that translate the list of dishes you're making and the list of ready-made food you're assembling into a list of every ingredient, and how much of it, you need to buy. Pause to scream at Mark, who is listening to a Deep Purple album in his bedroom upstairs, that the electric guitars are too loud. Pause to scream at Frank, who is watching TV in the next room, that *The Love Boat* is too loud. Wonder where Harry is, and when Dad will get home from the office, and circle certain items on the shopping inventory—the special-trip, specialty-store stuff like cannoli and *bocconcini*—to be assigned to Dad. Make a mental note to tell him that he should wait until Wednesday to pick them up, so that they're as fresh as possible on Thursday. Make an additional mental note to remind him on Monday and again on Tuesday that Wednesday is right around the corner.

T MINUS FOUR DAYS—Shop. Take the station wagon. Make sure nothing is in the far back, or in the backseat, or in the passenger seat, because it's possible you'll need all of this space. Make sure a stretch of about five hours is free and clear, because you'll need this much time for driving to and among all the right stores and shopping and circling home to unload the perishable items; nonperishables can be left in the car until the kids come home, at which point, with enough prompting, they might help. When the kids do come home, tell them there's some stuff in the rear of the car you'd like them to carry into the kitchen. When they haven't budged a half hour later, tell them again. When they promise to get on it "during the next commercial," commence strategic weeping. Thanksgiving requires you to use all the weapons at your disposal; besides, the stress is getting to you.

T MINUS TWO DAYS—Back to the stores. There were things you didn't get on the last trip, because you were worried about how well they'd keep. There were things you forgot. There were mistakes you caught when, on day T minus three, you spent two hours at the kitchen table reviewing your lists. Say to Dad, "You're all set for tomorrow?" Hear him answer, "What?" Say, "The cannoli! The mozzarella!" Hear him answer, "Sheesh, I almost forgot." Cry. He's kidding, and you half-know that, but you need everybody to be operating with a peak sense of urgency.

T MINUS ONE DAY—A new set of lists. A map, really. Plot a painstakingly detailed time line of what can be assembled in the hours before the guests arrive and what must be prepared after they arrive. So that you don't get thrown off track or confused on the big day, prepare Post-it notes to be put on different bowls and pans and packages. Each Post-it note is an appointment, a set of instructions signaling destination (top oven, bottom oven, burner) and time (10 a.m., 11:15 a.m., 11:55 a.m.) and temperature (350 degrees, 425 degrees, medium heat). Turn the refrigerator and the counters into a yellow thicket of Post-it notes, then worry that you won't be able to see and heed the individual trees for the forest. Look out the window, notice that Harry's skateboard is still in the middle of the driveway, though he's been told four times already to put it away, and scream at him that Grandma is going to step on it, break her hip and be rushed to the hospital, and if she dies it's all his fault. Think about a glass of Chablis. It really might be time for a glass of Chablis.

THANKSGIVING DAY, 11:30 TO 11:45 A.M.—The guests begin arriving, and you instantly begin feeding them. Pull two freshly made quiches out of the oven. Cut them into square-shaped pieces and put the pieces on platters and have Mark or Frank make himself atypically useful by passing them around. Have one of the children pass around a platter of chicken livers wrapped in bacon, too, and a separate platter of stuffed mushrooms as well. These supplement a tray of deviled eggs, another light beginning to a long day. Somewhere there's a plate of little balls of mozzarella known as *bocconcini*; somewhere else, some prosciutto and maybe some olives. Don't forget the chilled shrimp! You cleaned and cooked four pounds of them on day T minus one, and you're serving them with cocktail sauce you made at seven a.m., another lifesaver that could be prepared ahead of time.

NOON—Hustle Dad into the kitchen so he can begin the carving process. The carving process could take up to an hour, because you've made both a twenty-eight-pound turkey and a separate nine-pound turkey breast so that there will not only be enough turkey for the main meal but enough left over for sandwiches later in the day. You must serve sandwiches later in the day.

12:30 P.M.—Lay food on the buffet table. Somehow find space for separate bowls of corn, green peas, creamed onions, canned cranberry jelly (because some people prefer it to homemade), homemade cranberry sauce (because some people prefer it to canned), stovetop stuffing (same reasoning), real stuffing (ditto), mashed potatoes and pureed sweet potatoes with little marsh-mallows on top. Find additional room for two casserole dishes of manicotti. Then find more room for a broad tray of individual foil-wrapped yams, which you had to have in addition to the sweet potatoes (and the mashed potatoes) because, again, diners have very particular preferences within a given genre, even if the genre is as tangential as tubers. You must find yet more room on the buffet, because you're also setting down a basket of napkin-swaddled warm biscuits and of course the gargantuan platter of carved turkey, with the dark meat clustered in one section and the white in another. Put out the sliced baked ham as well. Though no one's bound to eat the ham dur-ing the main meal, it's going to be necessary for the sandwiches later on, so you might as well make it available now, too, just in case. Worry. Are there enough yams? Has Dad fallen behind on the carving? Amid all the worrying and arranging, use the turkey drippings to make gravy. Gravy is the final, last-minute flourish.

12:50 P.M.—Ring a bell. It's the only way to summon and speed sixteen to twenty vigorously chewing, loudly chatting Brunis to the buffet table and then into their assigned seats, and you need them to move and eat right away, lest the eating schedule be ruined. Collect and throw away loose Post-it notes that have fluttered into corners of the kitchen counter or onto the kitchen floor.

1:20 P.M.—Begin badgering guests to head back to the buffet table and help themselves to seconds.

1:45 P.M.—Begin clearing the buffet table. Clear guests' plates. Tell Harry to tuck his shirt back in.

2:00 P.M.—Begin making espresso. Put platters of melon slices and apple slices and grapes, along with bowls of almonds, in the center of the dining room table. This is the beginning of the official thirty-minute pause before dessert, but you still have to have some food around. You can't not have food around.

2:30 P.M.—Repopulate the buffet table with two pecan pies, two pumpkin pies, two apple pies and an assortment of ice creams. Vicki has made chocolate chip cookies: put those out. Carolyn has made some *pizza dolce* and some traditional Italian biscotti: put those out, too. Dad ultimately remembered to get the cannoli: put those out as well. Put out a chocolate cake with chocolate icing because that's Frank Jr.'s favorite kind and his birthday was a few weeks earlier, on Halloween. Put out a separate lemon-flavored cake because not everybody likes all that chocolate and the guests shouldn't have to suffer for Frank Jr.'s peculiarities. To Vicki's or Carolyn's compliments that "you've outdone yourself," laugh in a care-free fashion and say, "Oh, please, it was nothing!"

3:15 P.M.—Permit people to get up and leave the dining room.

5:30 P.M.—Summon them back. The buffet table now holds bread slices and rolls and carved turkey and ham and mayonnaise and cranberry sauce and lettuce and tomato and other fixings. It's sandwich time. But guests needn't feel confined to sandwiches. The quiche is back. The shrimp are back. Even the two kinds of stuffing and the manicotti are back. And, of course, the desserts.

7:30 P.M.—Begin making doggie bags for all the guests. Include composed sandwiches in these bags: What if someone gets hungry on the drive back to New York? Include containers of manicotti, because there's a lot of it left over. Do not include shrimp. They've been at room temperature too long and don't travel so well.

8:00 P.M.—Shoo Vicki and Carolyn out of the kitchen, where they're furiously working to help you clean up, and tell them that you've got it all under control, that it's going to be a snap, that the whole thing was a breeze and you've still got energy to burn. Hand guests their doggie bags as you kiss and hug them good-bye. Notice that only three yams went uneaten, and feel a knot in your stomach. Did you make too few? Might someone have forgone a yam for fear there wouldn't be enough for others? Make a mental note: next year, more yams. And maybe also some lump crabmeat to go with the chilled shrimp. The appetizer hour needed a little something extra.

Four

n the kitchen, Mom was a creature of habit, though the habits were sometimes short-lived. She would become fascinated for a span of months or maybe a whole year with a new dish, new sandwich or particular ingredient, celebrating it and toying with it until it finally bored her and she moved on to the next thing.

Picasso had his blue period; Mom had her shrimp period. There was shrimp scampi, of course, which she made with generous measures of butter, garlic and shallots and just a bit of lemon juice and cayenne pepper. There was shrimp Creole—a casserole of sorts involving shrimp, rice, onion and lots of tomato—and there was another shrimp and rice combination, which I liked better, called shrimp Harpin. Shrimp Harpin's superiority was easily explained. The recipe called for a cup of heavy cream, two tablespoons of butter, a half cup of slivered almonds and a half cup of dry sherry.

For a while Mom took to wrapping things in bacon. In fact she never completely stopped wrapping things in bacon, but there was definitely a phase of more aggressive, frequent, committed wrapping of things in bacon, and it was a happy phase indeed. If something could be wrapped in bacon, speared with a toothpick and broiled, she did precisely that, and usually served the results as canapés, disregarding the extent to which things wrapped in bacon might fill a person and diminish his or her readiness for the rest of the meal.

She wrapped chicken livers in bacon. Scallops, too. She wrapped water chestnuts in bacon, though I never really saw the point. When you had bacon on the outside of something, why put a vegetable on the inside? It struck me as a crucial loss of nerve.

She became obsessed for a while with club sandwiches, layered with bacon, and this was because of the pool that she and Dad decided to put in the forested yard behind our Avon house. It was a grand, ludicrous pool, out of sync with the family's usually sensible spending habits, a splurge exponentially larger than anything before it. It was twenty yards long, so that Mark, Harry and I could do meaningful laps in it if we wanted. It resembled a lake, its outline curvy, its deck punctuated with enormous boulders that jutted toward, and hung slightly over, the water. Given all the money that had gone into it, Mom all but demanded, from mid-May to late September, that we get ourselves out there and *enjoy* it, and so she developed what she considered pool-friendly cuisine: guacamole with chips, crudité with dip. And club sandwiches.

The fact that they had turkey in them allowed her to tell herself that she was making something healthier than hamburgers or hot dogs. She always bought freshly carved turkey or cooked turkey breasts herself and carved them. She carefully toasted the white or wheat bread (her choice depended on her mood and dieting cycle) so that it was firm and golden brown, discarding slices that emerged from the toaster too dark. Then she'd cut the sandwiches into triangular quarters, crucial to her insistence that this was just piddling poolside finger food. A person could have just a quarter sandwich—just a nibble. Who was she kidding?

No one in our family stopped at a quarter or even two quarters, and I usually didn't manage to put the brakes on before five or six.

I had more discipline and did better with other things: chemistry, American history, Steinbeck, Wharton. At Loomis Chaffee, the private school outside of Hartford to which Mom and Dad sent us, I got As in almost all of my classes in the tenth and eleventh grades. I had editing positions on the school newspaper and the school literary magazine, and, due to those activities and my continued participation in swimming, more friends than I'd ever had before. I was, as Mom and Dad had always prodded me to be, well-rounded. Only the rounded part—well, I felt that it applied to me just a little too literally.

I had either six or seven or twelve pounds that wouldn't go away: I never knew exactly how many, because at a certain point I just stopped getting on scales. I didn't like what they told me. I was about five feet ten, only three-quarters of an inch under what I'd grow to be, and according to those rigorous medical charts of ideal weights at certain heights, I should have been 170 pounds. But I often weighed above 180, and I could blame only some of those extra pounds on big bones and a genuinely broad frame.

During physicals in doctors' offices, I averted my eyes from the scale and instructed the doctor not to tell me the number. Usually the doctor just chuckled as he wrote it on his chart. Sometimes he said, "I'd like it if you lost five to ten pounds." He never said, "You're fine the way you are." I know because I listened for that—listened for some indication that I was wrong about myself.

Ten pounds: it wasn't a disaster. I recognized that. But it was aggravating. Maddening. It was the distance between me and some confident, enviable, all-American ideal that might well be mine if I could just turn away from yet another quarter of club sandwich, from the third buttered yam at Thanksgiving, from the second bowl of ice cream I'd carry up to my bedroom—in Avon I had my own bedroom, connected to Mark's by a shared bathroom—at eleven thirty on a weeknight when I was up late studying.

The extra weight was the confirmation: once a fat kid, always a fat kid, never moving through the world in the carefree fashion of people unaccustomed to worrying about their weight, never as inconspicuous. It was the stubborn thing I seemed least able to control, and I often felt that all my shortcomings flowed from it—were somehow wrapped into and perpetuated by it. If only I could fit into pants with a waist size of 31 or 32 instead of my 33s and 34s, I could walk briskly and buoyantly into a crowded school party instead of hovering tentatively at the door, unable to decide whom to approach and questioning whether my approach would be welcome.

With 31s and 32s, I could wear whatever color and cut of shirt I wanted instead of the vertical stripes and the dark blues, browns and blacks that Mom said flattered me most. I could wear the madras sport jacket I'd tried on in a Hartford department store, the one she had told me wasn't "particularly slimming," or the kind of red plaid flannel shirt that was also—according to Mom, and according to the mirror—a sartorial no-no.

One of my best friends, Adrian, a fellow swimmer on the Loomis team whom I regularly harangued into going along with me to late movies on Friday or Saturday nights, had a shirt like that. But then he also had a thirty-one-inch waist, even though he stood three inches taller than I did, with broader shoulders.

On some of those Friday and Saturday nights, I'd get home after midnight and, though I'd had dinner earlier, grab two or three hamburger patties from the freezer in the garage, put them on a broiler pan and shove them under the broiler, flipping them as soon as I thought I could get away with it and leaving them on that second side for maybe five minutes tops.

My preference for rare burgers, by then established, started out as a matter not of taste but of haste. Rare burgers came soonest off the grill or out of the oven.

Partly because I tried not to, I was always thinking about food. Mark was always thinking about Amy, his girlfriend during his senior year at Loomis, which was my junior year. And since he and I shared the car for the half-hour drive between Avon and the Loomis campus, I spent almost as much time around her as he did.

Actually, I spent most of that time with her best friend, Ann, who kept me company while Mark and Amy stole away somewhere. In Amy's house, Ann's house, or a house that Amy frequently watched for friends of her family's, Ann and I would listen to Neil Young's *Harvest* or *After the Gold Rush*, to Fleetwood Mac's *Rumours* and the Grateful Dead's *American Beauty*, and eat toasted bagels with melted Havarti on them. Ann had introduced me to Havarti, flecked with dill. Like most such introductions, it went well.

"Where's *your* girlfriend?" she asked me once. I sensed she could be trusted with the truth, which I hadn't told anyone yet. I didn't want a girlfriend, I confessed. I wanted a boyfriend.

"Mark doesn't know?" she said. It was more statement than question. She could pretty much tell that was the case.

"No," I said.

"Are you freaked out?" This one was a question, and she was asking about more than what Mark might learn and how he might react.

I said I wasn't. It was nearing the end of junior year. I planned to bide my time until going off to college in about sixteen months. And I was going to make sure to choose a college in a decent-size city or with a big student body: a place where I'd be guaranteed to find other gay guys and might even have a boyfriend, maybe someone tall and thin and able to wear a red plaid flannel shirt like Adrian's.

"And when you find him, are you going to hide behind the car to take your clothes off?" she asked. It was a reference to an episode she couldn't stop ribbing me about. She and Amy had been with Mark and me in a parking lot where he and I had to change our shirts before meeting the rest of our family for dinner out. While Mark took off his T-shirt and put on a button-down in front of them, untroubled by their presence, I walked to the far side of the car and squatted slightly so I was completely hidden from them. The parking lot wasn't a pool, and this wasn't a swim meet: I didn't have to let others see what paunch and love handles I still had.

The next fall Mark left for Amherst College, a sticker Mom was thrilled to put on the back window of her car. Harry joined me at Loomis as a freshman, becoming my new partner for the commute. He also became a new member of the swim team, of which I was now cocaptain, and decided to concentrate on diving instead of the other events: it suited his talent for solitary focus. But his real passion was *Star Trek*. He'd sometimes invite fellow "trekkies" from school to the house on weekends for all-night *Star Trek* viewing marathons.

I wrote letters to Ann, who had gone off to college in Washington, D.C. On weekend nights I hung out with Adrian, as much as he would let me. On weeknights at home I often tucked in Adelle, who was now eleven, and whose bed had a lacy, undulating canopy over it. I'd study that canopy as I snuggled with her and sang her my favorite slow songs from the radio. We'd been doing this for years and I could tell it was about to end: she liked it less than she had at eight. She was getting so much older so fast and in so many ways, including her growing worry about her weight, with which she struggled. That was part of our bond, part of what separated us from Mark and Harry.

But I couldn't yet talk to her about the things I'd shared with Ann, and with Ann gone I needed a new confidante. Soon after the start of senior year, I got one. She turned out to be more than just a confidante. She was my unofficial diet guru.

Beth came to Loomis as a senior, transferring from a public high school, to try to bolster her chances of getting into Yale, on which she'd set her sights. She was among the slight minority of Loomis kids who boarded there rather than living at home. She had to: her family's house in southern Connecticut was nearly ninety minutes away.

She was a swimmer, a good one, and that was how we got to know each other. But I was drawn to her mainly because of her appearance: the oddity of it, the way it didn't add up.

Her height matched mine: nearly five feet, eleven inches. Due to genes and sports, she had the broad shoulders and thick upper arms of a football player. The thighs, too. And though her stomach was flat, her waist was broad. That was the genes more than the sports. In some ways they'd been cruel to her.

In other ways they'd been magnificent. She had a gorgeous face. I once read a profile of the actress Elizabeth McGovern—I'm not sure if this was just before or just after I met Beth—and its writer described her as having skin so flawless a butterfly could skate on it. That was the skin Beth had. The curve of her jaw was sharp. Her cheekbones were high and the creamy flesh right below them slightly sunken. Her eyes were the color of a Tiffany box. And if she'd nudged her hair toward a pale shade seldom seen outside Scandinavian countries and strip clubs—well, didn't eyes like hers call for blondness like that?

I picked up instantly on her awareness of the discrepancy between how she looked from the neck up and how she looked from the neck down. I recognized the signs. Like me she favored loose clothing. Like me she spent less time than other swimmers strolling around the pool deck in a bathing suit and hustled from the locker room into the water, or from the water to wherever a T-shirt or warm-up suit was waiting. In the school cafeteria she assembled strange combinations of food or walked the length of the salad bar rattling off the calorie counts of everything in it, citing one of the many nutrition books she'd read. She was waging a war with her body, and obviously felt estranged from it. I knew how that was.

My own anger at not being naturally thin—and at having this hunger that threatened to tug me ever further from thinness—opened the door to grievances over not being so many other things. I was unwilling to accept how slowly and lightly I tanned, so I bought a tiny, cheap sunlamp, put it on the desk in my bedroom and sat closer to it than the instructions deemed permissible, feeling the bulb's fire on my face, which seemed to crackle. I sprayed store-bought bleaches in my hair, then blamed the brassy, uneven outcome on swimming pool chlorine. My class-mates bought the excuse, but Mom couldn't abide

For my high school yearbook,
I'm suddenly and magically blond.

the brassiness. She dragged me to her salon, saying that if I was intent on being a blond, I should at least be a credible, presentable blond, and she had her hairdresser frost my hair by pulling strands of it through this weird cap with scores of tiny holes. She dragged Beth along with us, having made the executive decision that Beth should have her own shade of platinum toned down.

One day Beth announced that she was starting a new diet, but not just any diet. I was intrigued.

"Let's *both* do it," I said, suddenly convinced that together we'd reach what neither of us had reached alone: the wondrous Xanadu of the willfully emaciated.

She told me she had a book in her dormitory room that was just what we needed, and later that day she put a thin paperback in my hands.

"Read this," she said. "Then we'll fast."

The book talked about the evil that sweets did to blood sugar levels, the spikes and valleys they created, the insatiable hungers they bred. It recommended a three-day cleanse—no food, only water—that would break the cycle, purify the body. It promised mental clarity in the aftermath, along with an ability to manage cravings, if they even returned.

"When do we start?" I asked.

We chose a three-day span that didn't nudge up against any important swim meets or tests. Then we embarked on our mission.

"You're doing what?" Mom asked when I refused dinner on day one.

"Fasting," I responded.

"That's ridiculous," she said. Even Mom had limits.

"This book Beth gave me says a person can last a really long time without food," I explained. "Longer than we think."

"If you want to diet," she said, "why don't you do low-carbohydrate?"

"I don't want to do Atkins," I said. "I need to purify myself." I imagined these little bubbles, each carrying a sign that said FAT-MAKING TOXIN, cascading from my body, oozing out my pores.

"We should go to Weight Watchers," Mom said, my own madness pushing her closer to sanity. "I'll pay for Weight Watchers. I'll do it with you."

"It won't cleanse me the way a fast will," I argued. I had gone without food for only about eighteen hours at that point, but I was suddenly an expert. A messiah.

"I'll broil you some chicken," she said.

"No."

"I'll take off the skin," she offered.

"I'm fasting."

"Just eat the white meat," she pleaded, "not the dark meat."

"I'm only going to have some hot water with lemon. I'm allowed to have lemon."

"Suit yourself," she said, and stormed away. She hated losing. I figured she'd do something mean, like make a fresh batch of brownies, just to get the better of me. But she let me be, no doubt figuring I'd cave soon enough.

On day two I struggled. The novelty of the experiment had worn off, and my stomach gurgled and seethed, like lava in an active volcano. I also began to feel light-headed, but chalked it up to euphoria, to the purge of those toxins from my sugar-racked body. I resolved to fast like this once a month. It would be the cornerstone of a thinner, better life.

At school I quizzed Beth. "You *really* haven't eaten anything?"

"Nothing," she said, but I wasn't sure I believed her. She didn't have the winnowed midriff that I was determined to believe I had already achieved.

"Not even a Diet Coke?" I asked. "You know that diet drinks aren't allowed!"

"Just water," she said. "With some lemon. And I don't feel hungry at all!" I saw her steal a nibble of a cuticle. Hmm. Was that cheating? Was it tasty?

At the beginning of day three, I slipped.

I snuck a few crackers around breakfast time. I drank some milk around lunchtime, because my stomach-volcano was poised for its own Pompeii. At dinnertime I accepted that I'd strayed from the plan and rationalized that I might as well stray some more. I ate a burger. But I didn't put the beef on a bun. I had to preserve some shred of dignity.

Although my clothes felt looser at the end of three days, I knew I couldn't do this fasting thing again. It was too grueling. I told Beth, confessing in the process that I'd cheated a little, and of course she had a plan B.

"Protein powder," she said, producing a new paperback filled with recipes for fat-burning shakes you could make with nonfat powders, water and a few low-cal flavor additives—some strawberries, say, or banana slices—in a blender. Over the following weeks we made a bunch of these, but they didn't really work, quite possibly because we kept sneaking things like vanilla ice cream and peanut butter into them, to obscure their chalky, yeasty essence.

Beth was like a mysterious witch doctor with a stock of potions that never ran out. Pills, too. She'd found someone in her dormitory with a pipeline to amphetamines, these tiny pale blue ovals with dark blue flecks. They looked like shrunken robin's eggs.

We swallowed them to stay up all night in advance of important exams. We swallowed them before some swim meets, along with capsules of bee pollen, which we'd decided was another energy booster. And we swallowed them to keep from eating. They did the job nicely. I was slimmer senior year than I had been junior year, and it was largely thanks to Beth and her little eggs.

Maybe because of Beth, I also set my sights on Yale. We both got in, and briefly fantasized about the eating pacts and years of leanness ahead of us. But I also ended up winning a merit-based scholarship to the University of North Carolina at Chapel Hill from the Morehead Foundation, which provided an entirely free education, plus spending money and other perks, to private-school students whom it wanted to lure away from the Ivy League and down to Carolina.

I took the scholarship. Although Dad and Mom had more than

enough money to pay for college and insisted that I not consider the cost, I couldn't ignore it. I figured Mom could live with a Carolina sticker next to the Amherst one. And I reasoned that a state school in the South would actually be more of an adventure for someone who'd gone to a Northeastern prep school than Yale would.

On top of everything else, the Morehead came with interesting, foundation-funded summer adventures: an Outward Bound wilderness survival course before freshman year, a "public safety" internship riding around with big-city police officers before sophomore year, foreign travel after senior year.

I left for the Outward Bound course—twenty-four days in the mountains of Oregon—a few weeks after my Loomis graduation. Right before I went into the wild I talked on the phone with Beth, who was back home in southern Connecticut. She told me she wished she could go, too.

"You wouldn't last an hour without your lip gloss," I teased.

"It'd be worth it," she said.

"Exactly *which part* would be worth it?"

"All of it."

"You mean the sleeping in a sleeping bag for weeks on end?"

"You're missing the point."

"You mean the lack of access to a bathroom or, for that matter, *toilet paper?*"

"All for a higher cause."

"What," I said, "are you talking about?"

"Aren't you going to be hiking up steep hills and mountainsides every day, for hours on end?"

"Unfortunately, yes! With a heavy pack on my back."

"How heavy?"

"I don't know. Someone told me it could be as heavy as thirty-five pounds, maybe forty."

"Perfect."

"Are we talking about the same thing? Earth to Beth! Come back, Beth!"

She laughed dismissively. "Hours of hiking, with a forty-pound pack, every day for several weeks," she said, going back through it all. "Think about it."

I did, and realized what she was getting at. "By the time I get back," I began, but she cut me off, finishing the thought.

"*You are going to be a rail,*" she said.

"There's no way that *won't* happen, is there?" I asked. "I mean, no way at all?"

"I'm drinking nothing but protein shakes the whole time you're away," she said.

"For twenty-four days?"

"Well, maybe every other day."

"OK, that's manageable. Lay off the peanut butter and ice cream."

I knew she wouldn't, because she was just like me.

On the seventh or so day of Outward Bound, I walked in soggy boots from the tarp under which I would be spending the night to the tarp belonging to Dan, one of the two instructors for my group of eleven campers. I told him I had something serious to discuss.

"At the start of this," I reminded him, "you said that there were ways—if someone in the group got hurt, for example, or if someone had another kind of medical problem or a really pressing need—to get that person out of the wilderness midcourse."

"Yes," said Dan.

"Well, I need to get out," I told him. "I can't do this anymore."

By that moment, I'd long stopped thinking about all the great exercise I was getting. If my scratchy wool pants were looser on me than when the course had started, or if there was a bigger pouch of excess material where my scratchy wool shirt hung over my stomach, I didn't notice or care. My misery blotted out anything else.

Its source? Well, let's start with the snow. *In late June.* No one had warned me about it. And somehow I hadn't processed the fact that the mountain-climbing element of my particular Outward Bound course, in the Central Cascade Mountains of Oregon, meant high elevations, and that high elevations meant snow, even in summer.

Snow, in turn, meant wet boots. And wet socks beneath them. Wet pants, too, along with cold fingers, chapped hands—the whole winter works. At night the temperature dropped low, and we didn't have tents, just these slanting tarps, which provided protection from anything falling straight down from the sky, like snow or rain, but not from frigid gusts of air coming in sideways. I turned my sleeping bag into a body bag, zipped all the way over my head. And if I didn't doze off right away I lay there in utter darkness, entombed, with almost no range of movement, listening to the wind shriek and the evergreens thrash. Fifteen minutes became a lifetime. An hour was an eternity.

On the first and second days of the course, and maybe on the third day as well, the temperature had been relatively pleasant, and we hadn't climbed high enough to hit snow-covered ground yet, so I could have chosen to sleep without the bag zipped up all the way. I zipped it nonetheless. I'd noticed that our wilderness area was home to a teeming population of ants, along with other, bigger, uglier bugs. And I'd convinced myself that they'd crawl all over me at night if I wasn't vigilant, if I didn't create an impermeable barrier between me and them. Never mind how hot it got in that sleeping bag. If I was going to feel something crawling down my leg, I'd take a trickle of sweat over the kind of hard-shelled, glittering, poisonous black beetle I'd seen several times along the trail. The poisonous part was merely a suspicion, but my philosophy about bugs had always been: assume the worst, and reach for the Raid.

In the wilderness I didn't have any Raid. Any shampoo, either, because there weren't any showers in which to use it, and there wouldn't be any showers for the entire twenty-four days. This fact I had indeed processed in advance, but I'd shrugged it off as unimportant, because I knew that a wilderness area would have streams at the least, and quite possibly narrow rivers or lakes, and I'd planned on dipping into one every other day or so and keeping sufficiently clean that way. I hadn't gambled on water temperatures well below sixty degrees. When I lowered my hand into the first stream we passed by, and instantly felt my fingers go numb, I realized I was going to have to get comfortable with a grungy, funky, smelly Frank.

But I couldn't. I just couldn't. My scalp itched from the way my oily hair was matted against it; my cheeks itched from the stubble of my incipient beard. My face felt as if it were not just caked with dirt but somehow calcified by it. By day seven I wasn't sure I even qualified as human anymore.

I had blisters on my heels. I'd never been a big walker, and my boots didn't fit quite right. At night I'd take them off and see dark brown spots on the backs of my socks: bloodstains. The stains got darker each day, even though I'd cover the blisters with adhesive bandages. I bled right through them.

"I'm sorry," I told Dan during my talk with him. "But I'm finished."

"What you are," said Dan, "is a spoiled brat."

"I'm spoiled?" I said, flabbergasted. "Spoiled? Because I don't enjoy walking for miles on end with bloody feet, wet clothes and close to fifty pounds on my back?" It probably wasn't that much—the kerosene stove and the rock-climbing gear and the sleeping bag and the too-few changes of clothes—but it was a lot.

"I've never been camping before," I continued, trying to make Dan understand how hard all of this was for me. "Not even in a Winnebago. And I've never, ever been able to tie knots." We'd had two knot-tying lessons already in the course, and there were more to come. And they mattered, not just because the right knots kept your tarp from fluttering away in the middle of the night. The right knots kept you from tumbling down a cliff to your death during rock-climbing exercises, of which we'd done several, God help us.

Dan had a big bushy beard, wore tiny spectacles and was short and scrawny. He looked a lot like a woodland gnome, or at least a woodland gnome with access to an optometrist, and at this particular moment he looked like a bespectacled woodland gnome in a put-upon, disgusted mood. He didn't speak for a good thirty seconds.

"Everything's always come easy to you, hasn't it?" he asked. Dan was aware that I, like one of the other ten campers in my Outward Bound group, was taking the course because of the Morehead scholarship. So he knew that I was a top student and athlete.

But did he appreciate the all-nighters that had gone into my grade point average? The five thirty a.m. workouts that had gone into being fast in the pool?

As if reading my mind, he added: "I'm not saying you haven't worked. But the things you've done well and been praised for, they were things you had the talent for, right? The natural potential? Now here's something that you really might not be suited for. That you might actually be bad at. And right away, you want to quit."

He was right. On all counts he was dead right. Whatever hard effort I'd put into most endeavors had been hard effort with an almost certain payoff, hard effort wed to considerable aptitude. That was an easier kind of effort than Outward Bound demanded. Outward Bound wanted me to struggle through something I really and truly found difficult, and hated.

Dan said, "There are some things you enjoy doing, and there are other things you enjoy having done. And that second kind of enjoyment lasts longer."

Then he turned away.

My appeal had been heard—and rejected.

I bumbled across the snow, back to my tarp, and crawled into my sleeping bag. I zipped it tight. I replayed the conversation for hours before I dozed off, and when I woke up, it was with a determination to show Dan that I wasn't spoiled, that I could get through this ordeal.

I just had to be resourceful. I just had to adapt.

While stream or river water was definitely too cold to be plunged into, I could bear pouring it over my head. So I began to sort of wash my hair every two days or so, using a water bottle and a bar of soap.

I swore off knots, making a deal with the two campers with whom I shared a tarp and daily chores. I told them that if they would take care of tying anything and everything that needed tying—from the ends of the slanting tarp, which had to be secured to stakes and nearby trees, to the harnesses we wore when rock climbing—I'd take care of all the cooking. I'd make any hot oatmeal breakfasts we had. At night I'd be the one to fire up our pathetic little kerosene stove and put the pot on it and wait for the water to boil and pour in the grits, the beans, the canned beef or whatever we were having. I'd even clean the pot afterward, so long as there weren't any more knots for me in this wretched adventure, and so long as my two coconspirators helped conceal my knot avoidance from Dan, who surely wouldn't approve.

"All the cooking?" one of my tarpmates asked. "All the cleaning?"

"Yes," I said, "and yes."

I'd never been, and wasn't, much of a cook. I'd never mustered the requisite patience for it. My rice and pasta were always too hard, because I always yanked them off the stovetop too soon. Whatever ingredients I assembled for a dish had a way of disappearing before I could use them, because I had a way of preempting the slicing, grating, pulverizing or molding of them by the consuming of them. If I set out to make three dozen chocolate chip cookies, I'd end up with nine, on account of all the dough I pilfered along the way.

But by volunteering to cook for my tarpmates, I not only sidestepped my knot problem but also got to be the chief meal planner, deciding which of our provisions we'd have one day and which the next. I could determine when we treated ourselves to the peanut butter, which we spread on thick crackers called pilot biscuits. I could also determine how much canned beef got mixed into the egg noodles, and just how much of the brackish liquid in the can with the beef should be poured over the noodles. I thought long and hard about these things, and it helped me forget that the blisters on my heels weren't healing and that there were still fourteen days and then thirteen days and then twelve left until I could have a proper shower.

With about eight days to go, each camper was situated alone on his or her own patch of forest to do a "solo." This was an integral, dreaded component of the Outward Bound experience: three whole days with no human contact whatsoever. You got a whistle, so that if you fell ill or encountered some other serious problem, you could blow it and summon the camper nearest you, who was theoretically within earshot. You got a sleeping bag. You got a miniature, individual-size tarp. You got a water bottle and, so that you could keep refilling it, proximity to a stream. And for food, you got three pilot biscuits and about two handfuls of "gorp," which was a mixture of nuts and dried fruits, including raisins. That was it.

You weren't, in fact, supposed to touch it. It was there for emergencies. Say the mercury dropped sharply, and your body temperature dropped with it, and you found yourself on the verge of hypothermia. In that case, our instructors told us, you should eat. You should most definitely eat.

But the solo was meant to be a purifying experience, and the idea was that while you were forgoing plumbing, heat, electricity, TV, music, reading material, interaction with fellow members of your species and just about anything else that makes life endurable, you should pass on food as well. If you were going to embrace this kind of asceticism, why not bear-hug it for all it was worth?

I concurred: I'd leave the gorp and the biscuits alone.

Eight hours later, I reconsidered.

Night was falling, and I was losing my mind, because I'd already sung my five favorite albums from beginning to end and made a mental list of everything I should pack for freshman year of college. I'd even spent an hour or two drawing crude pictures with a stick in the dirt. I was deeply in touch with my inner Neanderthal.

I was lonely. I was even a little scared.

And the effect of having been told I shouldn't touch the food in my possession was the endless repetition of a single syllable in my head. As I sat all alone in the gathering blackness, I didn't think, *wolves, wolves, wolves* or *bats, bats, bats* or *help, help, help.* I thought, *eat, eat, eat.*

I told myself I'd just have one pilot biscuit, and maybe the equivalent of a thimble's worth of gorp.

Five minutes later, my rations were gone, and I had sixty or so hours of my solo to go.

On the last day of Outward Bound, when we had descended to the base-camp area where we'd begun, our instructors had us trade our hiking boots for sneakers and sent us out on a thirteen-mile run: a half marathon. The point was to show us that after all the fasting, hiking and climbing, we were in fantastic shape.

I finished the run without pause.

The next day I saw a mirror for the first time in more than three weeks. I only half-recognized the person staring back at me. He was bearded, something I'd never been. And he was lean: yes, lean. His face seemed longer than mine. I liked the looks of him.

Back in Connecticut, I called Beth, telling her how horrible Outward Bound had been—and how it was the best thing I'd ever done. I prattled on about a genuine sense of accomplishment and about how true Dan's words had turned out to be.

She hurried me to the punch. "How much weight did you lose?" she asked.

I hadn't stepped on a scale, so I couldn't give her a number. But I told her: "I think I'm as close to skinny as I'll ever be."

There was a moment's silence. "I'm thinking of going out for women's crew," she said, talking about freshman year. "Imagine how many calories that must burn!"

A lot, I guessed. But *crew?* That seemed drastic.

To keep my newly lean Outward Bound form, I'd have to come up with something else.

Yo-Yo Me

Five

To be a successful bulimic, you need to have a firm handle on the bathrooms in your life: their proximity to where you're eating; the amount of privacy they offer; whether—if they're public bathrooms with more than one stall—you can hear the door swing open and the footfall of a visitor with enough advance notice to stop what you're doing and keep from being found out.

You need to be conscious of time. There's no such thing as bulimia on the fly; a span of at least ten minutes in the bathroom is optimal, because you may need five of them to linger at the sink, splash cold water on your face and let the redness in it die down. You should always carry a toothbrush and toothpaste, integral to eliminating telltale signs of your transgression and to rejoining polite society without any offense to it. Bulimia is a logistical and tactical challenge as much as anything else. It demands planning.

My preferred bathroom was in a back corner of the student union at Carolina, right above the office of the campus newspaper, where I was first a movie and music critic, then the assistant arts editor, and then—toward the end of freshman year—an editorial writer. It was a public bathroom with multiple stalls, but the stalls were a decent distance from the door, and the door opened noisily. Few people used this bathroom, anyway. I could walk to it in about three minutes from the university cafeteria, so neither lunch nor dinner had to sit in my stomach for long. I could get there even faster from the newspaper offices, where I spent many hours a day, and where I'd sometimes eat a slice of pizza or a half tuna salad sandwich too many. With a quick jaunt up the stairs, these excesses could be erased.

I thought that I was clever—that I was doing something lots of other people would if they just had the nerve, the poise, the industry. I knew it was supposed to be dangerous: I'd read stories in newspapers and magazines about this behavior, always characterized as a disorder, an affliction. It was these stories that had given me the idea. From them I concluded that people who threw up their meals tended to get carried away with what was an otherwise solid, tenable plan, especially if they fell prey to anorexia as well, and I was an unlikely candidate for that. Even a fast of merely three days had foiled me. But if a person just threw up the occasional meal, the meal that had gotten out of hand, well, what was the harm in that?

And consider the *benefits*. My willpower could waver, I could gobble down more than I had meant to, and I wouldn't have to go to bed haunted by the looming toll on my waistline, or wake up the next morning owing the gods of weight management even more of a sacrifice than I had owed them the day before. Throwing up was my safety valve. My mulligan.

It usually happened like this: I'd go to the cafeteria, begin to assemble my dinner. I'd get a salad, or something similarly virtuous. I'd pick at it slowly, hoisting the picayune cherry tomatoes and wan slices of cucumber into my mouth one at a time, in slow motion, and then chewing and chewing and chewing, as if there were some odometer rigged to my jaw and I could stave off hunger by pushing the numbers on it high enough.

There'd be a few jagged cubes of feta in the salad, each one an event

I would pause and savor for half a minute. They and the croutons, all four of them, were islands of excitement in a dead sea.

Upon finishing the salad, I wouldn't be anywhere close to satisfied. I wouldn't be in the same *hemisphere* as satisfied. And the sound of that dissatisfaction, like a drumbeat in the center of my brain, would grow louder and louder.

Pum-pum. I could have had a burger. I had seen the cafeteria workers cooking burgers on a griddle. There were burgers to be ordered. I could have had one.

Pum-PUM. Macaroni and cheese. There'd been macaroni and cheese. It looked sort of congealed and stiff at the edges. I love it when it's sort of congealed and stiff at the edges.

PUM-PUM. Remember the smell of the hot oil that still clung to the fried chicken on the food line? And the way the chicken seemed to have a *palpable* crispness? And yet . . . and yet . . . the breading didn't look all *that* thick. Could one piece, a breast, hurt so much? Hadn't Mom always said that white meat was less caloric than dark?

I'd go back to the food line. I'd get a fried chicken breast. I'd eat it, and then I'd worry—no, I'd conclude—that I'd miscalculated. That I'd eaten too much, and would have to get rid of some of what I'd eaten. This decision made, I'd get an ice cream sandwich. And a cookie. Two cookies, actually. If I was going to empty my stomach—if I was going to go through all of that messy, beet-faced trouble—I might as well make the most of the buildup, might as well acknowledge and address all my cravings and satisfy them. That way, I'd be less tempted the next day. I'd be less likely to need to throw up.

Off to the second-floor bathroom in the back corner of the student union I'd go. I'd walk in, listen for the sounds of anyone else, bend down and glance under the stalls to check for feet, making sure the coast was clear. I'd stop briefly at the sink, turn on the water and moisten the index and middle fingers on my right hand, so that they'd slide more easily down my throat. Two fingers were better than one. They brought the gagging on faster.

I'd enter one of the stalls and kneel down. I knew just how far down my throat to push the two fingers, just where and how long to tickle it. Once the food started coming up, I could pretty much will my throat to stay open and the food not to stop. Heaves built on themselves, one setting off another.

Sometimes I'd have to probe and tickle my throat a second time, sometimes not. I could tell when I'd purged enough, because I could taste the flavors of what I'd eaten in reverse. I could gauge whether anything was still left in my stomach.

Although I never persuaded myself that what I was doing was normal or meaningless, I was consoled by the fact that I seldom did it more than once every other day, and never twice on the same day. In a strange way I was consoled as well by my speed and efficiency when I did do it, by how undisruptive it was. It was a like a special talent, a nifty trick. I wondered: What other tricks might I try?

I'd read that bulimics sometimes took laxatives as well, and from those stories I'd wrung another unintended moral: managed correctly, this practice, too, could be useful. It could be smart—if deployed only in special circumstances, in emergencies.

An emergency came along. A big party was three days away, and the diet I'd vowed to start four days earlier hadn't quite come together. So I bought bars of chocolate-flavored Ex-Lax and took twice the recommended dosage. I knew that it would eliminate only waste—food already digested—but that meant there'd be less mass in my body. Wouldn't that make me look thinner? Or at least *feel* thinner?

It did, so I kept the Ex-Lax around for the next emergency, and then bought some more Ex-Lax for the emergency after that.

For this reason, too, it paid to know where the good bathrooms on campus were.

Before I'd arrived at Carolina, I'd vowed to stop doing one thing and start doing another. These twinned resolutions had a shared effect. My worry about my weight actually intensified.

What I was stopping was swimming. I just couldn't stare anymore through foggy goggles at that thick black line on the bottom of the pool. And while I promised myself that I'd find some replacement exercise, I wasn't sure what it would be, or how devoted to it I'd become. It certainly wouldn't absorb as many hours a week—and burn as many calories a week—as swimming had, so I'd have to eat much less.

Especially because of what I was determined to start: dating. In prep school I'd told myself that once I got to college, I'd be candid about what I felt—about who I *was*—and keep an eye out for other young gay men. I was sure I'd find at least a few at a school as big as Carolina. And I assumed that the chances of a romance with one of them boiled down to how heavy I was. It was Häagen-Dazs or love. I couldn't have both.

But in the first weeks at school, Häagen-Dazs wasn't easy to avoid. There was a Häagen-Dazs parlor on Franklin Street, the commercial stretch that ran along one edge of the university, and Häagen-Dazs pints were sold in freezer cases scattered around campus. Pizza was even harder to get away from: one or another student in my dorm got a delivery from Pizza Hut or Domino's seemingly every ten minutes after noon. On top of that there were fried-chicken biscuits, beer, egg and cheese biscuits, beer, pulled-pork sandwiches, beer, ramen noodles with jar tomato sauce, and beer. The freshman *fifteen?* By the end of two weeks of freshman orientation, I was on a pace to accomplish a freshman twenty-five, partly because the baseline of my post–Outward Bound weight was such an unusually slender one for me, but mostly because I was unsettled and anxious and seldom more than an arm's length from something tasty and filling enough to calm me down.

I signed up for a physical education class, a twice-weekly regimen of calisthenics that had the additional benefit of fulfilling some requirement. At the first meeting of the class, the teacher talked about something called a body fat index, then produced a contraption with pinchers to grab and measure any folds of fat around our waists. We had to roll up our T-shirts so the measurement could be made. I registered a higher body fat index than half of the other students. And dropped the class later that same day.

Then I became a vegetarian, figuring I wouldn't have to be vigilant about how much I ate if I limited the categories of food I allowed myself. When friends got hamburgers, I got grilled cheese. I ate plain pizza instead of pepperoni. Okay, so I sometimes ate five or six slices, but wasn't the food I was giving my body supposed to be easier to digest than meat, and wouldn't my body respond by digesting and getting rid of it more easily? I believed that for about four weeks, after which point it became clear that my particular approach to vegetarianism wasn't making me thin. The size 33 pants that were loose on me just after Outward Bound had worked their way to the far back of my dorm-room closet.

One night about midway through the fall semester, I sat alone in my room—my roommate was away somewhere—and reeled from a night of too many and too much of *everything*: plastic cups of beer from a keg at some outdoor mixer for Morehead scholars; pizza with a few of them on Franklin Street; ice cream (three scoops) from the Häagen-Dazs parlor where I'd gone by myself, on an eating roll that I didn't want to interrupt. I was angry at myself. I felt slightly queasy, the booze and the ice cream waging a little war with each other in my stomach. I worried that I'd throw up.

And then, a split second later, without any conscious transition, I *hoped* I'd throw up. It hit me: if I threw up, the evening's eating would be expunged.

I was already on the precipice of getting sick. With a little effort, could I get myself over the edge?

Yes, yes, I could.

By the time the semester was over and I headed home for the holidays, I was terrific at it.

D o you want lasagna?" Mom asked me on my first day back in Avon. "I don't really care," I told her.

"I bet Mark will want lasagna," she said. "Mark always wants lasagna." In fact Mom had begun making lasagna for the entire Amherst College swimming team. Anytime the team had a competition anywhere near Avon, she insisted that Mark, his teammates and his coaches stop by for dinner on the way back to school. She made lasagna for forty to fifty. By carefully mapping out the process and doing much of the preparation in advance, she was able to watch all but the last thirty minutes of the competition, race home ahead of the swimmers and have the lasagna ready for them within forty-five minutes of the team's bus pulling into our driveway. It was an impressive feat, and she knew it. She reveled in it.

"Lasagna's fine," I said.

"I'll make enough for leftovers," Mom said, "since you and Mark will be home for a while. What do *you* want? Do you want chicken divan? You must want chicken divan."

Mom had this ridiculous recipe for chicken divan—involving not just sherry and sour cream but also cans of Campbell's cream of mushroom soup and buttered Ritz cracker crumbs—that had an effect on me not unlike that of violin music on the Frankenstein monster. Whenever she made chicken divan, the rest of the family ate about half the pan. Over the course of dinner and then a snack two hours later and then another snack two hours after that, I took care of the rest. Chicken divan didn't have a shelf life in our house. I saw to that.

Since Mark and I were now in college and couldn't avail ourselves

Me, my parents and my siblings during my college years.
I'm suddenly and magically the thin one.

regularly of her food, Mom treated our holiday visits as Make-A-Wish Foundation moments, only all the wishes involved eating. She cooked anything and everything she assumed we wanted: lasagna, chicken divan, club sandwiches, chicken livers wrapped in bacon, scallops wrapped in bacon, and her newest experiment in bacon wrapping, *hot dogs* wrapped in bacon, which were arguably as close as she could come to wrapping bacon in bacon without being flagrantly redundant. Before she would wrap the hot dogs in bacon, she'd use a knife to carve grooves in them and fill the grooves with cheese. Her pig-on-pig action apparently needed a little cow.

Something else, too, had joined her repertoire: homemade Egg McMuffins. One of the glories of Mom's approach to cooking was that she could get just as excited by lowbrow dishes as highbrow ones, bringing as much passion and precision to a faithful, by-the-numbers replica of a fast-food classic as to something torn from the pages of Julia Child. Although her beef Wellington was superb, her *coquilles St. Jacques* estimable, and her manicotti so fluffy and light they were fit for angels, she felt no greater vanity about these dishes than about her chicken divan or her bacon-wrapped hot dogs.

Or her Egg McMuffins. She thought it was a kick on weekend mornings to have an electric warming basket—the kind used for dinner rolls—filled with the foil-wrapped egg and Canadian bacon sandwiches associated with on-the-run, on-the-road breakfasts of extreme convenience.

"Aren't mine *better*?" she'd ask my siblings and me or our friends— she especially liked to make Egg McMuffins if friends had slept over. She'd note that the English muffins on her Egg McMuffins were crisper than those on the ones at McDonald's, and the egg in one of hers was less flat and dried out, as if besting a fast-food chain were a laudable triumph. Sometimes she'd offer to poach the egg to order, so that it had a firm yolk or a soft, runny one: take your pick!

"You don't have to have one of the McMuffins from the warmer," she'd tell an overnight guest—overnight guests always got extra-special culinary treatment—as she gestured to the basket in which the already-made McMuffins sat. "I'll make a fresh one!"

While waiting for an answer, she'd tilt her head back and take a long swig of Diet Rite, from her third can in two hours.

Dad, overhearing the conversation from his desk in the nearby study, would shout: "I ate *my* McMuffin from the warmer!" He was shading the truth. He hadn't stopped at just one McMuffin.

Mom would pretend not to hear him. "Soft yolk or hard yolk?" she'd ask the guest, sometimes adding, gratuitously: "McDonald's doesn't give you that choice."

After the guest departed, as Mom tidied the kitchen, she'd say, "I bet your friend doesn't get McMuffins like that at home."

Dad, taking a break from his work in the study, would wrap her in a hug and say, "Nobody has a mom like your mom, huh? Nobody."

Then he'd ask her if she'd decided what we were having for dinner. It was already ten a.m., after all. How could he plan the day's eating if he didn't know?

On my winter break from Carolina, I ate whatever Mom made, because this was vacation, and because the bathroom that connected my and Mark's bedrooms was a very safe place. I'd lock the door on his side, so he wouldn't walk in. I'd turn on the stereo in my room and set the volume to a level slightly louder than usual, to conceal any gagging or choking, but not so loud that Mom would show up to complain. I'd heave to the strains of Duran Duran's "Hungry Like the Wolf"—the cheeky choice was deliberate—or Tom Petty's "Don't Do Me Like That."

At Grandma's house on Christmas Eve, she asked me if I missed her all the way down in North Carolina.

"Constantly," I said.

She put another cutlet on my plate.

Aunt Vicki asked me how I liked my roommate.

"He's OK," I said.

She gave me a tin of brownies for the road.

Aunt Carolyn asked me what I was going to major in.

"English, probably," I said.

She wrapped up an assortment of Christmas cookies for me.

Almost a month into the spring semester, by which time I'd almost forgotten about him, Scott called.

I had met him—sort of—just before the Christmas break, at a party in the offices of the *Daily Tar Heel*. He'd come with two of the women on staff, and all night long we'd thrown looks at each other, but we'd never managed to talk. I'd subsequently learned his name from the women, and he'd apparently learned mine, along with my phone number. Because here he was, on the other end of the line, asking me if I wanted to come over to his apartment for a drink sometime.

I did, and made a point of setting the date a solid week into the future, so I could get ready for it. Every day leading up to it, I went to the track, and each time I ran more than two miles, pushing myself up to three, even three and a half.

I took Ex-Lax. One day I took too much—nearly quadruple the recommended dose—and a few hours later, while walking across campus, had to stop, steady myself against a tree and press every relevant muscle into the service of warding off catastrophe. This was crazy, I told myself. I had gone too far. I had to shape up. From now on, I pledged, never more than three times the recommended dose.

With the date approaching, I didn't just want to be smaller. I *had* to be smaller, because if I got my wish and got to see and feel another person's body in the way I wanted to, I'd have to let him see and feel mine. I'd be more exposed than I'd been in a Speedo; I'd have no floppy T-shirt or billowing towel to run to. I was as terrified as I was excited.

By date night I didn't feel as thin as I'd hoped to, so I wore a bulky black Windbreaker over my clothes.

"Let me take your coat," Scott said.

"That's OK," I said, insisting that I was cold.

We went into the kitchen to pour ourselves some wine. I kept the coat on.

We sat down on the living room couch to talk, me still in my coat.

We stretched out on the living room carpet and started kissing.

"Aren't you going to take off your coat?" he asked, maybe noticing the sweat along my hairline.

I mumbled something about being cold, though there was clearly no reason I should be. We were indoors. The heat was on. Scott and his roommate weren't behind on their utility bills.

I willed him to stop asking about the coat. As long as I kept it on, he couldn't get a good sense of my body and possibly discover that I wasn't as trim as he'd hoped I was and as I meant to be.

He fumbled with the coat's zipper. I escaped briefly to the bathroom. He tugged at the coat's arm. I swatted his hand away. After an hour and a half I couldn't stand the heat and the awkwardness anymore. There was no alternative: I left. I figured I'd never hear from him again.

I did. We went back to his apartment and this time the coat came off, partly because I'd been better about eating and exercising in the interim, mostly because I was an eighteen-year-old male and my desire for sex won out over my desire to conceal whatever that calisthenics-class pincher had grabbed hold of and measured.

We dated for a month, after which I dated Joe for two weeks, then Mike for three. And the rapid-fire sequence of Scott and Joe and Mike meant that I ate less. I ran more. And in a pinch I threw up: sometimes every few days, sometimes just once a week. It depended on my excesses, and on how soon my next sleepover with Scott and then Joe and then Mike was. I believed—no, was *certain*—that a pound too many could change everything, and that some crucial junctures demanded a special effort. At those junctures, not throwing up would be nothing less than defeatist.

I often ate dinner with Abigail or with Jared, or with Abigail *and* Jared, my closest friends during freshman year. Abigail was my stand-in for Beth, another looker adept at weaving an air of melodrama around her. In her case, that skill was being honed for professional use: she planned to major in theater. She spent much of her time at auditions and rehearsals for campus productions. She spent much of the rest of it telling Jared and me about those auditions and rehearsals.

She had delicate moods and a way of making grand pronouncements about them. One night she pleaded for a change in our plans to go to a late-night movie, saying she would rather just drink some wine in one of our dorm rooms and talk.

"I'm just so *emotionally fatigued*," she explained, and the phrase stayed with me for months—for years—because I wasn't sure how emotional fatigue differed from garden-variety exhaustion, or a hangover, except that it was what people as sensitive and soulful as Abigail suffered.

So we talked: about how well her face, which was like a prettier version of Kelly McGillis's, photographed; about how lucky she was to have such long, dark, wavy hair; about how unlucky she was to have hips slightly wider and thighs slightly bigger than those of the scrawny blond graduate student who got an ingénue part that Abigail had gone after.

"I think she's sleeping with the director," Abigail said, parroting the plaint of frustrated actresses since the Stone Age.

Jared was the gay man I wanted to be: quick with a quip, confident in his charms, slight enough to wear plaids and horizontal stripes. I was too intimidated by him to want more than his friendship, but I wanted that desperately. I wanted his insight and inside knowledge: over the fall semester, he had learned and retained a library's worth of information about seemingly every openly and secretly gay student. He'd point to a waiter in a restaurant on Franklin Street and tell me about another waiter in a nearby restaurant who was sleeping with him. He'd point to an effeminate sophomore strolling across the main quad and tell me which black diva he'd dressed up as for the annual drag pageant at the gay bar near campus that I frequented—that *we* frequented, together. Jared had been the one to introduce me to it. Whenever we went, he made a dozen new friends and left with a half dozen promising phone numbers. I was lucky if I screwed up the courage to talk to the bartender.

Our dinners with Abigail happened about twice a week, usually somewhere on Franklin Street, where a meal could be cobbled together almost as cheaply as in the student cafeteria. Whether we ate Chinese, pub grub or Mexican, Jared picked at his food. Abigail could go either way—eating a lot, eating a little—and always explained why she was veering in one direction or the other. There are unexamined lives and examined lives, and then there are actors' lives, examined in real time, out loud and ad infinitum, provided that there's an audience at hand. Jared and I were an obliging audience.

But it wasn't an obligation. It was a privilege, to be sitting in a booth at Sadlack's, a deli on Franklin Street that served gigantic submarine sandwiches, with Jared and Abigail, each so commanding, each so self-possessed. I felt bigger around them, but in a good way.

"Be right back," I said one night, clambering out of our booth and heading to the bathroom in the back of the restaurant.

I'd eaten too much: a whole tuna submarine, when half would have been more than enough. No way was I going to let all of that linger in my stomach. The bathroom at Sadlack's was for one person only, and it locked, so I had the privacy I needed. I ran water from the sink to camouflage any sound I might make. I got to work immediately. I kept getting speedier and speedier at this.

Within forty-five seconds the sandwich was gone. I flushed the toilet, then went to the sink and scooped some cold water into my mouth to rinse it. I splashed some water on my face. I studied myself in the mirror. I needed to wait a bit longer before returning to the booth. I was still too red.

After a minute, I made a fresh appraisal: pink now. Much better. Almost there.

Thirty seconds later, I was good to go. My eyes were still watery, and faintly bloodshot. But how much of a giveaway, really, was that? Eyes could look the way mine did for any number of reasons. Allergies. Dirty contact lenses. Those were two reasons right off the top of my head.

Jared and Abigail weren't talking when I returned. And they were looking at each other in a puffed-up, purposeful way. Then they were looking at me.

"So," Jared asked, "did it taste as good coming up as it did going down?"

"What?" I asked, going through his words one at a time, twice over. Could they have a meaning other than the obvious one? Could he be asking about something other than what I'd just done in the bathroom?

I didn't think so, but I didn't cop to anything right away. I feigned confusion.

Jared rolled his eyes.

Abigail threw back her hair, all Rita-Hayworth-in-*Gilda*-like. "Do you really think we don't know what's happening when you disappear into the bathroom the minute you stop eating?" she asked.

"When do I do that?" I asked, trying for a tone of indignation, because that's how the falsely accused were supposed to sound.

"Um, I don't know, maybe *half the time we eat with you*," Jared said.

"So I go to the bathroom!" I said.

"And come back looking like you've been hit by food poisoning," Abigail said. She emphasized and drew out the words "food poisoning." Abigail didn't just speak; she delivered lines.

I slumped. "You know," I said, "it's not such a bad thing."

"Tell that to Karen Carpenter," said Jared. She'd died that February. I'd read some of the articles. I'd actually taken a weird sort of comfort from them, because they included details like her possible use of ipecac to make herself vomit. I'd never even heard of ipecac before. The articles included pictures of her looking cadaverous. I'd need another *two* Outward Bound courses and a week of protein shakes to close in on bony.

But, truth be told, the articles—or, rather, the accompanying sidebars and television chatter about eating disorders—did spook me a little. They went through the effects this bulimia thing could have on your skin (bad), hair (worse), gums (eek!) and fingernails (nasty). For me the whole point of throwing up was to look better, and I was having trouble ignoring the prospect of looking worse if I kept at it long enough. A slim worse, true. A worse with—potentially—a thirty-two-inch waist. But worse all the same. That wasn't my intent.

And now Jared and Abigail were telling me I wasn't even succeeding in keeping my throwing up a secret. This was an additional problem. Not necessarily in terms of my relationship with the two of them: I suspected that at some level they found my bulimia interesting, and found me more interesting because of it. It was the kind of neurotic flaw in a person that amused Jared and the kind of personal mini-drama that mirrored Abigail's own tumultuous sense of self.

But if the two of them knew about me, who *else* did? I apparently didn't have full control over that, and that wasn't okay with me at all. No one was going to admire or want to sleep with a person known to be thin only by dint of regular vomiting. That person was destined instead to be the object of tittering, the butt of jokes.

"It's really pretty gross," Abigail said at one point, and I couldn't quibble. I'd persuaded myself that it was resourceful, but I always knew that it was disgusting. And at this point it was, indisputably, a habit. I hadn't planned on letting that happen.

So that was that: I'd stop. And I did, for the most part. Although there'd occasionally be a pig-out so preposterous that I couldn't let it be or an imminent event so skinniness-demanding that I had to draw on every skinny-making tactic available, I threw up less and less, until I wasn't throwing up at all anymore. I also stopped keeping a store of laxatives around. It was impossible to acknowledge the grossness of the vomiting without acknowledging that this other waste disposal project wasn't so pretty, either.

Six

You could see the movie *Flashdance* and marvel at the moxie of the single gal, welding steel by day and stoking lust by night. You could see *Flashdance* and wonder at the ability of a Giorgio Moroder score and an Irene Cara theme song to hold together a threadbare, derivative plot: the distaff *Rocky*, *Cinderella* with a blowtorch.

Or you could see *Flashdance* and think, *a bicycle! I need to get a bicycle!* That's what the Jennifer Beals character used to propel herself through smoky, gritty Pittsburgh, burning calories and developing muscle tone all day long. The movie didn't exactly present her mode of transit as a considered beauty regimen; what *Flashdance* was telegraphing was her scrappy determination to make do on a budget too tight for a two-door hatchback. But I detected an additional message—and a profoundly useful one at that. Jennifer looked that good and danced that well because of that bicycle. No doubt about it.

So I bought one toward the end of the summer between freshman and sophomore year, the summer when *Flashdance* ruled the box office. I saw the movie three times, in part to be sure I was fully processing the immense life wisdom it had to share, and in part because I was doing a summer internship in Minneapolis, had somehow ended up in an apartment in a sleepy suburb and was going bonkers with boredom. The internship involved observing police officers at work—the Morehead scholarship administrators thought this would help us understand society better—and I spent hour upon tedious hour riding in the backseats of police cruisers that responded to 911 calls. The cops I accompanied never seemed to catch a homicide or anything like that. They caught domestic disturbances, and left me in the car as they entered yet another home for yet another session of marriage counseling that, as they practiced it, involved handcuffs, headlocks and restraining orders.

The bicycle I bought upon returning to Chapel Hill had ten speeds. It was deep purple and sleek. It had a cradle for a water bottle, because I'd be needing big restorative gulps of fluid to stay hydrated as I pedaled and pedaled, traveling everywhere on the strength of my ever-pumping legs, a metabolic furnace with no off switch. Although I brought my father's old four-door Mercury Grand Marquis, more tanker than sedan, to school with me that year, I intended to use it only for select nighttime excursions, or long weekend trips, or major shopping, the kind that entailed large objects or bags. Otherwise, I'd be on the bike. I'd be all about the bike.

I was living off campus, in an apartment instead of a dorm room, with a theater major I'd met through Abigail and a computer sciences major I'd met through Jared. Our building was just under five miles from campus: a totally workable bike ride. Just outside the building's entrance stood a bike rack where I could park and lock my bike. Part of the route from there to campus was a bona fide bike trail. Everything was falling into place.

But on the first day of class, I had a bonehead's epiphany: North Carolina's late-summer, early-fall weather—as steamy as a Turkish bath—wasn't well suited to a bike ride of more than a few blocks, not unless you were okay with arriving at your Shakespeare class looking like someone had just taken a hose to you.

So for the month of September I parked the bike, trading it for Dad's old tanker. I took the bike out again in October, when I was educated in another of its drawbacks, one unrelated to weather: helmet hair. I had untamable helmet hair. And while such an unruly tangle had worked for Jennifer Beals, it looked laughable on me.

So much for the bike. Onward I went, but not on two wheels.

That was the story of college: one obsession after another; an advance followed by a retreat; a breakthrough dissolving into a setback. It was a reprise of the years preceding it and an omen of the years to come. It could be broken down into the forces and schemes that propelled me toward thinness and the obstacles and quirks that tugged me in the opposite direction.

Into which category did Mom fall?

She and Dad came to visit sophomore year. Mom had seen Carolina before, when she'd dropped me off freshman year. Dad hadn't. Mom had probably made him feel guilty about it, in accordance with one of the tried-and-true dynamics of their marriage. She would volunteer to relieve him of some burden concerning us children, then make him feel guilty about not being as attuned to our lives as she was. He would snap to, and she would gloat about having made that happen.

In a telephone conversation before their visit, she said to me, "Don't mention it to him, but I told your father." She didn't need to be any more specific. This was the latest chapter in an ongoing and, by this point, comical saga titled, "Mom Takes Control of Frank's Being Gay."

She had figured out the truth about me shortly before my high school graduation, or rather she had read the truth about me in a letter from Ann that I had made the mistake of leaving out on my bedroom desk. ("I was cleaning your messy room because you never do," Mom said, turning the tables so that she was the aggrieved party, "and the word 'gay' just *leapt* out at me.") After her discovery she had told me that while she could deal with it, she wasn't so sure about my siblings and father. She made me promise that I wouldn't test them with this information just yet.

Then, during a phone conversation about a month into my freshman year, she announced: "I saw a window of opportunity, and I told your brother Mark."

A few months after that, she had an update.

"There was a good moment," she reported, "so I told your brother Harry."

But she remained steadfast: Dad must not-not-not be told. Until, that is, she simply went ahead and told him, after which point she instituted a new rule. I must not-not-not force Dad to engage in an actual conversation about what he now knew.

In any case, Mom's main alert in advance of their visit to Carolina sophomore year wasn't about that. It was about her and Dad's diets. They'd lost a lot of weight, she crowed.

They both looked significantly slimmer than when I'd seen them months before, and they had brought with them some of the little snacks and props to which they attributed their progress: that edible cardboard known as Wasa bread, which Mom convincingly pretended to enjoy, and some weird yellowish powder that the diet center they were attending recommended as a seasoning for vegetables and skinless, fatless meats. It was supposed to emulate salt and butter without transmitting their sins.

"Salt is *terrible* for you," Mom said. We were in a restaurant on Franklin Street, a nicer, more expensive restaurant than the Chinese place or Sadlack's or my other usual hangouts. She made a grand gesture of pushing the salt shaker to a far corner of the table. Dad's eyes followed it as if he were watching a golf putt go astray or noticing that one of his stacked television-time Eskimo Pies had melted before he got to it.

"Just *terrible* for you," Mom reiterated, and then she elaborated, as if answering a question I had not, in fact, asked.

"One, salt bloats you," she explained. "Two, it makes you thirsty, and thirst can be confused with hunger, and in any case you wind up drinking or eating more than your body needs or even wants to. That's why they have pretzels and salty nuts on bars. That's why there's so much salt in McDonald's food."

So she had banished salt. Well, she had *mostly* banished salt. This diet center she was attending also prohibited diet colas, on account of their sodium content, but telling Mom she couldn't have diet colas was like telling an aardvark "no more ants." It just wasn't going to fly.

She had also taken up aerobics. This I'd seen firsthand during a recent visit home, because she'd lassoed me into going to a class with her, no doubt wanting an audience for the various leg kicks and abdomen crunches, at which she'd become shockingly adept. Even so, she was closing in on fifty, had carried and delivered four children and had ridden her own roller-coaster of weight gains and losses. It showed. And watching her do her squats and squeezes in a leotard—well, there are experiences even the closest of mothers and sons shouldn't share.

We were indeed close, and she was indeed a sharer. When I was thirteen and fourteen and fifteen, she passed along steamy Sidney Sheldon novels and lurid serial-killer books as soon as she finished reading them, raving about what page-turners they were. We'd debate the relative merits of *The Other Side of Midnight* versus *The Stranger in the Mirror* versus *Bloodline*. When I was fourteen and fifteen and sixteen, I made her take me to R-rated movies, and sometimes, during the sex scenes, she'd nudge me and tell me what she found plausible and what she didn't.

We always argued over which movies we'd go to, she wanting something melodramatic and escapist, I wanting something gritty and "slice-of-life," as the reviewers said.

"I don't need slice-of-life," she'd protest. "I *live* slice-of-life." Her particular slice wasn't one of noteworthy hardship, though Mom had always taken on so many volunteer assignments, done so many favors for our school classes and swim teams, typed up so many of our term papers and handled so much of Dad's personal business that her days were crammed with obligations and deadlines. In fact, she usually had to limit herself to five hours of sleep in order to get her pulp fiction in.

During her and my father's trip to Chapel Hill my sophomore year, she and I breached a new frontier in sharing: she actually tried to get me a date. She stayed on a few days longer than Dad, and she and I had lunch one afternoon at Pyewacket, a vegetarian restaurant where I'd been introduced to the glories of hummus. Mom and I ate a vegetarian lasagna, made with spinach noodles and a béchamel sauce. As we did, she noticed the way I was looking at our waiter.

She leaned across the table, motioned me to lean in, too, and whispered: "You think he's cute, don't you?"

I nodded.

"Me, too," she said. Mom loved stuff like this. She loved entering into conspiratorial modes and confidential pacts about topics normally outside the bounds of a parent-child relationship.

I started to lean back, figuring we were done. She motioned me forward anew.

"Is he?" she asked.

I played dumb. "Is he what?"

"You know," she said. Although we were whispering, she was nonetheless wary of speaking the word "gay." She may well have thought she was respecting my privacy; it would take her a long time to understand that I really didn't care. But she also had objections to the way "gay" had become a synonym for "homosexual." She occasionally complained that a once-innocuous term had been hijacked and turned into something freighted. And she sometimes refused to participate in that.

I thought about pressing on with my charade of confusion and making her utter the dread syllable, but I relented.

"I'm pretty sure he is," I told her.

"How do you figure something like that out?" she asked.

"There are signs," I said. "The sway in his walk. The floppy wrists."

"Stop it," she said.

"There are telltale birthmarks," I said.

"I'm serious!" she protested. "How?"

"Every time our eyes met," I said, "he held the gaze for a good four to six seconds. I figure anything over three seconds can't be an accident. I figure the odds are very, very good that he doesn't have a poster of Farrah Fawcett in a swimsuit on his bedroom wall."

"But *you* once had a poster of Farrah Fawcett on *your* bedroom wall," she reminded me.

"That was when she was an icon," I explained, "and that was about her hair."

Mom shook her head and sighed. Her children's worlds confused her. My world in particular.

At the end of lunch, when she was about to pay the bill, she noticed that the restaurant's credit card form had not only a line for a signature but also a line for a phone number—some sort of security measure. She pushed the form, the credit card and the pen toward me.

"You sign it," she said. "That way you can write in your phone number. And he'll have it, in case he wants to call." She said all of this in an excited voice, immensely proud of herself.

I rolled my eyes, as if the possibility of a call from the waiter was immaterial to me and I deemed her little scheme ridiculous. I didn't. Signing the form and writing out my number, I grew exhilarated at both the prospect that he might get in touch with me and at the goofiness of Mom having a role in it.

He never called. But the lunch at Pyewacket did have a payoff: Mom found a recipe for a vegetarian lasagna similar to the restaurant's and started making it, though her version was cheesier, runnier—in sum, more caloric. I once came home from college to a whole pan of it. It was gone within two days. As good as it tasted warm, it tasted even better cold, around two a.m., slid quietly from its shelf in the refrigerator so that no one would know that I was still up, so that no one would know that I was still eating.

In my off-campus apartment that sophomore year I never made anything as ambitious as vegetarian lasagna. I never really cooked. I toasted bread for Swiss cheese sandwiches, which I slathered with mayonnaise, and I popped popcorn in butter-flavored Crisco, a method one of my two roommates taught me. These were my late-night snacks, the possible compensations for—or add-ons to—whatever food I'd avoided or surrendered to during the day.

It was a year of drift. I lost touch with emotional-fatigue Abigail, who sank deeper and deeper into the subculture of theater rats as I cast my lot with the would-be Woodwards, Trillins and Kaels at the newspaper. Jared was still good for weekend trips to the gay bar in Durham and for weeknight conversations about guys pursued, guys surrendered, guys beyond reach and guys spotted buying pore-minimizing makeup at the Clinique counter. But I saw less of him, too: he'd moved farther off campus than I had and made frequent trips home to a rural area in the southern part of the state.

As an English major I slogged wearily through *Beowulf*, *The Canterbury Tales* and *The Faerie Queen*. At the campus newspaper, I focused on writing editorials, promulgating opinions I didn't know I had until I was called upon to have them. And, periodically, I ate too much, my vigilance waning, my willpower faltering, my waist expanding.

I hadn't replaced my aborted bike riding with a different form of regular exercise, and by the end of spring semester I was down to just two pairs of pants that fit me: burgundy corduroys, their color fading fast, and forest green corduroys, their color fading faster.

What awful timing. This wasn't the summer to be fat, to look frumpy. The Morehead Foundation had arranged an internship for me in New York City, where I'd be working as a fact-checker and sometime reporter for writers at *Newsweek* magazine. *Newsweek* magazine! In New York City! I'd hobnob with real journalists, real *magazine writers*, writers whose names were known to millions of readers around the country, writers who granted movies their acclaim and books their best-seller status and politicians their moments of glory. At night, I wouldn't be hunkered down with Jennifer Beals at a suburban multiplex. I'd be lining up outside exclusive nightclubs. I'd be seeing Broadway plays.

And I'd be doing all of this, it seemed, in burgundy or forest green corduroys.

What *now*? Buying new pants was out of the question, because that would mean buying bigger pants, and *that* would mean reconciling myself to a heavier, broader me, and the heavier, broader me would be gone in a week, wouldn't it? I'd do a three-day fast, and I'd do it better than I had with Beth during senior year at Loomis. Or maybe a two-day fast. Or at least a juice fast, every other day. Or five straight days of protein-powder shakes, with no ice cream in them and no peanut butter, or only a tablespoon.

But for the first month of my internship at *Newsweek*, before I crammed into a Downtown Manhattan loft with six other Carolina students doing summer internships in the city, I commuted to Midtown Manhattan from White Plains, where I stayed with Uncle Mario and Aunt Carolyn. And Uncle Mario and Aunt Carolyn did what Brunis playing host to guests always do, even if the guest is a close family member who ostensibly doesn't need to be impressed, and even if the guest doesn't budge for nearly a month. They fed me, constantly and lavishly.

Taking a page from Grandma, Aunt Carolyn did much of her serious cooking in a separate kitchen that she had installed in the basement of her house. It was there she would go, this blond-haired, blue-eyed, all-American girl from a farm in Indiana, to dredge chicken cutlets through bread crumbs and Parmesan and then lower them into sizzling oil. The cutlets would be waiting for me when I returned from a day at *Newsweek*, and they were better than Grandma's, better than Mom's, though I kept mum about that. I was a glutton, not an imbecile.

Aunt Carolyn had asked my mother for the recipes of some of my favorite dishes, and she made them for me: chicken divan, beef Stroganoff. Uncle Mario would open a bottle of red wine, and after a glass or two, I'd have an easier time convincing myself that a third helping of the chicken wasn't such a bad idea. Grandma might drop by, or we'd pay her a visit: the drive was about ten minutes. On those occasions the quantity of food expanded, because neither Aunt Carolyn nor Grandma could let the other woman run away with the show.

My corduroys were getting snugger, and they were still all I had. I would march into *Newsweek*—into these offices filled with writers whose work I revered and whose approval I craved—in the burgundy corduroys on Tuesday, the forest green corduroys on Wednesday, the burgundy corduroys again on Thursday, and so on. With them I wore ridiculously blousy button-downs so that the way the corduroys cinched my love handles wasn't so obvious. And I walked hurriedly past mirrors, to avoid any visual confirmation of my worst fears.

I spent most of that summer working for one writer, David Gates, who was in charge of a feature of the magazine called "Update." He had big eyeglasses, a sprawling mane of frizzy hair and a talent for speaking in slowly unfurling, irony-inflected, gorgeously sculpted sentences that instantly sealed my admiration for him. When I learned more about him—or rather one detail in particular—that admiration turned to awe. He had been married to Ann Beattie, whose short stories, every single one of them, I'd read when I was avoiding Chaucer, Petrarch and Coleridge.

He was now involved with another writer, Elizabeth Kaye, who did long celebrity profiles for *Rolling Stone.* Could a couple be any cooler? When they asked me to dinner one night, I was light-headed with glee, until it hit me: while there might, among the clothes with me that summer, be a button-down nicer (albeit tighter) than the ones I'd been wearing regularly to the office, my choice of pants was, well, the burgundy or the forest green corduroys. I cursed every oversize meal I'd eaten on every day of every week of the last month. I made an irrevocable, unequivocal decision not to eat another oversize meal for the rest of the summer.

And then I sat down in a Chinese restaurant with David and Elizabeth and had multiple helpings of one of the dishes in front of us. How could I not? The dish was cold noodles in sesame paste. It looked like spaghetti sauced with peanut butter. It tasted like that, too, and if chemists had gone into a laboratory to hatch a calorie-ridden Kryptonite just for me, this is precisely what they would have come up with: a sort of pasta, my vulnerability to which was encoded in my genes, smothered with an analogue to peanut butter, my vulnerability to which was documented by a trail of empty jars in the cupboards and waste bins of my childhood.

Before that night with David and Elizabeth, I'd never eaten this, but I would eat it again and again in the months and years to come. I'd eat it with strands of cucumber on top, because some Chinese restaurants served it that way. I'd eat it with chopped peanuts on top, which was the way of other restaurants. I'd eat it with scallions in the mix, and I'd eat it when the sesame paste was really more of a sesame splash, pooling beneath the noodles instead of clinging to them. Restaurants that served the dish in this overly wet fashion were restaurants I didn't patronize again.

I also tried to hook Beth on cold noodles with sesame paste, at least the few times I saw her that summer. With so much distance between Carolina and Yale, we weren't doing a good job of keeping in touch, but I met her for dinner after leaving the *Newsweek* offices one night. I suggested Chinese. She suggested some macrobiotic nonsense. I relented. Later, when I returned to my Downtown loft, I called for Chinese delivery. And I ate the cold noodles in sesame paste straight from their paper carton, which I emptied.

The noodles were the real legacy of my first internship with *Newsweek*. The legacy of my second internship with *Newsweek*—I returned the next summer—was different, and in fact didn't involve food. It involved the murder of Mary Tyler Moore.

I was floating through the magazine that summer, which meant I was contributing reporting to, and doing fact-checking for, different sections on different weeks. My best buddy among my fellow interns was a bubbly, chirpy young woman named Karen. She enjoyed playing the naïf, so I enjoyed playing tricks on her. One week, when she was doing fact-checking for the magazine's Transitions page, I played a foolish one.

Fact-checking the Transitions page involved rounding up, for the page's writer, the most important biographical milestones of the week: which famous people had given birth or won big lawsuits or celebrated a wedding or, most important of all, died.

"If there were any deaths this week I don't know about, make sure to tell me!" Karen said to me via an electronic message from her computer terminal to mine. I couldn't tell if she was serious. But even if she was, I decided, I'd have a moment's fun.

"Well," I wrote back, "Mary Tyler Moore died this morning, but of course you know that." Mary's name just came to me, from nowhere. I plucked it from the air.

Karen asked if I was kidding.

I said I wasn't.

Then I waited for what I was sure would be one more inquiry, via electronic message, about my seriousness, upon receipt of which I'd admit the joke.

Five minutes later, I hadn't heard back from her.

I sent her a new message: Just kidding, pulling your leg, I'm sure you know that, please tell me you got this, please please please.

A minute passed. No response.

Another minute. No word.

I picked up the phone and dialed her extension.

No answer.

About a minute later, I heard a rumble at the far end of the corridor along which my cubicle sat. The rumble became more of a thunder: the sound of several people walking heavily and hurriedly in my direction. I poked my head out of my cubicle and saw them: Karen and Elsie, who was in charge of all the fact-checkers for the features sections, bearing down on me. Each of them was riffling through and staring at a long roll of printed Associated Press and United Press International copy that unspooled from her arms. Each of them looked frantic.

"Where," Elsie asked me, "did you hear that Mary Tyler Moore died?"

I did a quick survey. I made a mental measurement. And to my considerable distress, the space just under my computer keyboard was not quite tall and broad enough for me to crawl into.

"Um," I said, trying to make my voice sound bright and unbowed. "Nowhere! I was just playing! Come on, you know I was just playing, don't you?"

Elsie actually smiled. She poked Karen in the ribs. "I *told* you," she said. She laughed.

Karen, her face reddening, laughed, too.

They went away, and I went back to work, oblivious for the next two hours to the full chain of events I had set off.

Before appearing at my cubicle, Karen had messaged the Transitions writer to alert her to Mary Tyler Moore's death. That writer had messaged or called some midlevel editor. That editor had in turn notified the top brass, who sent word out to the Los Angeles bureau that the magazine might have to open up a few pages in its coming issue for a major story, something like "Death of an American Icon."

Word of Mary's passing had left the building, reaching enough reporters at enough news organizations who made enough calls to some publicist of Mary's that the publicist began reaching out to news organizations that hadn't called to deny this metastasizing rumor and make clear that Mary was alive and well.

I learned most of this as I received a stern talking-to in the office of the editor in charge of summer interns. The rest of it I pieced together from various other sources, including the next morning's *New York Post*. It contained an entire article about Mary having to dispel some strange rumor that she had died.

I figured my career was over. I figured my *life* was over. They were done with, wasted: all the hours at the Carolina newspaper, both summer internships at *Newsweek*. Some High Central Committee of Journalism, learning of my irresponsible behavior and taking special offense at its injury to *an American icon*, was going to ban me from the profession forever more. No newspaper work. Certainly no *Newsweekly* work. I'd return to college without a backup plan, without direction, another superfluous English major who could rattle off lines of Shakespearean sonnets but had no social utility or marketable skill. I'd fall victim to a fatal case of purposelessness and, unlike Mary, die an early and unmentioned death.

But as the *Post* story made a point of noting, Mary and her publicist had no idea where the death rumor had come from, and that turned out to be my saving grace. I hadn't directly embarrassed *Newsweek*. In a few days' time, I was forgiven.

Before it was entirely clear that I would be, as I wondered if it weren't too late to tailor my classes at Carolina for a new career in telemarketing or taxidermy, I took advantage of a day off to get out of the city and away from *Newsweek*, journalism or any reminder of either. I went to Grandma's summer house in Madison, and I ate. I ate pizza she baked in the oven and steak that Uncle Mario cooked on the grill and anything else put in front of me.

I would have gone even farther, all the way to Avon, and let Mom tend to me, but she and Dad weren't there anymore. Between my sophomore and junior years at Carolina, Dad had been transferred from Hartford to San Diego, far enough from the Northeast that they were no longer dependable attendees of family holidays and other get-togethers. They settled in La Jolla, a wealthy oceanfront community about a twenty-minute drive north of the city center. The house they bought there was a stunner. It should come as no surprise that the most stunning room in it was the kitchen.

Seven

"The wallpaper has to go!" Mom told me during the first of our many telephone conversations about the house in La Jolla, which absorbed her attentions like no house before it. She was referring to the wallpaper in the kitchen, which absorbed her attentions like no other room. "It's hideous," she said. "Garish! Purple, turquoise, shiny, metallic. Very dated. Very *seventies*."

It was only the mideighties, mind you, and Mom had never before focused on interior design. The financial demands of four Bruni kids and six Bruni stomachs hadn't left her and Dad with a lavish budget for keeping current with décor trends. In our living room in Avon the furniture was the same set that my parents had purchased for, and used in, the first house they had ever owned. It was very *fifties*. Mom and Dad didn't drive fancy cars or wear fancy clothes or take especially fancy vacations. They paid the high mortgages on spacious houses with individual bedrooms for each kid. They paid private school tuition and swimming-related travel costs. And they bought enough food for a small country: Liechtenstein for sure, and quite possibly Andorra. They didn't sweat the bathroom fixtures.

Until La Jolla. Dad's transfer was a big promotion accompanied by a big salary hike and a sizable housing allowance, and Mom suddenly went real estate mad. "Suddenly" isn't quite right: she had always had a voyeuristic curiosity about other people's houses, floor plans and asking prices, and there was a period in Connecticut when, on weekends, she'd tote me with her to open houses, telling the Realtor at the door that we were relocating to the area from Cleveland or Kansas City or Saint Louis. She'd always cite a city in the Midwest, perhaps reasoning that the Midwest was regionally vague enough that we could pass as Midwesterners. Sometimes she'd even invent a new profession for her absent husband: doctor, lawyer, nuclear physicist. If we spotted someone we knew upon entering the house, she'd switch strategies and say she was there on a scouting mission for a doctor, lawyer or nuclear physicist who was a close family friend and about to relocate. Upon leaving, she'd turn to me and commence her review: the master bath was too cramped, the family room too remote, the marble tiles in the foyer too imperial. But the second-floor laundry room? She craved one of those. Life, she frequently said, would be complete with a second-floor laundry room, just outside the master bedroom, eliminating the need for a hamper or for hauling armfuls of dirty socks and bedsheets down a flight of stairs.

The house in La Jolla was all on one level, a contemporary beauty with all sorts of neat facets and tricks: a fireplace that lighted itself; blinds that could be raised or lowered with the flicks of switches; "central vacuum." The kitchen was gadget central. On the vast center island, there was a separate sink with a special faucet for instant hot water, and there was an appliance dedicated solely to the constant production and storage of ice, a production attended by a faint whirring and plopping and crunching that never quite ceased. On a long counter nearby was an "appliance dock," into which you placed the specially designed can opener and the specially designed blender, neither of which needed to be plugged into sockets. And against the wall separating the kitchen from the family room was an old-fashioned soda fountain, with bays and spigots for different syrups, a wand that produced carbonated water and deep, temperature-controlled compartments for tubs of ice cream.

Mom and Dad weren't about to let this soda fountain lie fallow, so they'd go to the local Baskin-Robbins and get the workers there to cut those broad cylindrical columns of ice cream beneath the glass display cases in half. They'd lug home these squat, frozen tree stumps and, with much huffing and moaning and griping about back strain, lower the stumps into the proper recesses of the soda fountain. There was room for three kinds of ice cream: usually Rocky Road (Dad's favorite), Pralines 'n Cream (Mom's favorite) and one other (Peanut Butter 'n Chocolate if I was visiting). To get at this treasure, you had to reach deep with a real ice cream scoop, as if you were at a real ice cream parlor.

Mom adored this kitchen, which was so spacious you could run laps around that island and sleep on the counters that skirted it—they were that long. The actual countertops, though, weren't acceptable. While Formica had been good enough for Connecticut Mom, it wasn't for California Mom, who coveted Corian, a matte marble-emulating synthetic that had just come into vogue. One of its selling points was that if it got nicked or dinged badly over time, its top layer could be sanded down, and it would be good as new.

"You can cut on it!" Mom exulted, a detail that so transfixed her she couldn't stop mentioning it. Talking for the umpteenth time about the various color options she was considering for her new countertops, she'd pause to interject: "You can cut on these countertops, did you know that?" Yes, yes, I did. And I began to worry: given her apparent zeal to exploit this virtue of Corian, would we henceforth stand in a phalanx at the kitchen counter to eat plateless steak dinners, so that we could just slice right through the gristle and sinew to the sandable surface beneath?

In fact Mom seldom cut on the snowy white Corian she chose, because it soon occurred to her that while she *could* sand it down to repair it, she'd be a fool to incur that mess with any frequency, to have Corian dust coating the new wallpaper—eggshell-colored, with subtle gray-blue stripes—or the new dark wood cabinets with which she'd replaced the turquoise metal ones or the wood-paneled surface of the mammoth Sub-Zero refrigerator she'd installed. Back then almost no one had a Sub-Zero, but Mom did. She said she needed the storage capacity, even though she continued to keep an additional refrigerator and freezer in the garage and even though, during the La Jolla years, her household was usually just three people. Mark was finishing up at Amherst and would then take a job in Boston. I was halfway through Carolina and spent summers away, honing my journalistic skills and offing American icons. Harry was doing a senior year at Loomis as a boarding student, after which he would head to Dartmouth.

With just her, Dad and Adelle around the house most of the time, she cooked less frequently, more simply and, this being southern California, with more of an eye toward balanced, healthy meals. She tossed spaghetti with broccoli, olive oil and almond slivers. She made enormous salads. I got the sense that Mom had become so practiced at cooking for larger numbers of people that she couldn't muster any enthusiasm for putting together elaborate meals for a household of three. A meal for three was child's play. It was beneath her.

Christmas was pretty much the only time of year when all six of us reliably converged on La Jolla and were together there. We were determined to come up with a special ritual, because we were no longer within driving distance of White Plains and couldn't descend on Grandma's Fifth Street house for *strascinat* and the birth of baby Jesus. We replaced the Christ child with twenty-four-ounce cuts of prime rib. Medium-rare beef—along with medium-rare veal and oceans of lobster bisque and baked potatoes the size of Nerf footballs—became the God and the cynosure of our holy night.

Dad had discovered this restaurant, Remington's, that he revered. It was in Del Mar, where it catered in large part to the big spenders who laid down big money on the ponies at the nearby racetrack. And it catered to them with mind-boggling portions. Even we had never seen anything like them.

The smallest cut of prime rib was a pound, and the options went up, up, up from there. The veal chop was Flintstonian. An appetizer portion of the lobster bisque could fill a punch bowl. Remington's was the upscale restaurant world's equivalent of a big & tall shop, except it needed more extreme adjectives: titanic & alpine.

We treated it as a dare. How much of his prime rib would Mark get through? Would Harry do better? Would I polish off my entire veal chop, and if so would I be able to handle the quintuple scoop of cappuccino crunch ice cream with which a meal at Remington's typically ended? Mom would get a fillet of salmon or swordfish, just to be perverse. It easily weighed more than twelve ounces.

In the weeks before this meal, it was all any of us could talk about on the phone.

"All pumped up for the Remington's munch?" Mark would ask me, calling down to Chapel Hill from Amherst.

"Eight days and counting," I'd say.

"Are you thinking veal chop?"

"Maybe," I'd answer. "Or the pepper steak." It was a solid pound of sirloin encrusted with not only peppercorns but also bacon. It appealed to me more than prime rib, which to my mind didn't have enough tender-crisp contrast—it was too cushiony and flabby through and through.

"I'm going with the prime rib," said Mark. He always went with the prime rib.

On the big night, we'd gather in the living room for a cocktail hour and we'd make vodka-and-tonics, less because they were our favorite drinks than because they gave us something to garnish with lemon and lime from trees in the backyard. We couldn't believe we had actual citrus trees in our very own backyard. Plucking fruit from them just minutes before we sliced it for the drinks was a way to embrace the strange experience of California, where Christmas was always snowless and what we'd see outside the house's windows weren't little children riding sleds but teenagers lugging surfboards.

Cocktails in hand, we'd call Grandma around six p.m. West Coast time. We'd reach her just as she and our uncles and aunts were finishing their long dinner. Whoever talked to her first would confront a brief, palpable frostiness: if moving to Connecticut had been a cruelty, moving to California was an act of such florid hostility that, to Grandma's thinking, she had every right to disown us, and never to press thumb to pasta dough for our benefit again. But of course she never exercised that right.

Mom or Dad would pass the phone to Mark, who would pass it to me. I'd pass it to Harry and he'd pass it to Adelle. Each of us would say "I love you" to the same sound track of Grandma's sobs.

"I pray for next Christmas," she'd tell whoever happened to be on the phone at the moment when she was catching a breath between those sobs, and what she meant was that she was praying she'd be around, because she was sure the chances were slim. Her conviction was unshaken by the fact that she'd survived what was by this point at least a decade of such predictions. She wasn't about to surrender the drama of it all.

After the call it was off to Remington's, where we always had the same waiter and always shocked him by how much we ordered: the bowls of bisque; the hunks of meat; the potatoes, slathered with sour cream; onion rings, deep-fried; corn, just scraped off the cob; ice cream. It was Christmas Eve! A time for unbound revelry!

Mark and Harry would dig in to the feast with every bit as much enthusiasm as Dad and I did. They were Brunis, after all, attuned to the imperative of going overboard on special occasions, and when they chose to, they could just about keep pace with Dad and me. They just didn't have my habit of bingeing in between these big nights, my way of turning everyday eating into a warped science experiment.

By both swimming and playing water polo at Amherst, Mark was staying in decent shape. He'd get a little chunky one semester, then wouldn't be chunky at all the next. But he was only barely conscious of these fluctuations. He had his girlfriends, he had his fraternity mates, he was easily getting Bs and As in his courses: Why worry about anything else? A mirror was what you consulted when you had to shave or comb your hair. Otherwise, there wasn't much cause to look into it for long.

Harry was getting buff. Over the course of high school his interests had moved well beyond *Star Trek*, and as those interests expanded to include girls, he decided to put more muscle on what had been a slender, unimposing frame. Around the time Mom and Dad moved to La Jolla, he'd started lifting weights. In the La Jolla garage, which Mom and Dad never used, he set up a gym of free weights and inclined boards for sit-ups, and he spent hours there on holiday and summer breaks from school. He set a fitness goal of passing the grueling physical test required to work as a public beach lifeguard in La Jolla. And he indeed passed it, doing that job for a summer during which his skin turned bronzer than it ever had— both he and Mark, unlike me, could tan—and his hair turned blond.

Mark sometimes joined Harry in the garage gym, but I didn't. I found it too dark and depressing. I also knew I'd never manage even half as many sit-ups as they did, and I knew each of them would cock an eyebrow at the other as they watched me struggle. So I wouldn't give them the pleasure. Instead I'd head down to Mexico, where I'd found my own, different antidote to the Remington's munch.

In addition to its ocean breezes, gorgeous sunsets and seemingly limitless reserves of guacamole, San Diego had the virtue of proximity to Tijuana. I'd made it a point to head there on one of my first visits to La

Jolla, because I'd heard that in Mexico the kinds of drugs that required a prescription in the U.S. could be bought over the counter. I dipped into a pharmacy and asked for diet pills, not sure what I'd get but certain that it was at least worth trying. The ones the pharmacist gave me were small and yellow and—*woooooeeeee!!!*—made my scalp tingle and my heart thump faster and louder. They were speed, pure and simple. I remembered it from high school, and I put it to renewed good use, stocking up on the pills whenever I visited La Jolla and could make my way south of the border.

Back at Carolina, I'd take one in the late afternoon or early evening, on a day when I'd eaten little or nothing, so that I could quiet my hunger and simultaneously summon the energy for a four-mile run.

If I did this just two or three days a week, I balanced out the overeating on other days. At one point toward the end of my junior year, I jammed my way into size 33 pants. I'd been up to 35 that first summer at *Newsweek*.

Thank you, my Mexican speed! I love you, my Mexican speed!

But I was wary of it, and not just because I knew that it wasn't going to serve as a permanent solution to my eating and weight problems, that it wasn't a viable, or at least sensible, long-term strategy. I was wary of its side effects in real time. I had to develop and abide by certain guidelines for my Mexican speed.

GUIDELINE ONE: Do not take it on a day of heavy coffee drinking. If I did, I noticed that the scalp tingling became, instead, a burning, flushing sensation suffusing the entirety of my cranium: what I imagined a hot flash would be. I had to take deep breaths, splash cold water on my face, close my eyes, say a calming mantra, ride it out. My heart seemed not merely to beat but to do jumping jacks in my chest.

GUIDELINE TWO: Do not take it after nine p.m. I enjoyed nighttime runs—enjoyed the sense of no one getting a good look at me as I lumbered down the road, love handles jiggling—and was indeed temped to do this.

Me (upper right) *with my parents and siblings at Remington's on Christmas Eve. The Mexican speed is working.*

But I learned my lesson fast. My Mexican speed didn't just quit when I wanted it to and couldn't be dissipated with a concentrated burst of activity. It lingered, and so there was the risk of being bright-eyed and bouncy at three a.m. My close friend Nancy, with whom I lived off campus during both my junior and senior years, could always tell when I'd taken my Mexican speed too late in the evening. The apartment would be miraculously clean the next morning, because I'd take to vacuuming floors and scrubbing counters in the dead of night, just to channel, and get rid of, my extra energy.

GUIDELINE THREE: Do not take it on a stomach that feels volatile, or after spicy food, or after large quantities of cheese or milk, if it's to be followed by a vigorous run. Certain urgent needs could present themselves during that run. Certain involuntary, convulsive and exceedingly embarrassing things could happen.

So I followed my guidelines, paced myself and reassured myself that this was a healthier alternative to throwing up. It was also just a temporary measure, intended to whip me into a state of fitness and thinness so rewarding I would discover the discipline to maintain it without any pharmacological assistance. My Mexican speed would get me there.

My Mexican speed, that is, and my Metamucil. I noticed Metamucil in a drugstore during my senior year and I read the packaging, which identified it as a gentle, "natural" laxative. *Maybe*, I thought, *this was what I should have been using instead of Ex-Lax.* And maybe it was something I should use now, a way not of falling back into old habits but of resurrecting whatever good there had been in them while steering clear of the bad. I started buying Metamucil or Fiberall, both fiber-rich, orange-colored powders that dissolved—less thoroughly than one might hope—in water. And I started drinking these grainy concoctions regularly, though never too close to the time when I might take some of my Mexican speed and go out for a run.

I berated myself: Why hadn't I paid attention to fiber before? Fiber was obviously crucial, and fiber was going to save me. By making sure there was an unusually high concentration of fiber in my system, I'd feel too full to overeat, and anything I did eat would be digested too quickly to become fat. I deemed this science no less compelling for the fact that I'd more or less invented it.

With fiber as my focus, I ate the following dinner, night after night: a sludgy glass of three times the recommended dosage of orange Metamucil or Fiberall and four pieces of toasted Branola bread, slathered with low-cholesterol Shedd's Spread, a pathetic butter imposter marketed as less fattening.

The ritual appalled Nancy but also amused her.

"Your dad called," she announced one night when I came in from a late run.

"What did he want?" I asked.

"He has some business trip near here," she answered, "and he said he wanted to come into town and take us to dinner. He asked me about restaurants. He asked me what your favorite food was."

She paused, clearly for effect.

"I told him," she continued, "that he should just mix you some Metamucil and toast you some Branola. I apologize: I forgot about the Shedd's Spread."

Of course she hadn't said that, and when he came he took us to the nicest French restaurant in town. We had steak au poivre—the portion, he and I both noted, wasn't anything like the one at Remington's—and roasted duck. We had chocolate mousse.

It was a terrific meal, and I relished it for a while before ruing it for a whole lot longer. The next afternoon I took a little yellow pill and a four-mile run. And hours after that I ate a dinner of Metamucil, Branola and Shedd's Spread, though I applied the Shedd's Spread in a portion much more stinting than usual.

The fiber got boring. The speed, like the throwing up, started to scare me. But I wasn't out of ideas, not nearly. I had this theory that repetitive eating was potentially dietetic eating: that if I ate the same abbreviated spectrum of things over and over again, my body would become so practiced at digesting them that they would be less fattening than their caloric equivalents. It was a reprise and refinement of my vegetarian logic, and was seductive in part because it suited me so well. Unlike most other people I knew, I could consume a boring, set meal—Branola toast with orange-flavored Metamucil, for example—day after day and night after night for weeks on end.

And that's what I often did on my first trip to Europe, which I took shortly after my graduation from Carolina. In a land of thrilling culinary traditions and vibrant produce, I subsisted for a period on bread alone. In an eater's paradise, I elected a purgatory of feta and tomato followed by tomato and feta.

I was in Europe on a three-thousand-dollar grant from the Morehead Foundation, a reward, given to most of the Morehead scholars, for finishing school with a respectable grade point average and for completing prior Morehead-related summer activities and internships with distinction (the foundation didn't know about Mary Tyler Moore). To get the money you just had to come with up with an edifying script and educational justification for your proposed journey, and mine was this: I was going to trace, loosely, the voyages of Aeneas as described in *The Aeneid*. The plan reflected—or, rather, was superimposed on—my desires to visit Italy and Greece. To make the proposal credible I threw Tunisia into the mix, because that was where Aeneas had shacked up with Dido, lighting her fire (somewhat too literally, as it were).

Although Aeneas had hit Greece before Italy, I wanted to proceed in the opposite order, and couldn't see the harm in rewriting his itinerary ever so slightly. Although Aeneas had never made it up to Florence or Venice, at least not according to my research, I decided that those cities were spiritually of a piece with his other stops and could in good conscience be visited. I began my adventure in Venice and went from there to Florence and then to Rome, by which point I realized I had to find some remedy for all the spaghetti alla carbonara, *bucatini all'amatriciana*, pizza and gelato I'd been consuming, some method for managing Italy from that point forward. The one I adopted was born in part of penury, or at least thrift.

To save money, I limited my dinner one night to a variety of breads purchased from a brick-oven bakery in Rome. I loved them all, the crunchy and the soft breads, the salty buns and the rolls flecked with seeds, and so I went back to the same brick-oven bakery the next night and got another array of bread. The bread was all I ate, no cheese or meat or butter or oil on it.

The morning after, my stomach felt emptier than usual, and my jeans were loose. Was I on to something here? Sure, I had walked at least ten miles each of the previous days—from the Baths of Caracalla to Saint Peter's; up and down Via del Corso and Via Venti Settembre and Via Veneto—and that might have a little something to do with my feeling of newfound litheness. But I was crediting the bread. I was crediting a virtually no-fat, monochromatic meal that must have been a breeze to digest.

So I did an all-bread lunch the next day, followed by an all-bread dinner. And I just kept on going like that, for at least a week. I made just one alteration, adding beer to the nightly routine. I figured beer, like bread, was made from grain, so I was essentially *drinking* bread while I ate bread and keeping the meal both fat-free and confined to a strictly limited group of ingredients. A strictly limited group of nutrients, too. Halfway through the week, I began to experience periodic moments of dizziness. By week's end the moments weren't so periodic, and I was forced to acknowledge the good sense of an occasional hunk of mozzarella or bite of veal *saltimbocca*. Bread couldn't give a body all that it needed.

But could Greek salads? That's what I ate, meal after meal, in Athens and on Santorini and on Mykonos. For the classics scholars now crying foul, I admit I had no proof Aeneas docked on Mykonos, nothing I could point to in the historical or literary records. But it's a beautiful island and a crazy amount of fun, and Aeneas sailed the seas nearby. He surely *would* have hit Mykonos, if the weather had been right and the winds had been advantageous and there had been half-price cocktails during happy hour at Super Paradise Beach that day. I felt certain of it.

The Greek salad in our country tends to get distracted with vapid and unnecessary lettuce. But in its birthplace it sticks for the most part to juicy cucumbers and juicier tomatoes and a sheep's worth of feta, which isn't crumbled but presented in thick rectangular slabs. If there are olives, they're dark and robust. It's as much a cheese and crudité plate as it is an actual salad, and if it's large enough, it can definitely pass for a meal.

I made sure it did and, during about three weeks in Greece, ate at least two dozen Greek salads. I washed them down with Dutch, Belgian or Italian beer. There weren't any Greek beers to speak of, and retsina and ouzo weren't my thing.

The Greek salads served me well. Near the beginning of my week on Mykonos I spent a night with a good-looking Scotsman from Glasgow; toward the end of it I spent two nights with an even better looking Frenchman from Lyon. My good fortune didn't go to my head: when the Frenchman suggested, in between those two nights, that I accompany him to the nude gay beach on the island, I made a slew of excuses—shopping to do, clothes to wash, postcards to write, a hard-to-get appointment with a local oracle to attend—and told him to enjoy himself, though not too much. I wasn't about to disrobe in public in the bright Mediterranean sun, even though all the walking and monochromatic eating I'd been doing since Rome had definitely reduced my weight.

Which was . . . *what?*

As always, I didn't know, and as always, I didn't want to find out. I had my guesses, based on the one or two times over the past four years when curiosity—or dread—had got the better of me and I had tentatively stepped on a scale. I was no doubt somewhere in my usual 180-to-195-pound range, and likely toward the bottom of it. I certainly wasn't the 177 pounds that those medical charts said a five-foot, eleven-inch man—I was now nearly that tall—should be, because I'd never managed that. Maybe that's what I'd been right after Outward Bound, but I hadn't checked then, too fearful of disappointment.

And I wasn't going to check now. I preferred not knowing. I preferred assuming from the attentions of the Scotsman and the Frenchman that whatever the number, it was low enough not to be an embarrassment, though surely higher than it should be.

"I think Jill Eikenberry is just terrific," Mom said. "Don't you?"

"She's fine," I answered, taking another bite of one of the avocado and Cheddar sandwiches we often had for lunch in La Jolla. We got them from a sandwich shop just six blocks away. "But I'm more of a Susan Dey person."

"And if I'd singled out Susan Dey, you would have gone with Jill Eikenberry, because you always have to contradict me," Mom said, sounding genuinely wounded. She was right that I liked to contradict her, wrong that I could switch positions so easily on this particular matter. For one thing, I took *L.A. Law* very seriously. For another, Susan Dey was a prior Partridge who had reportedly had an eating disorder, wore her blond hair in a sleek cut, and was involved onscreen with Harry Hamlin. Jill Eikenberry wore her hair in a blandly voluminous style and bestowed her affections, in both the show and real life, on a short, balding mensch. There wasn't any contest here.

I was back in La Jolla, having decided to hang out there for the eight months between the end of my European travels and the start of journalism graduate school at Columbia University in New York in the fall of 1987. Mom had taped all the *L.A. Law* episodes I'd missed while in Europe. And as I caught up on them, she watched them a second time, if not a third. When she loved something, she loved it passionately and without any possibility of boredom, whether it was the prose stylings of Sidney Sheldon; Giorgio Beverly Hills perfume, which became as essential to California Mom as Guerlain's Shalimar had been to Connecticut Mom; linguine with a basil and pine nut pesto, her default pasta dish of this particular period; or the legal and romantic melodrama performed by Jill Eikenberry and Susan Dey, among other actors and actresses, on *L.A. Law*.

We tended to watch the videotapes at lunchtime, because my days were free until about four p.m., when I would head to a French bistro where I'd landed a job waiting tables. It served the smoothest, creamiest chocolate mousse I'd ever tasted, and every time I hustled to the kitchen to drop an order ticket, I stopped en route to steal a gigantic spoonful of it from the refrigerator along the path. I caromed between the tables in the dining room with mousse on my breath. I went home at night with mousse coming out of my pores.

Mom and Dad would be asleep by then, but Adelle would usually be up. She was in high school, and the hours between eleven p.m. and one a.m. were crucial telephone time, though she'd sometimes take a five- or ten-minute break between calls to acknowledge my existence and ask me for a bit of advice, sometimes something involving guys and sex. Mom had taken it upon herself to clue Adelle, too, into my sexuality. (In fact the only close family member Mom shied away from telling—and I was glad for this—was Grandma.) Adelle treated the news as an interesting opportunity. She wasn't about to let an older gay brother—and any knowledge about dealing with men that he might have picked up—go to waste.

She had a tall, handsome boyfriend and a place in the most popular posse of girls at school, and she carefully watched her eating in the interest of holding on to both. Broad-shouldered, big-chested and barely five foot three, she was never going to look willowy, but she had accomplished something close to slenderness. It hadn't been easy. Like me she had a way of tumbling headlong into tubs of ice cream or bowls of pasta, a tropism toward calories. Like me she'd been fat between the ages of four and eight. And like me she'd emerged from that experience with an anxious, nervous relationship with food, which she alternately surrendered to and swore off, almost always going to one extreme or the other.

Were there reasons beyond our shared histories of heaviness—and beyond, possibly, our genes—that she and I approached food differently than Mark and Harry did, and worried more about being or not being thin? I wondered if there was something to the fact that she and I both sought the romantic favor of men, and that movies and magazines and so much else signaled that the most powerful, handsome, magnetic bachelors responded, in a fashion much narrower than the most desirable women did, to a potential mate's looks. If you wanted your pick of men, beauty was your best weapon, and beauty began with thinness.

Adelle had followed Mark's, Harry's and my lead into swimming, but hadn't been as dedicated to it, in part because Mom hadn't pushed her. She also played basketball and dabbled in a few other sports. Her shortness and thickness prevented her from being a standout at any of them in an athletic sense, but she would nonetheless find herself voted the team captain, because she had Mark's charisma. As a student she more closely resembled me. She was better with words than with numbers.

And she had a wicked sense of humor, which came out whenever Mom, in a down mood, went on about all she'd sacrificed and done for us: the laundry, the traveling to swim meets, the marathon cooking.

"I've come up with the title of the biography of Mom you'll write someday," she told me, with Mom listening in. "You should call it 'My Mother and Other Christian Martyrs.'"

One weekend day Adelle and I neglected to get up from watching television as Mom, grunting theatrically, hauled grocery bags from the car into the kitchen.

"Don't help!" Mom facetiously instructed us. "Please don't even think about helping!"

"Maybe," Adelle observed, "the book should be called 'My Mother and Other Beasts of Burden.'"

But she revisited and revised the title once more when Mom, furious about our lack of appreciation for some errand she'd run or meal she'd made, launched into an uncharacteristically foulmouthed tirade.

"You people," Mom bellowed, "just shit on me and shit on me and shit on me some more!"

"I have a new title for the book," Adelle interjected. "Call it 'My Mother and Other Flush Toilets.'"

Mom rushed out of the room, because even she had started laughing, and she didn't want to let go of her outrage and let us off the hook.

Eight

New York suited me better than California. It had seasons, which I appreciated less for the variety they presented—the coming and going of foliage, the possibility of snow—than for the wardrobe options. In New York it was cold enough at least six months of the year for coats, which covered a multitude of sins. In New York I wasn't surrounded by so many tan, blond, shirtless rebukes to my own appearance. I felt thinner.

The journalism program at Columbia was only nine months long and seemingly over even before it began, an uneventful whirl of practice deadline writing and roasted cashews from the bodega nearest my dorm room, of lectures in journalism ethics and Middle Eastern delivery in the one-bedroom apartment where my best friend at school, Elli, lived. While I was one of the youngest students in the program, Elli was the oldest, two decades my senior, a tenured history professor at a Maryland university who was using her sabbatical to study journalism. We spent at least three nights a week together in her apartment pretending to do homework but really watching TV, especially *L.A. Law*. I turned her into a surrogate Mom.

I took advantage of my proximity to White Plains to see Grandma more often than I'd been able to during the previous few years, and I could always count on her response to my arrival to dissipate any anxiety I was feeling over pretty much anything, including my weight. Her excitement was so enormous, it didn't leave room for darker emotions.

Sometimes she wouldn't even speak for the first few minutes, because she had to get through the kissing, a fusillade of twenty smacks on the nearest cheek, and then she had to proceed to the scurrying. She'd scurry to a cabinet to get a bag of M&M'S with peanuts, which she knew I loved, then to the side-by-side refrigerator/freezer, where she kept parfaits of vanilla ice cream, crème de menthe and Cool Whip in tall, fluted glasses. She'd put the M&M's and one (or two) of the parfaits on the table, then scurry back to the refrigerator for something else.

Yanking open the refrigerator door, she might pluck out a shell steak and hold it high. Steak was fancy. Steak was a statement.

She'd beam.

"I'll make steak?" she'd ask.

I'd look at the M&M'S and the parfait, and I'd think about the *frits* that I knew would appear any minute. Inwardly I'd groan but also rejoice.

"Well," I'd say, pointlessly. "I don't know . . ."

"I'll make steak!" she'd decide, the offer becoming a command. Within ten seconds the meat would be on a broiler pan in the oven, and two minutes later she'd produce the *frits*, cooked in—and retrieved from—the basement kitchen. As she got on in years, Grandma's smorgasbords became less coherent but no less abundant. I'd never be entirely sure which item on her menu to tackle first, and I'd find myself moving dishes and platters this way and that, a food traffic controller arranging food-planes on a food-tarmac.

I'd usually wind up favoring the *frits*, because she'd usually make only stuffed ones for me.

"They came good?" she'd ask, as preposition-challenged as ever.

"Mmmm," I'd murmur as I continued to chew, as if too focused on the food to pause.

"*Quanto sei bello!*" she'd yelp. It meant, "How beautiful you are!" Then she'd cup my face in her hands and commence another fusillade of kisses.

When my nine-month program at Columbia ended in the late spring, I got an internship at the *New York Post*, which was then trying to change its image in the media world, to be less of a racy tabloid and more of a comprehensive—although spirited—newspaper. The internship morphed within weeks into a full-time job, compelling me to look for an apartment, because my Columbia dorm room was being taken by someone else. I searched the *Village Voice* listings, went to a building on West Eightieth Street near Columbus Avenue and met Martin, who needed someone to share his two-bedroom apartment with him.

We didn't get to talk much at the start of our first meeting. He was distracted by the disappearance of his cat.

*Me with Grandma
at my Columbia graduation.*

"Is she there?" he yelled out an open window and up toward the sky. I assumed there was someone searching for the cat on the roof, though I couldn't see the other person. In fact I couldn't see much of Martin, either. His head was all the way out the window.

"Areeeeeeeeetha!" he bellowed, and at this point I assumed he was addressing not the cat searcher but the wayward roof-clambering pet herself.

So his cat was named Aretha?

Promising.

I agreed to split the rent with him, took the extra bedroom and got to know this Aretha, a calico with a relatively placid disposition, along with Sasha, a black Labrador retriever mix. And within a matter of months I met and got to know Audrey, also a calico, found wandering across the grass outside the American Museum of Natural History, where Martin took Sasha for walks. He just came in the door with Audrey, plopped her on the carpet and informed me that our family had grown. He chose the name Audrey because he liked the assonance of "Aretha and Audrey," but when he addressed the two cats directly, he just said "you young ladies," a real kindness to Aretha, who was getting on in years and had lost her girlish figure.

Martin sometimes seemed determined to stock our second-story walk-up with as many living organisms as possible, returning home one night from work—he was a food purchaser for a small group of restaurants—with four crawfish. They'd been a dinner special, apparently not a popular one. Martin found these dwarf lobsters adorable and thought they'd make a kooky, festive addition to his living room aquarium, stocked with eight fish.

A few days later I counted seven fish and said something to Martin, who expressed confidence that the one I couldn't see was just obscured by an underwater plant or the ceramic scuba diver. Later I counted six, then five, the aquarium's inhabitants disappearing like characters in an Agatha Christie novel. And was it just my imagination, or were the crawfish looking strangely robust?

When Martin finally figured out what was going on—it took him about a week—he grew so enraged about the murders that he sentenced the killers to a flight out the window, down two stories and into a concrete alley. The hideous crunch reverberated in my nightmares for weeks.

Martin's silliness made me feel relatively sane. But an even bigger reason I enjoyed and got along with him was our shared weakness around food, accompanied by our shared vows, relentlessly articulated and repeatedly abandoned, to get ourselves into shape.

Martin had blue eyes and blond hair and a lightness of spirit as well as coloring that drew people to him. He was a few inches shorter than average, with shoulders that stooped slightly. And like me he toggled between being as little as five or as many as fifteen or so pounds overweight. Together we entered into short-lived exercise pacts in an effort to stay at the low end of that range.

We went to a local gym together. We got on side-by-side stair-climbing machines, not the StairMasters that would become popular a few years later, but those truncated escalators to nowhere, whose steps descended and disappeared and then circled back around, forcing you to walk up and up lest you be dragged down. The machines measured the number of stories you supposedly rose in your ascent to the top of some imaginary building. You could set a goal. Both of us always chose a hundred stories. Martin seldom made it past sixty. I usually quit around forty.

Sometimes we'd run in Central Park, sometimes at nine or ten p.m., when we knew it wasn't smart or safe, though we'd tell ourselves that by bringing Sasha—the least aggressive, sweetest love muffin of a dog ever to unravel a rawhide bone—we were taking care of our protection. We'd let Sasha off her leash, and as Martin and I circled the reservoir in the middle of the park, she'd dart toward and away from us, spending most of her time in nearby clusters of trees, where she could be heard but not seen.

I'd take advantage of her invisibility to cast her in a more ferocious light, just in case muggers were lying in wait and listening.

"That's a good girl, *Psycho*," I'd say. "That's a good, good Doberman pinscher."

At least three nights a week we ate Chinese delivery, almost always the same meal: cold noodles in sesame paste, broccoli in garlic sauce and either chicken with cashew nuts or kung pao chicken, which had peanuts. We congratulated ourselves because this meal didn't have any red meat in it. Come to think of it, it was practically vegetarian! Pleased with our imagined virtue, we rewarded ourselves by calling the corner bodega and having ice cream delivered.

For the year and a half we lived together, which was the year and a half I worked at the *Post*, neither of us really dated much. I'd had a boyfriend for most of my spring semester at Columbia, and had grown attached enough to him to feel bitter about the breakup, the reasons for which hadn't been clear to me, and to avoid men for a while. But occasionally I'd drop into a bar for a drink, and on one of these nights I met Arthur, a strapping Australian with a chiseled jaw, sandy hair and pale blue eyes framed by the kind of slight, happy wrinkles that don't suggest age so much as time outdoors, staring at waves and squinting at sunsets. He was about ten years older than I was, and I assumed my youth must be compensating for my flaws, chief among them my untoned body.

About three weeks after we met, on Valentine's Day, he gave me a box of chocolates.

"Where is it?" asked Martin when I told him about the gift. I'd just come home from Arthur's and was giving Martin a rundown of the date.

"Oh, I threw it in a trash can on the way home," I said.

"You *what?*" Martin yelped, incredulous. "Why did you do that?"

"Well, I didn't want to eat it," I said. "If I'd brought it back here and put it on the kitchen counter, five minutes later you and I would have been drinking bourbon and scarfing down chocolates while we surfed the channels for a show with bird sounds." Audrey loved television nature programs with bird sounds. She'd jump up to the arm of the chair nearest the TV, stare at it and meow.

"But that's so rude," Martin said. "What are you going to tell Arthur?"

"That the chocolates were delicious."

"Maybe I would have liked one," Martin said.

"Maybe you would have eaten ten," I said.

"Maybe you would have, too!" he said.

"I rest my case."

Of course the chocolates wouldn't have been any worse than the ice cream we would surely order in on one of our next Chinese delivery nights, but that wasn't the way I thought things through.

I hadn't trusted Arthur before the chocolates; I trusted him even less after. He obviously wasn't seeing me clearly—how could he give someone like *me* a present of chocolates?—but at some point he might start to, and I didn't want to stick around for that. I broke it off before March arrived.

And then questioned whether I should have.

"I miss Arthur," I told Martin.

"But you blew him off," Martin said. "You threw away his chocolates." He made those two acts sound like equal sins. Actually, he made the throwing away of the chocolates sound worse.

"I shouldn't have broken up with him," I said, but that wasn't my real regret. My real regret was that I wasn't fitter, in which case I wouldn't have had to break up with him. I'd been at least six pounds lighter during that spring semester at Columbia. That's when I'd had a boyfriend who lasted months, not weeks.

I needed to pull myself together. And there was a perfect starting point for that: the move I was set to make. Eager to write longer stories about a broader range of topics than I could at the *Post*, I'd accepted a job at a more conventional newspaper in a different city. I hated leaving Martin. But I vowed to compensate for it by leaving behind some of our sloppy, reclusive ways as well.

Sometime around 1990 several concerned citizens of Detroit launched a major initiative to improve the city's fortunes, and it was based on a curious premise. According to these citizens, Detroit's problem wasn't its crime rate. Detroit's problem wasn't whole neighborhoods of abandoned and crumbling houses, thousands upon thousands of them. Detroit's problem wasn't the absence of a full-service, full-scale department store anywhere within the city limits, or the fact that the only first-run movie theaters were so deep inside the impenetrable maze of the downtown Renaissance Center that almost no one who found his or her way to them could find the way back out.

No, Detroit's problem was an epidemic of naysaying. Residents simply talked too much trash about it. So this bold urban initiative exhorted them to do the opposite. Placards, bumper stickers and the like were emblazoned with the slogan SAY NICE THINGS ABOUT DETROIT.

I'll say this about Detroit: there wasn't a lot of traffic in the city center. Also this: the Detroit River, cleaned up in the 1970s and 1980s, was bluer than anyone who hadn't seen it could imagine, and Detroit's main public park, Belle Isle, was smack in the middle of that river, rivaling the main public park of any other American city in terms of picturesque setting. I was grateful for that, because it motivated many a run of about five miles, the island's circumference.

I moved to Detroit in the spring of 1990, when I was twenty-five, to start work as a metropolitan desk reporter with the *Detroit Free Press*, the most respected daily newspaper in Michigan and the one with the highest circulation. I found a spacious loft-style one-bedroom apartment with eighteen-foot ceilings and windows that were more than six feet tall in a former paint factory, and I paid less than six hundred dollars a month for it, including parking for the used red Ford Tempo I bought. In Manhattan I'd been paying seven hundred dollars for half of a two-bedroom that wasn't much bigger and didn't have any light. A very, very nice thing I'll say about Detroit is that you get a lot of apartment for your money there.

Then again, my neighborhood had its shortcomings. It was a redevelopment zone on the edge of downtown that still lacked some fundamental services. It lacked fundamental *foods*. I couldn't locate a proximal source of cold noodles in sesame paste. I didn't even dare to dream of pad Thai. Pretty much the only dinner I could order by telephone and have deposited at my doorstep was pizza, and that, over time, wasn't enough. I couldn't live on delivery the way I had in New York.

So I took up serious grocery shopping. I could drive just a half mile to the relatively new Harbortown Market, which gleamed in the way that optimistic bellwethers of an intended urban renaissance gleam, and which was reasonably well stocked. I'd bring home salad greens, other salad fixings, asparagus, broccoli, scallops, shrimp, turkey burgers—all sorts of sensible, responsible food. In my airy, dashing apartment, without Martin around to enable me, I was going to make my own dinners and make sure they were healthy, low-fat, and low-cal.

The problem was, I remained an impatient cook. Once I'd embraced the thought that dinner was in the offing I didn't want the offing to mean ninety minutes or even thirty minutes down the road. I didn't want an offing at all.

Then I noticed, or rather focused on, the precooked Tyson chicken pieces in shrink-wrapped packages that spread out across an enormous refrigerated case in the market. These called to me in a way that roasted whole chickens in supermarkets didn't, because a whole chicken was messy, and purchasing a whole chicken might increase the possibility of *eating* a whole chicken. Pieces were better. I could eat just one or two, or at least start out with that intention and without having already stacked the deck against myself.

This wasn't great chicken, or even good chicken. I knew that even then. But it had a thick, fatty layer of skin that had been marinated in, or brushed with, some sort of vaguely sweet sauce. It had a barbecued-but-not-really quality that I liked. And it was meaty, in an unnatural but not altogether unappealing way: the breasts looked and felt as if the chickens they'd come from had been given silicone implants. It called to me and somehow demanded that I answer right away.

I would typically hurry from the checkout line to the parking lot, slip into my car and, before I put the key in the ignition, use it to puncture and peel off the shrink-wrap. Then, using only my left hand to steer, I'd use my right hand to eat one of those suspiciously gigantic breasts. I almost always started with a breast, and almost always finished it in less than a minute. And then, before the three-minute drive from the supermarket to the parking deck opposite my building was done, I'd confront a sequence of difficult decisions.

Should I go for another of the shrink-wrapped breasts in the grocery bags clustered on the passenger seat beside me? Or should I try a thigh? Or a drumstick? Or maybe a thigh *and* a drumstick? It was only chicken, after all: no starch, no carbohydrates, except maybe just the barest traces of them, in whatever was coating the skin, and that was just a *coating*, just a seasoning, like salt.

Nine times out of ten, I went for another piece—usually another two. With the car in motion and the key in the ignition, I would use my teeth to bite through the shrink-wrap. If I needed to liberate both hands, I used my left knee to steer.

Then there'd be a final question, a final complication: What to do with the empty packages, and more precisely with the bones on top or inside of them? I wouldn't want to put them back into the bags with the other, unused, unsullied groceries. I didn't have a trash bag in the car, despite the number of times I'd reminded myself to put one there. So I'd sweep them onto the floor in front of the front passenger seat. And I'd make a mental note to get them later, certainly before someone sat in the seat.

A few months after these chicken runs began, I volunteered to be the chauffeur for a movie outing with my friend Renee, an editor at the *Free Press*. She opened the passenger-side door, began to step into the car and recoiled.

"Um," she said, backing up another step.

"You know," she said, still at a loss for words.

"I think," she said, an expression of confusion and utter revulsion on her face. "Um, I wonder . . ."

I looked where she was looking, at the floor of the car, and winced. I had somehow forgotten about the pile of skeletons in my little chicken graveyard.

"Oh!" I said. "That's just chicken! I mean it was chicken. I mean I ate it."

"Obviously," Renee said.

"It's just sometimes I snack on chicken when I'm driving," I explained.

She said nothing.

"My apartment's pretty clean," I said, trying to salvage some dignity. It was true. There were no chicken bones lying around, though if you looked deep in the cracks between the cushions of the living room sectional, especially on the day right before my weekly cleaning lady came, you'd find some stray kernels of buttery stovetop popcorn.

Without a trash bag I couldn't sanitize the car for Renee, who lowered her body into her seat carefully, leaving her legs outside of the car until the last moment, then pulling them in just far enough to close the door, but not so far that they brushed against the bones.

"Sorry," I said, and meant it. I was also mortified.

Two weeks later I happened to offer a ride to another friend, Robin, a fellow writer at the *Free Press*. And as soon as we reached my slovenly Tempo, I realized my mistake. The graveyard wasn't gone. It was more populous still, and even if Robin kept her legs far, far to the side, pressed hard against the door, she wasn't safe. She rode with her feet up on the dashboard. It was the only sure way to protect her shoes, and Robin wore nice shoes. She was the newspaper's fashion critic.

Years later her work as the fashion critic for the *Washington Post* would win her a Pulitzer Prize in criticism. And I'd tell people: I've known her for many years! We used to hang out in Detroit. She came over all the time to watch *L.A. Law*!

I'd leave out the part about how she refused, after a time, to set well-shod foot in my car.

One morning I stumbled out of bed, walked groggily to the kitchen, started to make my morning coffee and, as I poured water into the machine, realized that something wasn't right. The kitchen was a sty, and there wasn't any reason or explanation for that. I hadn't cooked the night before, or the night before that, and my cleaning lady had been around—when was it?—just yesterday morning.

And yet there, in the sink: the colander I used for draining pasta, with a few strands of linguine glued to it. And there, on the stove: the big pot I used for boiling pasta. The white stovetop and the patch of white Formica counter beside it had a Pollock's worth of tomato red streaks, smudges and swirls: marinara expressionism.

The only one who could have created it was me.

I thought hard: *When had I done it?* I took several hasty gulps of coffee, trying to understand.

And then I did, sort of, in a fractured way, images flashing in my brain: I'm getting out of bed, roused by the certainty that I need to eat. Now I'm staring into the refrigerator. Now I'm at the stovetop, where I can feel heat rising and hear water boiling. Now I'm sitting cross-legged on the sectional, an enormous bowl in my lap, the insides of my legs warmed by it, my mouth full of sauced noodles. Now I'm chewing. Now I'm chewing some more.

Each flash was like a piece of a puzzle that, fragment by fragment, became easier to put together. I took a look at the living room and, sure enough, the bowl from one of those flashes was on the coffee table, and it was empty. As I looked at it I knew, which wasn't quite the same thing as remembering. At some ungodly hour between bedtime and dawn, I had prepared and consumed a gigantic, if one-note, meal. I'd done this in some state of quarter-consciousness that had left me with these fragments but without a fluid narrative of events.

Over the next year this sort of thing happened again and again. Sometimes I'd conduct these middle-of-the-night binges in something closer to half consciousness, dimly aware of my actions but feeling more like a witness to them than their perpetrator. I wouldn't pause in what I was doing or question it or even realize I had any alternative. It was motion without volition, and it had a drugged, liquid, underwater quality to it.

And when I'd wake to the mayonnaise-smeared knife in the sink or the open can of tuna atop the garbage or the stray cornflakes that had fallen to the kitchen floor or whatever else it was, I'd be surprised and yet not surprised. I'd travel in my incrementally dawning, incomplete memory to a point hours earlier and retrieve anything from a tiny fraction of what had happened to the whole of it, accompanied by the unequivocal knowledge that I hadn't decided on—hadn't chosen—the fumbling, makeshift meal I'd assembled. It had chosen me.

As far as I knew, I'd never sleepwalked in the past. But I guessed that what I was doing now was akin to sleepwalking, and that it was best described as sleep-eating, a phenomenon I later saw mentioned in an article or two but had never heard of at the time.

My sleep-eating, in fact, encompassed sleepwalking, inasmuch as I had to get to the kitchen, along with sleep-toasting, sleep-slicing, sleep-chopping and sleep-broiling, all required for the tuna melts I made during a few of these episodes. It encompassed sleep-boiling and sleep-stirring, in the case of pasta, which seemed to be a favorite of my somnolent self. Sometimes it confined itself to sleep-pouring, the only requisite for a bowl (or two or three) of cereal with milk. It never branched out to sleep-cleaning. The dirty instruments and leftover ingredients of my dreamtime feasting always awaited me in the morning.

The sleep-eating alarmed me only slightly, because I knew what was prompting it, the same thing that prompted those driver's-seat chicken feasts. Both happened when I'd gone too many hours, or even a whole day, eating next to nothing, or when I'd markedly ramped up my exercise without permitting myself anything close to the necessary calories to fuel it. Both underscored my inability to find any balance or moderation in my frequent pushes to be lighter for an imminent family photograph, an upcoming beach vacation or, of course, a date.

During my first years in Detroit, I went out on plenty of dates. I was in my midtwenties and horny, and guys recognized my name from articles in the newspaper. My apartment, with its ceilings and windows, impressed visitors. But I certainly dated less than I might have and with more petty melodrama than most people do, because dating while flabby, no matter what percentage of that flabbiness is real and what percentage mental, isn't a smooth, easy process, and that first date with Scott in college wasn't a one-time example of extreme neurosis.

It was foreshadowing.

Nine

You meet a cute guy at a Sunday night barbecue that an acquaintance is having. He glances your way more often than strangers typically do and, when you glance back, holds your gaze longer than he should. Then he cuts in on a conversation you're having with two other people. In response to a comment you make to one of them about a restaurant you want to check out, he says, "I'd totally be up for going there." Point is: he's flirting. He's interested. Only a moron would miss that. You're not a moron, at least not in that way.

He calls two days later. You're thrilled. You're panicked. When he asks if you have plans for the coming weekend, you tell him you have an out-of-town friend visiting, even though you don't. You just can't see him this weekend. More accurately, you can't let him see you. The weekend is only three days away, four if you sign up for Saturday as opposed to Friday night, and that's not enough time. In four days you might be able to lose three pounds, tops, and that's assuming several five-mile runs. You'd like to lose four to five.

You tell him you'll give him a call next Monday, about doing something that week.

You mention to one of your best friends—let's call her Renee—that you met someone promising and that you'll probably be seeing him again soon.

"Have you asked him to do something?" she says.

"No, he asked me," you say.

"So you've scheduled a date?" she asks.

"Not exactly. I told him I'm busy this weekend."

"What are you doing this weekend?" she asks.

"Not much," you say. "Do you want to see a movie?"

She's confused. It's understandable. She's a thin person. She's always been a thin person. Thin people—God bless them, God curse them—don't get it: if you're not thin, you need to be careful and conscious about when and how your suitors initially see you. You should never, for example, start dating somebody in July or, worse yet, August, because in August you can't wear as much clothing as in other months. Your wardrobe options are the most limited, and the few that exist aren't good at disguising little pouches and protuberances. August is a hell of a lot crueler than April. August is a sadist.

Right now it's October. But the issue is your distance from your goal weight, that mythic land to which you've been traveling as directly and expeditiously as Odysseus on the voyage home. And the distance is too great.

Renee says what you know she'll say, because it's the inevitable response: "But he's already seen you. He asked you out after having already seen you. Why do you need to lose weight?"

You're ready for this, and glad for the opportunity to educate her. "He wasn't looking at me as closely as he will be next time out. For starters, it was a big party. It wasn't just me and him. I was framed in an entirely different way. There were visual distractions." You don't entirely believe this, but you believe it could be 15 percent true, and even if it's just 10 percent true, you want to factor it in.

"In addition," you add, your voice growing louder as your case grows stronger, "I was wearing these brown brushed-cotton pants that are the single most flattering pants I own, at least three pounds more flattering than the next most flattering pair, and of course I've searched high and low to find them in another color, in two or three or even *five* other colors, but I haven't, and so I've shot my most-flattering-pants wad, and I can't wear those pants a second time, in case he's the type of person who notices that stuff."

When you take a breath she almost butts in.

"Not finished!" you admonish her. "Also, when he saw me at the barbecue, there wasn't the possibility of sex in just a few hours, the way there would be on a date, so he might not have been sizing up my body the way he will next time out." This last part you believe to be at least 80 percent true. And maybe as high as 95 percent.

"*On top of which*," you continue, rushing the phrase out because you're on a roll, "he wasn't thinking: 'boyfriend material or not boyfriend material?' I just piqued his curiosity. On an honest-to-goodness date, he's going to be looking a lot more closely and assessing a lot more critically." You're 100 percent sure of this.

"Brilliantly reasoned," Renee says. "Wow. I'm blown away. You *do* know, by the way, that the company medical insurance provides partial reimbursement for therapy?"

"What's playing at the Eastland Mall multiplex?" you say, ignoring her.

On Wednesday, the day after his call, you're supposed to be doing one of your healthy, I'm-being-good-today lunches, maybe a sandwich of turkey, lettuce and tomato on whole wheat, no mayonnaise, no chips on the side.

But the special at one of the popular lunch places near the office is the chicken Caesar salad, which is more like chicken Caesar soup, on account of how heavily it's dressed. It's an unconscionable chicken Caesar. You worship it.

And since you're not always in town or in the office on the day it's a special, shouldn't you have it? After all, you've pushed your date back to next week, which will probably turn out to mean that weekend, which means you have something like ten days—eleven if you schedule the date for Sunday instead of Saturday night—to lose the four to five pounds you hope to.

You eat the chicken Caesar.

You get stuck in the office until nine p.m., ruining your plan for a run around six thirty. Two colleagues are leaving the building as you are, and they suggest dipping into a nearby bar for a few beers. It's past dinnertime and it's not wise to drink on an empty stomach, so you allow yourself a hamburger and fries. Tomorrow will be all about turkey and running.

Tomorrow comes. It *is* all about turkey and running. It's a good day, a great day, but at this point it's merely compensation for a bad day, so by Friday you're sort of back to where you were on Wednesday. You've got eight or nine days until the likely date. Better get cracking.

Renee suggests that before the movie on Saturday you stop by her house for a bite. She's made a big batch of pesto. She's always making pesto, and it's a damned fine pesto, nearly as good as Mom's, and pesto happens to be one of your Top Five Most Beloved Ways to sauce pasta, especially if the pasta is fusilli, because the pesto works its way into the grooves of the corkscrew and there's more pesto per noodle. Renee often uses fusilli.

You stop by for a bowl. You wind up having two. It's not the very end of the world—you skip dessert, and you don't have popcorn at the movie. But it's also not the deprivation plan you had hoped to follow, and that's pretty much how the entire weekend goes, so by Monday morning you haven't made much progress. If you're any lighter than you were on Friday, it's by half a pound at most.

You call him on Tuesday. It's a day later than you said you'd call, but that's intentional: it conveys the proper air of distraction and aloofness. You're prepared to ask him about the coming Sunday night, which you now wish wasn't coming quite so soon, but something ghastly and unthinkable happens.

He says, "What are you up to tonight?"

"Tonight?" you repeat back to him. You're buying time. He's wandered off script, and you have to get your bearings.

"Yeah," he says, "I'm going to this cocktail party fund-raiser and I have an extra ticket."

"That would be fun," you say. "But I have to work late tonight." Having to work late is the only excuse that comes to mind. Having to work late seems credible, unimpeachable.

"On what?" he says. It's not a challenge. It's more like an effort to express interest in what you're doing. What a sweet, good guy. What a catch. That cinches it: he's not seeing you until you look as close to perfection as possible.

You mumble something about a "boring feature story due tomorrow," taking care to be vague enough that he won't be able to connect anything you've just said to anything that does or doesn't appear in the newspaper over the coming week, in case he's a reader. Then, to move the conversation elsewhere, you bring up Sunday night.

"Are you free?" you ask.

He's not. In fact he's leaving Friday afternoon on a two-week vacation. So when he says that he could have a drink or dinner on either of the next two nights, Wednesday or Thursday, you're stuck. You have to be able to produce two excuses at once, serial lies, and you don't have them ready. Even if you did, you'd then be pushing the date more than two weeks away, and you realize that that may be too heavy a tax on his patience.

"Thursday," you say, "could work."

But can it?

It's eight p.m. You took a run at six thirty p.m. But you ran only 2.5 miles, because you just weren't feeling it. You should have run another two. You *will* run another two. You get back into shorts and a T-shirt, grab your Walkman, rewind the mix tape with the Psychedelic Furs and Madonna, and off you go. You do the same 2.5 miles all over again.

In the morning you feel lighter. You feel like helium! You skip breakfast and you gnaw on an apple and a pear for lunch and you're feeling a bit woozy by the time you get out of work. When you factor that into the stiffness you feel from running twice the previous night, you decide against another run. You don't need it tonight. Your calorie count for the day is tiny. You just need to keep any eating before bedtime to a minimum. You'll just make a salad or something.

When you get home you realize there's nothing in the fridge. You're too tired and lazy to go out, so you treat this as an opportunity: you're done eating for the day. And what a net-loss day it's been, or will be. Just two pieces of fruit.

By nine forty-five p.m. you're crazy starving. All you can think about is how empty your stomach is. It's so empty it's forlorn. Angry. Your stomach seems to have its own range of emotions, all negative and needy.

You call your favorite pizza delivery place and order the smallest pizza, which isn't really that small, but you resolve not to eat the whole of it, then do.

And then it's Thursday. Dear God, it's Thursday.

You call an editor at work to say you have an important personal errand and will be in late. You say this in a tentative, embarrassed, please-don't-pry voice, eliminating any chance you'll be asked what the errand is. The errand is a run. You have to take a last-ditch run.

You do, and you overdress for extra sweating. Then, at work, you're turkey-sandwich virtuous at lunchtime. At about three thirty you go into the bathroom. You look in the mirror. You're wearing khakis, and you'll surely find something darker in your closet for the evening. You're wearing a button-down chosen more for comfort than midriff flattery. But still. You don't look thin, and you're not going to look thin in four hours, with a change of clothes.

You suck in your gut. It does not produce as striking an effect as you had hoped.

You call his home number, not his work number, because it's easier to tell a lie to a machine.

"I can't believe this and I can't tell you how bummed I am about it, but I've been sneezing all afternoon and I can feel that my head's really stuffed up," you say. You're using the clogged-nose voice just about anyone can affect when necessary. You're hoping yours doesn't sound too fake. "I think I'm getting sick, and I'd hate to get *you* sick." No, no! That last part was too much. It could be read as a presumptuous assertion that major germs would be exchanged.

You can't go back and delete the words, so you forge ahead. "As much as I hate to kick this too far into the future," you conclude, "I guess we'll have to wait until you get back into town. Let's touch base then."

That night you join friends at a Middle Eastern restaurant, where you set world records for hummus consumption. No reason to diet tonight. Any rescheduled date is more than two weeks away.

They're a relatively disciplined two weeks: Frequent runs. Infrequent binges. You don't shed four to five pounds, but it's possible you shed two.

You think, *If he calls, I'll go out with him. Whichever night he suggests. No chickening out.*

But you leave it to him to call. His call is the necessary proof that he's interested enough to overlook your physical flaws. His call is the reassurance you need.

What a surprise: it never comes.

Somehow, some way, thanks to unpredictable bursts of determination and unexpected stretches of levelheadedness, I did manage to date, and my desire for those dates to go well—along with my hope for additional dates beyond them—kept me in decent shape. It propelled me out to Belle Isle for long runs. It helped prevent binges too frequent or florid.

But I achieved actual, indisputable slimness only twice, and in neither case did the credit belong to better habits or more rationally marshaled willpower. It belonged to a minor war and a major athletic endeavor.

A few days after Christmas 1990, the newspaper sent me to Saudi Arabia to write about soldiers, sailors, pilots and marines who were there in preparation for the first Gulf War. I arrived in Dharan, Saudi Arabia, in time for New Year's Eve with the troops, and stayed for nearly three months.

Using my hotel room as a base, I'd take day trips and overnight trips out into the desert, near the border of southern Iraq, to spend as much time as military officials would let me interviewing the men camped out there. I'd sleep the way they slept, on hard cots inside tents, and eat the way they'd eat, which often meant those prepackaged, processed wonders known as Meals Ready-to-Eat. MREs were designed to provide maximum calories with minimum substance. They were compact energy bombs for soldiers on the go, with envelopes of rice stews or ham slabs or meat-flecked gruels. I was horrified, and not on epicurean grounds. I couldn't believe I was having extra-fattening food forced on me, especially when I was doing nothing more aerobic than scribbling in a notepad and banging on a laptop.

It was food so charmless that even I couldn't get through more than about half of an MRE a day. And when military officials finally permitted me more than overnight trips, assigning me to a cavalry regiment positioned along the tall sand berm separating northern Saudi Arabia and southern Iraq, MREs were the sum and summary of my diet. I picked at them joylessly as I waited for the ground war to begin.

When it did, I was given an empty seat in the rear of a Bradley Fighting Vehicle that had four soldiers inside, instead of the usual five. Our regiment was on the leading edge of troops moving into Iraq, and I might have been petrified had I not been too cramped, knotted and achy to feel anything else. A Bradley Fighting Vehicle isn't designed with such niceties as leg room and lumbar support in mind. It's a heavily fortified steamer trunk on wheels, with more room for armaments than anything else. I sat with my knees against my chest and my head banging against the low, hard ceiling. My only view of the landscape was through a small, smudgy rectangle of bulletproof glass. It was like watching *Lawrence of Arabia* on a microscope slide.

I ate less than ever as we trundled toward whatever awaited us, my appetite killed by my discomfort and something else: a determination not to go to the bathroom much. Because of the Army's concern about land mines, we were forbidden to step out of the vehicle, which didn't have a toilet of any kind. The solution was to lower the Bradley's rear hatch, crouch on its far edge and aim for the desert floor. I didn't have the thigh muscles for it. Or the immodesty.

We drove across the desert for five days without seeing combat, then got the news that the ground war was over. Brief as this trek was, it thinned me even further than my prior months in Saudi Arabia had, and when Renee met me at the Detroit airport in mid-March, she jokingly wondered if I'd been away at a spa. I suggested we head straight for a pub that had an oversize cheeseburger I loved. I'd never found a decent burger in Saudi Arabia and figured I was due and could afford one, calorically speaking.

Many months and more than a few regained pounds later one of my editors asked me if I'd be willing to pedal a bicycle across the breadth of Michigan. The newspaper was a principal sponsor of a group ride that publicized the Rails-to-Trails project, a campaign to turn train tracks that were no longer being used into bicycle routes. To chronicle the bikers' adventures on the first annual ride, the newspaper had sent a fit staffer along for the six-day trek from the edge of Lake Michigan eastward to Detroit.

For the second annual ride, the newspaper needed a new staff recruit for the assignment. The editor who approached me knew that I was a regular runner. Was I also, by chance, a biker? I wasn't, my emulation of Jennifer Beals having been brief and long ago. But I was in my late twenties and in decent cardiovascular health, and the ride was still three weeks away. I'd get a bicycle and I'd train. No problem.

Right away I got the bicycle, a clunky-looking one suited for off-road biking, because much of the ride entailed that. As for the training, well, I got sidetracked. I went out for a ride around Belle Isle, but found that I didn't enjoy biking as much as running, so the next day I went back to what I liked. I reasoned that as long as I was exercising and staying in shape, the method didn't matter. Besides, while the cross-state ride averaged about forty-five miles a day, I would have most of the day to do it. I could take my time.

As it happened I had to be slightly more attentive to speed than other riders did, because while they simply had to make it to a given night's base camp by dinnertime, I had to be there by three thirty p.m. so that I could write and file a story by six p.m. But that would still give me a good six hours to cover the requisite distance if I started out by nine a.m.

On the first day of the ride, it took me less than five hours to do the fifty miles or so, some of it across dirt and grass rather than pavement. On the second day, it took me only slightly longer, because I stopped more frequently for breaks. At various points along the route, the organizers set up refueling stations stocked with drinks and cookies, and I found I could eat seven or eight cookies without feeling at all stuffed. My body just burned them up. This was heaven.

On the third day, I woke up, began to get out of my bed in the school dormitory that riders were using, and shrieked. I couldn't straighten my legs. When I tried, my knees felt like they were being stabbed. I sat on the bed and breathed deeply, hoping this was just some postsleep stiffness. How could it be from the biking, which hadn't felt difficult at all?

I tried a second time to straighten my legs. This time I whimpered instead of shrieking, not because the agony was any less intense but because some pride had kicked in.

With halting movements I finally managed to get out of bed, get dressed and make my way outside, where I found one of the ride's organizers. He wondered how much bicycling I'd done in advance of the ride. When I told him I'd stuck to running, he remarked that the bicycling was stressing and straining a different set of muscles and joints, which were now voicing their complaint.

He reminded me of a truck that followed us from stop to stop and said I could ride in it, with my bicycle in the back. This would have been an excellent solution, but for one small problem: I'd already charted my journey and my thoughts in the newspaper for two days running, establishing a ritual of daily chronicles. If I stopped riding now, I'd have to own up to my failure to hundreds of thousands of readers.

One of my fellow riders had some ibuprofen. I took four of them for starters, and another two every two hours thereafter. And I biked. At first I biked as slowly as a human being could without tumbling sideways or going backward. Each time I pressed a pedal down, it seemed to me that shards of broken glass were scraping the inside of my knee, and I had to clench my jaw to get through it. On any incline of more than about three degrees, I got off the bike and pushed it forward. I started composing paragraphs for that day's story in my head and tried to memorize them. At the pace I was riding, I wasn't going to get to the next base camp by three thirty, so I was going to have to type like the wind.

By the end of that day I was doing much better, my agony eased by some combination of ibuprofen, vanquished stiffness and pure will. By the end of the next day I was, miraculously, close to fine. I completed the ride, all 250 miles of it, going so fast on the last day of it that I glided across the finish line well before the vast majority of other riders. I felt lighter than usual, but was actually less focused on that than on how much prouder than usual I felt. Sometimes I could grit things out. Sometimes I surprised myself.

Ten

The thrill of unusual adventures like my captivity in the Bradley Fighting Vehicle or my stupidity in biking across Michigan had a lot to do with sharing them with Mom. It felt like a proper return on the investment she'd made in us.

"I would have just held it in," she said when I told her how I'd had to go to the bathroom in the Iraq desert during the truncated ground war, at least the one time I couldn't avoid it. "I would have. For days if necessary!"

Regarding my Biker's Knees, she said, "I'm sure it wasn't that bad. You've always been a big baby about pain." She wasn't one of those mothers who rushed a child to the doctor at the sound of the slightest sneeze or kept him home from school if his temperature was just 99.8. She stuck a few aspirin in him, told him to buck up, sent him on his way and went back to the grocery store. She was always going back to the grocery store.

I reminded her of her unwarranted skepticism in the past. "Remember when I broke my back," I said, "and you didn't believe me?"

"I knew you'd bring that up," she said. "You always bring that

up! You think I'm just the most terrible mother. Fine: I'm a terrible
mother!"

I hadn't technically broken my back, but during my years at Loomis,
after jumping from a classmate's tree house rather than climbing down,
I'd experienced twinges and stiffness a few inches above my tailbone.
When I informed Mom, she was convinced I was making it up to get out
of an upcoming swim meet that I'd already said I didn't want to go to.
Weeks later, when the twinges got markedly worse and I found myself
walking in herky-jerky steps, Mom at last decided we should consult an
orthopedist, who did a special kind of X-ray called a bone scan. It turned
out that I had fractured two vertebrae. I spent the next three months in a
canvas and steel brace that went from my pelvis nearly to my underarms
and kept my lower back from bending.

From college forward, my phone calls to Mom had been frequent,
but while living in Detroit I called her just about every day, the two of us
having our morning coffee together over the phone, the calls lasting up
to an hour. I never cut them short. If she seemed to be enjoying them, I
didn't want to disrupt that, and if she was filling me in on the latest news
from her doctors, I wanted to hear it—wanted her to know that I was
paying attention and not oblivious to what she was going through.

You see, I've skipped over something, as reluctant to dwell on it
now as I was to accept it then. Just before I moved to Detroit, Mom was
diagnosed with cancer.

None of us in the family knew quite what to make of it, because
the hard facts of the diagnosis contradicted how healthy she seemed.
She had uterine cancer, but of a rare kind that acted more like ovarian
cancer, which was bad. We knew that even without having to educate
ourselves: there had been extensive news coverage of Gilda Radner's
struggle with ovarian cancer and of her death in 1989, the very year of
Mom's diagnosis. Pressed to make a prediction, Mom's doctors told her
she might survive for two years.

Almost immediately there was surgery, and then she started what would become round after round of different chemotherapies. She soldiered through them without suffering the worst of the fatigue and nausea chemo can cause. She soldiered through them without complaint. She was the same as ever: chatty, silly, impulsive, excitable and of course ornery, but not about the cancer, never about that. Occasionally she got a panicked, haunted look in her eyes, and her hair went from straight to curly, the chemo acting as an unflattering perm. But she made jokes about that.

And she had distractions. Harry was engaged to be married, beating Mark and Adelle to the altar, giving Mom her first opportunity to fuss over a child's wedding and giving her a daughter-in-law, Sylvia, whom she adored. Sylvia was thin, fine-boned, long-necked, tall. She looked nothing like a Bruni, and my favorite part of the wedding ceremony and reception was seeing her pose for pictures next to Grandma, who barely cleared her navel, even in her high heels and even with her high, stiff wedding-day hairdo. My second favorite part was watching Uncle Jim and Uncle Mario help Grandma out of the reception hall and across the parking lot at the end. She had danced so much that her feet were blistered and swollen, and she'd had to ditch those heels.

Soon after the wedding Mom was consumed by all the pesky domestic details surrounding Dad's latest transfer, from San Diego to New York City. Although rounding up new doctors and making sure her medical treatment didn't suffer in the transition gave her plenty to worry about, she still found time to sweat the usual stuff: whether the houses lined up by her real estate agent had kitchens that would pass muster; whether she should stick with Corian or switch her countertop allegiance to granite, which was then in vogue; whether Dad would survive the separation from Remington's.

The house they ended up buying was in Scarsdale, which was adjacent to White Plains but more exclusive, a way of simultaneously returning to a patch of turf they knew well and feeling they'd moved up in the world.

Not long after she and Dad settled into the Scarsdale house, she called Grandma several times one day and didn't get an answer.

This was strange: she'd talked to Grandma just the day before, and Grandma hadn't said anything about any plans to run errands, shop or do anything else that might take and keep her out of the house for hours. So Mom drove over to Fifth Street.

She found Grandma unconscious on the floor outside her bedroom. An ambulance rushed her to the hospital, where it was determined that she had suffered a major stroke.

While she was still in the hospital, I flew from Detroit to see her: perhaps the only visit with Grandma during which she wasn't hurling food at me and I wasn't idly protesting that she stop. She barely had the strength to kiss me and mumble the few words she said.

There was a good chance she wouldn't be able to live alone anymore, so Mom began sizing up the Scarsdale house, figuring out if it could be made suitable for someone with limited mobility. It had an odd layout, with many half flights of stairs between clusters of rooms, all these steps and more steps. But Mom determined that ramps could be installed, and she concluded that it made more sense for Grandma to live with her and Dad than with Uncle Jim and Aunt Vicki or with Uncle Mario and Aunt Carolyn, because she and Dad were the only ones whose kids were grown and gone. Mark, Harry and I had graduated from college and begun working; Adelle was finishing up at Princeton.

Those ramps never had to be installed. Grandma died soon after her stroke. She was eighty-one.

Toward the end of the visitations at the funeral parlor, Uncle Jim took out a camera and snapped several pictures of her in her casket, which was open, in accordance with family and southern Italian traditions. The pictures were for her relatives back in Puglia, to whom Grandma had sporadically sent documentary evidence of her good fortune, visual support for her written assertions that life in America was going well. More than a half century earlier she had photographed my father as a newborn, wanting to present her distant sisters with proof that she had been the first among them to produce a son. In the picture she had sent them he was naked.

In the picture that Uncle Jim took of Grandma at the funeral home she was wearing an elegant dress, and her hair and makeup were flawless. The point was that she looked regal and affluent in death, like a woman who had talked on a gold phone. What would *the people* think? That she had lived a good, gilded life. Her relatives back in Italy needed to be assured of that.

Back at Carolina I'd taken a psychology class with a professor whose mantra, only tangentially connected to what we were studying, was that life was ultimately about adjusting to loss, about letting go. He meant life after a certain point in time—after a certain age—and I wondered, with Grandma's death, if I was already there. Yes, new people would come along, but none who might loom anywhere near as large on the landscape of my life, of my whole identity, as she had. With luck a few of these people would love me, but none with the fierceness and pride that she had.

My world had just become irrevocably smaller and colder, and it threatened to become smaller and colder still. But I pushed that thought away.

Mom looked fine. Mom *was* fine. It was Mom who had been poised to care for Grandma.

A truly sick person didn't step up to play nurse.

I felt lonely in a way that I hadn't before. Back in Detroit I toted up the men I'd dated over the past few years and started worrying that I'd called it quits with some of them for dubious reasons and had maybe missed out on something. I realized, too, that I'd almost always called it quits precisely at the one-month mark. I had a pattern.

Then Greg came along.

Robin, my fashion writer friend, fixed us up.

"Solid job," she said in describing him, because he made decent money as a marketing executive for a chain of hardware stores.

"Handsome," she added, because he stood more than six feet tall and had a striking combination of strong Greek features with soft, non-Greek coloring.

"And I really think he'll like you," she concluded, because she knew something that she kept from me but that Greg later confessed. For him it wasn't a blind date. He'd seen me give a speech about my work at the *Free Press*.

Maybe that had somehow made me seem important. Maybe on our first date I wore something with astonishing thinning powers. For one reason or another, Greg decided right away that I was the guy he wanted, and he constantly made that clear—so clear that I could shelve some of my physical insecurity around him. I felt safe, and that feeling, coupled with my determination to break the pattern I'd only just identified, carried me into a second month with him, then a third.

Around Greg I could eat. I didn't do what I'd done around other men, didn't pretend to be full after five bites of an appetizer and seven of an entrée and then wave away dessert, saying I didn't know how I could possibly find the space, when my stomach was nothing *but* space, a McMansion of stomach, with laundry rooms and powder rooms and walk-in closets and in-law suites that other stomachs didn't have. Around Greg I hankered out loud, assenting without pause whenever he offered to make me a big dinner of penne alla vodka, meat loaf or, on special occasions, tenderloin with a creamy horseradish sauce. I cleaned my plate. I had seconds.

And it wasn't just that he made me feel safe—made me feel I had a margin of error when it came to my eating and my weight. It was less rosy than that. Although I would come to tell him that I loved him and on some level believe it, I never felt that he was the key to my happiness, that I'd be crushed if he went away, that I had to worry and work to make sure that never happened. I could live without him. And I figured that if he wouldn't stick by me plus a few extra pounds, I probably *should* live without him.

Both of us adored restaurants, for the theater and civilized pampering and pure deliciousness of eating out. And over time I'd become a better restaurant-goer. I hadn't eaten Chinese with Martin *every* night in New York; there were visits with other friends to some of Manhattan's most buzzed-about restaurants, like Arizona 206 and the Union Square Cafe. And when Dad had taken business trips to New York from La Jolla, he had treated me time and again to the Four Seasons, where I first tried duck. One bite of its crunchy, fatty, glistening skin and I was a goner. At the Four Seasons I never ordered anything but the duck.

Greg and I cycled quickly through all of his favorite restaurants in the Detroit area and all of mine, then cycled through them again. We had Vietnamese food just across the Detroit River in Windsor, Canada, at the Mini, where I'd first been educated in the silky, starchy wonder of congee. We had Middle Eastern food at Café La Shish in Dearborn, salmon seared in butter with capers at Joe Muir. For pasta we went to a restaurant called Little Italy in the far-flung suburb of Northville or to Lepanto in the nearby suburb of Royal Oak.

We logged hundreds of road miles chasing restaurant food, because that was the nature of the Detroit metropolitan area, which didn't really have a center of gravity, and because that was the nature of our appetites, which also sprawled. We had comfortable cars with cruise control and CD players, and we had our priorities.

Greg wasn't as prone to gaining weight as I was, and in the beginning I exercised enough to stave off the ravages of our adventures. But then

I got sloppy. Bit by bit I let my guard down—with eating, with sex. With previous boyfriends I'd been hyperaware, even when drunk, of every aspect of every sexual encounter: the brightness of the room; the angle from which the other person was getting a glimpse of me; whether those conditions would conspire to expose and underscore my flabbiness; how far from reach my T-shirt and underwear were. I'd want them back on as soon as we were done.

But not with Greg. I didn't always insist on darkness; I didn't instantly reach for that clothing. The difference was significant, but what exactly did it signify? I wasn't certain. So I initially resisted when, about four months after we met, Greg started lobbying me to give up my apartment and move into his small house just beyond the city limits.

He plotted a course around my resistance. He got sneaky.

"How about we pass by the pound?" he said one weekend day as we drove around doing errands. "Just to look."

He knew that I loved dogs and longed for one and that my family had had a frustrating, sad history with them: an Alaskan malamute that kept tunneling under the fence in Avon, despite all our measures to prevent that, and disappeared forever one day; an English setter that darted out the side door in La Jolla one morning and ended up under the wheel of a car. He also knew that my apartment building didn't allow pets.

"OK," I said. "Just to look."

"To look," he echoed. A few beats later he added: "My backyard *is* fenced in."

An hour later we pulled out of the pound parking lot with an eight-pound fur ball named Chester. From that night forward, I slept only at Greg's house. Within two months I'd moved in.

Black with tan patches, Chester had been labeled a "shepherd mix" by the pound. In fact every dog with his coloring had been labeled a "shepherd mix," a phrase whose ubiquity signaled either a disproportionate libidinousness among the German shepherds of southeastern Michigan or a lack of imagination among pound employees when it came to matters of nomenclature. As Chester got bigger it became clear that he was mostly Rottweiler, with some terrier thrown in. This wasn't a propitious mix.

Chester ran in a demented fashion around the living room. He ran in a demented fashion around the backyard, fast and furious and over and over, a doggie perturbed, a doggie possessed, a doggie impervious to my pleas that he stop and my stratagems to get him to by brandishing fistfuls of raw ground beef. He was seldom still and seldom sweet, and when he took to snarling at Greg, Greg had had enough. He wanted to get rid of Chester.

Out of loyalty and stubbornness, I insisted we give Chester one more chance, and I took him to obedience school two nights a week.

Other dogs learned to sit on command.

Chester didn't.

Other dogs came when called.

Chester wouldn't.

On the way home from class he'd sit in the front passenger seat next to me, and I'd say, "Do you know how disappointed I am in you? Do you know how embarrassed I was in front of all the other daddies and mommies?"

He wouldn't so much as cock an ear.

"Your days are numbered, you know?" I'd say.

He'd bark at a dog in a passing car.

About six months after Chester came into our lives, he was out of our lives, successfully pawned off on a gullible, optimistic family with more time and a bigger yard for him. We replaced him a few months later with Midas, an eight-month-old purebred golden retriever relinquished by his show-dog kennel because of some medical condition that made him a less-than-ideal sire.

By that point Greg and I were in a center-entrance three-bedroom brick colonial in the old-money suburb of Grosse Pointe Farms. The mortgage was in both of our names.

My pattern was officially broken.

And my weight was inching upward.

Greg was the first boyfriend I brought home to meet my parents and my siblings, and he accompanied me, too, on one of our family's vacations in Hilton Head, South Carolina, which had gradually evolved into an annual tradition. Hilton Head had golf courses that Dad loved. He and Mom would rent a house near the beach with at least five bedrooms, and Mark, Harry, Adelle and I, along with any significant others or spouses of ours, would pile into it for a week of rest, relaxation, competition and food. We focused in particular on the competition and the food.

There was almost nothing we couldn't turn into a contest, a race. If we went bodysurfing, the talk between waves hinged on who had caught the biggest one and who had ridden it the longest distance toward the shore. If we went miniature golfing, someone shouted out an update of everyone's scores after each hole, so that there was never any doubt about who was in the lead, who was in the rear and how many strokes separated them.

And then there was Oh, Hell, something of a cross between bridge and hearts, with trump cards and bids and ten successive hands per game. The optimal limit of players for it was five. We usually had about ten. So we created a system in which two games occurred simultaneously, one in a "major league" and the other in a "minor league." At the beginning of the night, players were assigned at random to one of the leagues. But at the end of each successive game, the person with the worst score from the major league was sent to the minors, while the person with the best score from

Mark (far left) *and his wife-to-be, Lisa,*
with Mom and me in Hilton Head.

the minor league ascended to the majors. By the fifth or sixth game, the league a player inhabited indeed reflected how well he or she was playing.

Sometimes the two leagues were just at opposite ends of the same long dining room table, sometimes at different tables in the same room or in adjacent ones. They had to be within talking distance of each other, to allow for scripts like the following, typical one.

Harry, sitting in the majors, to Mark, beside him: "You've got to be looking around right now, seeing who's up here and who's down there, and thinking that justice has prevailed. The elite players are grouped as they should be."

Mark, who had started in the minors: "You know what's amazing? It's more *comfortable* here. The chairs feel softer. The air's cleaner. Breathe that in! That's major-league air."

Lisa, Mark's fiancée, in the minors: "Someone might be sleeping on the couch tonight."

Me, sitting beside her: "Someone should be hit in the head."

Mark, to Harry: "Shouldn't there be some rule that the minor leaguers have to refresh the major leaguers' drinks? I'm due for a new beer."

Mom, in the minors: "You people are obnoxious. I can't believe I raised you."

Some nights we'd eat in, but a few nights we'd eat out, making a big, boozy, beefy production of it. One of our go-to restaurants, Stripes, a steakhouse, served oversize portions that guaranteed leftovers, designated for lunch the next day and maybe even the day after that. Sometimes, though, they disappeared first.

"Where's the rest of my rib eye?" Mark would say when he peeled back the aluminum foil around what was a suspiciously tiny slab of beef.

He would look at me. So would Harry and Lisa and Adelle and Dad. It didn't matter that, the night before, at one a.m., when I'd gone from my and Greg's bedroom to the refrigerator, I'd tiptoed. Everyone knew anyway.

"Are you sure that's *your* leftover steak?" I might say, feebly. "Maybe it's someone else's."

"I don't think so," Mark would answer.

"Maybe Tom ate it," I'd counter, referring to Adelle's boyfriend, who would eventually become her husband. As a newcomer to the family, he could be used as the fall guy. And he was a more credible culprit than Sylvia, whose weakness was sweets, or Lisa. Lisa was a mincing, birdlike eater, and had turned Mark into one, too. Since meeting her, he'd developed this odd habit of cutting his food into minuscule bites and chewing each one some two dozen times. His eating had become as seemingly joyless as any eating I'd ever witnessed. As a weight-loss mechanism, it didn't tempt me in the least.

He and Harry loved to call me out on my late-night refrigerator raids because it affirmed that their willpower was superior to mine: another competition they were winning. After listening to them rib me about the leftovers I'd pilfered or the disproportionate number of tortilla chips I'd dragged through the salsa or the extra scoop of ice cream I'd put in my bowl, I'd skulk away to read a book—or I'd throw on some running clothes and huff through two miles made harder by the rib eye and the chips and the ice cream. I'd wear a baggy shirt out to dinner that night, hoping to cloak my excesses.

Greg sometimes questioned the make, cut or color of the shirt. He sometimes questioned the rest of my outfit, too. But the eating? Unlike my brothers or the voices in my own head, he didn't judge me for—or tease me about—that.

"We should go clothes shopping," Greg said one morning back in Grosse Pointe Farms, as I poured myself a cup of coffee and unfolded the day's *Free Press*, which I'd just fetched from the front stoop. I was going to scan the first few paragraphs of the front-page stories, then take Midas for his morning walk. I almost always took Midas for his morning walk. I liked the way neighbors and random passersby stopped me just to tell me how gorgeous he was. I'd swell with pride, as if his lustrous coat was actually my genetic bequest to him.

Greg pressed: "What if we go shopping after work today?"

He went clothes shopping all the time, toting me with him whenever I would let him. He'd done wonders for my wardrobe, which hadn't previously existed as anything complete and distinguished enough to be called a wardrobe. When we'd met I was down to one pair of shoes other than sneakers, these shapeless once-brown clunkers that were now mottled with orange spots in all the places where the dye had faded. I wore them with dress slacks as well as with casual pants. I wore them with my only *suit*. Vanity's an erratic ruler, governing some things so ruthlessly that others escape its scrutiny altogether.

But after a half year with Greg, I had Ferragamo dress shoes, Bally loafers, Joan & David boots. I liked shopping for shoes, because trying them on didn't involve any kind of measurement or determination of where I was on the trimmer-to-heavier spectrum. Arches and toes had a constancy that love handles didn't.

But at this particular juncture, Greg wasn't proposing that we shop for shoes.

"Don't you think you should get some new pants?" he said, his voice as gentle as he could sculpt it.

I did need new pants. I was down to a pair of jeans and a pair of Army green chinos that fit, and they fit only because I'd worn them so frequently and stretched them so much. They were so faded and frayed that the numbers indicating their sizes weren't readily discernible. In any case, I wasn't trying to discern them. Wasn't that one of the benefits of being in a relationship with someone as devoted as Greg—that I didn't have to look? My memory was that the chinos were 35s. So I guessed I needed 36s, and I guessed I could live with that, but only until I lost a few pounds.

"OK," I told Greg. "But just a pair or two, because whatever we buy now isn't going to fit me a month from now. It's just to tide me over."

He didn't argue.

"And we should go to a discount place," I added. "T.J. Maxx or Marshalls. It's not worth spending money on something so temporary."

He nodded.

We went to T.J. Maxx. The narrow aisles and jammed racks depressed me, but then this shopping excursion wasn't meant to be fun, just functional. I found the men's section, then the slacks, then oriented myself in terms of those round white number signs on the horizontal poles, the signs with waist sizes. I dawdled briefly at the 32s, just in case anyone was watching—just for show.

Then it was on to the 34s, though there was no sense looking through those, either. I went grudgingly to the 36s, which would probably fit. Or would they? I realized I was unsure, and wondered for a few instants if in fact the pants that had become too small were 36s. No, no. Impossible. I'd remember if I'd purchased 36s. I'd definitely remember.

From the limited selection of 36s, I plucked a dark green and a dark blue pair. Dark colors were more crucial than ever now. I walked to the dressing room, tried on the green pants. They barely cleared my hips. There wasn't any point in seeing if I could get the zipper all the way up or button the pants closed. I wouldn't be able to walk in them.

I tried on the blue pants. They cleared my hips and . . . *oof! sheesh! ouch!* I stood ramrod straight, a guard at Buckingham Palace, as I tugged at the zipper so hard that its metal edges dug like spades into my fingers. I sucked in my stomach. I sucked harder. I held my breath. I could wear these pants, but only if I was willing to part ways with oxygen.

"These are cut really, really slim," I told Greg when I rejoined him outside the dressing room. "It's crazy how slim they're cut."

"Maybe," he said, "you should look in the 38s." He said it like he was expecting this all along.

"They'll be too baggy," I argued, suddenly unconvinced they would be.

"It's no big deal," he said. "Just try them."

"Fine," I said, and grabbed the first two pairs I came across, even though one was a too-light golden color. The other, more acceptable one was dark brown.

Both fit perfectly.

I strode right past Greg on my way out of the dressing room and toward the cashier, the pants not draped over one of my forearms but scrunched up in my clenched hands. As far as I was concerned Greg could catch up with me at the register, beside the car—wherever.

"What's your problem?" he asked as we left the store.

I was ready to unload on him. How had he let me gain this much weight—however much weight it was—without diplomatically directing my attention to it? How had he not gingerly noted that I wasn't running as frequently as before and nudged me out the door? Shouldn't he have stepped in?

But just before I began a tirade, I realized that what I was mistaking for fury at him was really epic embarrassment—outsize shame. I had not only plumped up rounder than I usually let myself get but had done so in front of a witness as near and ever present as I'd ever had, a witness of a more intimate kind. Although I had wanted a margin of error around Greg, this was way more than a margin.

"Midas better be ready," I told him. "Starting tomorrow, he is going to be taking some long runs with me." And so he did—with pauses, of course, so other runners could duly admire him. The 38s got looser, and then I retired them, actually threw them away. But they suggested how far I could slide. As it happened, they soft-pedaled the possibilities.

Greg and I scouted furniture stores for the right couch to put in the living room and carpet stores for the right rug to put in front of it. Together we took Midas to the vet. We went to his Aunt Margaret's house for her lasagna and then bickered amiably about it, him defending the way she added cinnamon to her tomato sauce, me crying foul. We signed both of our names on the cards accompanying gifts to the friends we now had in common. As a couple we went to dinner parties, and as a couple we hosted dinner parties. When Mom called, he and she would chat for a good ten minutes before she thought to ask for me or he thought to pass the phone along.

And for my thirtieth birthday, he secretly organized it so that Mom and Dad, Mark and Lisa, Harry and Sylvia, and Adelle and Tom all flew in for a surprise party. He organized it so that even Elli, my grad school coconspirator, who was then living in the Catskills in upstate New York, flew in. About two dozen of my closest friends in Detroit rounded out the crowd.

Many were from the *Free Press*, where I'd come to know just about everyone, because I'd changed assignments so often and because some of the stories I'd done had attracted a lot of attention. Following my stint in the Persian Gulf, my editors had given me an unusually long leash, letting me do ambitious, detailed feature pieces, one of which, a profile of a convicted child molester, had been a finalist for the Pulitzer Prize in feature writing. It had even led to a book, written with Elli, about child sex abuse by Catholic priests.

After that, I swerved again, indulging an interest in films—I'd seen plenty of Coppola and Malick in addition to *Flashdance*—to become a movie critic for the newspaper. I went to as many as a half dozen movie screenings a week. I flew regularly to Los Angeles, Chicago and New York to interview directors and stars, and I toted home great cocktail party stories: about Sandra Bullock insisting that I stay in her trailer on the set of *While You Were Sleeping* and listen to the brand-new song "You Gotta Be," by Des'ree, while she changed in the back for her next scene; about Mel Gibson summarily shutting off my tape recorder and launching into a foul-mouthed rant when I asked him about past characterizations of him as a homophobe and archconservative.

Even so, I was restless, wanting new challenges and adventures, feeling too young to stand still, thinking and often talking about leaving Detroit. Whenever I mentioned that, Greg and I fought. He was the only child of two aging parents who lived in the Detroit area. His other relatives, best friends, favorite haunts and most cherished memories: all revolved around Detroit. He wanted to stay there. And he demanded to know why, if I loved him, I couldn't at least entertain that possibility.

It was a fair question, prompting me to ask myself others. Was the steady contentment I felt with and around him love, or was it comfort? Where was the dividing line between the two, and how could you ever trace it? Was Greg a solution to my physical insecurities, or just a way to hide from the problem?

I hadn't found any answers when I got a call from a good friend of Elli's working as a deputy metropolitan editor for the *New York Times*. I'd apparently been on the newspaper's radar ever since the Pulitzers, and Elli's friend wanted to know if I was wedded to movie criticism or if I'd consider a general reporting position on the *Times*'s metropolitan desk. I said I'd consider it, and then I was on a plane to New York, and then I had a job offer, and then I was telling Greg he should move with me to New York, even though I wasn't sure I wanted him to.

For a while he toyed with the idea, but he couldn't get past his anger that I'd decided to take the job without making sure it was okay with him. He railed about how inconsiderate I was. How selfish. By the time I packed up my footwear and the rest of my expanded wardrobe, it seemed unlikely he'd be following me. I reached New York feeling guilty, crummy and empty.

·THREE·

Ipso Fatso

Eleven

or Harry's wedding, Mom and Dad had been relatively
restrained. They had hosted only 55 of the wedding's 130
guests at the previous night's rehearsal dinner. And they had
held the dinner at a restaurant more charming than showy,
a sweet country inn of sorts.

For Mark's wedding to Lisa, which took place in Dallas, her
hometown, in the late spring of 1994, Mom and Dad had gone bigger,
brasher, Bruni-er. The rehearsal dinner was held in a private club near
the top floor of one of the tallest skyscrapers downtown. There were
ninety-six guests, because Dad felt that all of Lisa's closest Texas relatives
should be there and of course Uncle Jim and Uncle Mario and their
families should be there and, come to think of it, shouldn't anyone
who was traveling from the Northeast all the way to Texas be able to
look forward to a fancy meal in addition to the one at the wedding? An
additional fancy meal is what Dad gave them, and he insisted that there
be a continuously open bar not only in the room where the cocktail hour
took place but also in the nearby dining room, where the more serious
eating occurred, because he didn't want people to have to walk all the

way across the hall to freshen their drinks. What kind of host, he asked, would allow that?

But Adelle's wedding to Tom, in Scarsdale in the fall of 1995, let Mom and Dad seize control of the actual wedding reception itself for the first time. They didn't let the opportunity go to waste.

Their worry that people be adequately fed was reflected less in the sit-down meal—a four-course affair, because there had to be a pasta course between the appetizer and the main course—than in the cocktail hour that preceded it. For starters they decided that this hour should be extended to ninety minutes—it *had* to be ninety minutes—because

Harry (far right), *Mark* (next to him)
and me with Adelle at her wedding.

anything shorter wouldn't allow the 175 guests to size up and visit the food stations that would exist in addition to the passed hors d'oeuvres, of which there were nearly a dozen.

There was a station where a carver stood poised to press his knife through various kinds of meats. There was a pasta station offering different noodles and different sauces. There was, naturally, a cold seafood station, and there was a cheese station as well. And then there was something more eye-catching than anything else, with its glittering glassware and its blocks of ice: a vodka station, with several brands of vodka and several flavors of vodka and pony glasses and Champagne flutes and a half dozen fresh fruits to be used as garnishes, mixes or little nibbles on the side.

"Jim, did you get to the vodka bar?" Dad asked Uncle Jim, leading him in that direction. Dad was the first of his brothers and cousins—the first of his generation in the Bruni and Mazzone families—to throw a wedding for a daughter, and he wanted everyone to see that he was doing it in style.

"Carolyn, did you have some pasta?" he asked Aunt Carolyn, nudging her pesto-ward.

He directed one platter of hors d'oeuvres toward Grandma's brother Agostino and another toward Grandma's sister-in-law Florence, saying to them, "Ma would have loved this, don't you think?" She would have. Not a minute of the event went by without my thinking that, and I didn't have to check with any of my uncles, aunts or siblings to know that not a minute went by without their thinking that, too.

Dad was part conductor and part shepherd, his mission to make sure people got as much food and drink as they could handle and then got some more. Bunched up in his dark tuxedo, he moved in abrupt bursts, his upper body tilted slightly forward, the way it always did when he was nervous or rushed, and his hands balled into fists.

He was a creature of such fierce, fierce pride, so clearly his mother's son, hypervigilant about the face he showed the world, keenly attuned to what the world might be thinking of him and his family. When I'd been in school and he'd insisted on As or betrayed disappointment at a slow time in a swim meet, he wasn't just trying to make sure I did my best and got as far as I might want to in life. He was also mourning an aura of perfection I'd just sullied.

And yet his attention to that aura didn't extend to how I looked, or rather to whether I was showing the world a figure as handsome and fit as I could be. Unlike Mom, who chose not to recognize or reconcile the contradiction of shoving food at me one day and a diet book the next, Dad never nagged me about my eating and never said much of anything when I gained weight. He never nagged Adelle, either. I always wondered: Was it because the notion of plenty was so central to his conception of taking care of people—of having the economic wherewithal to do so? Because he saw a joy in my eating that he couldn't bring himself to challenge? Or because he understood what it was like to be weak around food, which was what he often used to relieve all the pressure he put on himself?

For a man so image-conscious, he was an awful dieter, still carrying around appreciably more weight than he should. He didn't try to hide his zest for food. And he goaded the people around him to demonstrate the same kind of enthusiasm.

"Did you have enough to eat?" he asked a business associate he had invited to Adelle's wedding. He unclenched one of his balled fists to pat the associate on the back. "Have some more, before we get called in to dinner."

"This isn't the dinner?" the business associate asked.

"Of course not!" Dad said, feigning surprise at the question, which was precisely the question he expected and wanted to get.

I parked myself near the vodka station, where Mom whizzed by me at one point. I nodded toward it and flashed a confused expression at her.

Mom, gaunt from the cancer and chemotherapy,
with Dad at Adelle's wedding.

"We're suddenly Russian?" I teased.

"Look how many people are crowding around it!" she shot back. "Vodka's what all the young people drink." I could tell she was feeling very with-it and in-touch and of-the-moment and maybe a few other hyphenated phrases connoting keen, boundary-traversing generational empathy.

She looked fantastic, her smile turned up as high as it went, her dark green dress bringing out the steely blue of her eyes, which were aglow from the privilege and power trip of being the mistress of ceremonies, the mother of the bride. Actually, she looked fantastic and terrible at the same time, but the terrible part we all tried to edit out of our mental pictures of her, because the terrible part was the cancer's doing. She was thin, too thin, by any standard: a good five pounds shy of anything healthy. Her face was gaunt and her arms were spindly, and that hadn't been the case after the first or second or even third round of chemo. But all of it was catching up to her now, six years into the two years her doctors had said she could hope to live.

She was exhausted, she was defiant. Here she was celebrating a family milestone that she wasn't supposed to be around to see, and another milestone was within reach. Sylvia was pregnant, and it was beginning to show: Mom's first grandchild was on the way. She was determined to hold that baby and confident that she had a will steely enough to guarantee herself the experience, but she wasn't sure about much after that. With increasing frequency she reminded me that I'd promised not to let her suffer if things were headed in that direction, to make sure it was fast at the end. I murmured the proper assurances and nodded the proper assent, though I had no idea if or how I could follow through, and Mom hadn't mapped out any kind of scenario. It was just this vague, chilling understanding we had.

I paid the vodka station more attention than anything else at the wedding, trying to find a Dostoevsky-esque grandeur in my apprehension and sadness, wondering how many glasses of vodka on the rocks erased a parent's terminal illness, and how many more erased my own fickleness (had I been fickle?) and disloyalty and selfishness (was I guilty of these, too?) in beating such a decisive retreat out of Detroit and away from Greg. And what about the worry I felt every time I walked into the *Times* building, a worry that never wholly abated and was with me even now? How many glasses of vodka for that?

On the work front, the three months since I'd left Detroit had been miserable. I arrived at the *Times* having not handled a concise, straightforward news story in about three years, but these were the kinds of stories that I'd signed up for and that were instantly thrown at me. I reported and wrote them in a state of dread, and after filing them, I sometimes watched as an editor recast the first sentences and lopped off every other sentence after that and made the fifth and sixth paragraphs the tenth and eleventh paragraphs and then struck the last two hundred words, dismissing them as long-winded effluvium. The newspaper published a few articles under my byline that bore only an oblique relationship to what I'd actually handed in.

Assignment after assignment seemed like an invitation to failure or an exercise in near-catastrophe. I was sent out to the Hamptons to cover raging wildfires and told to interview homeowners either fleeing from their homes, refusing to budge or coming back in tremulous states to appraise the wreckage. But every time I got near a neighborhood in the fire zone, I encountered a police barricade and was turned back. Radio reporters and wire service reporters, however, were getting precisely the sorts of scenes and interviews I wasn't—what trick wasn't I figuring out? When I finally did reach a threatened neighborhood and set foot on the front lawn of one of the houses, a large, snarling dog rushed at me and sank its teeth into my right thigh before I could back away. I limped into the newspaper's offices back in Manhattan that night with ripped, bloodstained pants. I went into the men's room, looked in the mirror and thought: *That's about right.* The way I looked matched the way I felt. I was a mess through and through.

For a few weeks after I landed in New York, Greg and I talked on the phone as often as every other night. Not talked: negotiated, needled, nitpicked and ultimately shouted. Tense discussions about who should get which lamp and how much he should pay me for my equity in the house led to pettier, nastier dissections of our sex life or of our friends, he claiming never to have liked most of mine, I claiming in return never to have liked any of his.

And if these interchanges came at the end of one of my more

nerve-racking days at the *Times*, I'd find myself rushing out the door afterward to a nearby bodega—for beer, for chips, for ice cream, for all of it—or riffling through a stack of delivery menus. Delivery menus! Manhattan was the mother lode of them: Chinese, Vietnamese, Japanese, Lebanese, any *-ese* there was. Also Mexican and Italian and Thai, not to mention Indian and Peruvian and Cuban. Every day a new menu appeared just inside the front door of my Uptown apartment near Columbia University, slipped through the crack underneath the door by unseen underminers, a multipaged message for the shut-in binger: *Psst. Have I got something delicious for you!* I called the numbers on the menus, counted the minutes until the doorbell rang and then opened the door wide to enchiladas and empanadas, satays and spring rolls.

It was a fast, easy, certain source of pleasure, not dependent on the assent or participation of anyone else. I'd spread the cartons and tins of food on the living room coffee table so I could survey and size up the bounty. I'd put on sweatpants and a baggy sweatshirt: nothing that could cinch or cling. I'd put something trashy and brainless on television, maybe one of those women-in-peril movies starring Veronica Hamel or Markie Post. And the world would shrink to just a few square feet around me and to the warm, uncomplicated, unremarkable ripple of gratification running through me.

Sometimes I bopped from my apartment down to Chelsea, where my old roommate Martin had moved and was now living with a new roommate but without his menagerie, its members having either died or gone to live with friends. But as much as I wanted to, I couldn't tap back into the silliness that had always been our special glue. I didn't go to gay bars and didn't date and didn't think about doing either. The ugliness of those final conversations with Greg—before we finally agreed on the lamps and the money and declared a truce—put me off the very ideas of sex or romance the way being stung by a jellyfish puts a toddler off the ocean. I now knew the perils and the price. I wasn't about to dip in again anytime soon.

And I used this break as an allowance to eat more, which in turn became an added reason to extend the break. I wasn't really thinking so much as pressing forward, day by day, not letting things get completely out of hand but not taking charge of them, either.

Central Park was close enough that I went for occasional runs there, even pushing those runs to as many as six miles on rare, guilt-stricken occasions, usually the mornings after I'd assembled and worked my way through an especially large coffee-table feast. I joined a gym four blocks from my apartment, but it was a tiny second-floor room with only a small assortment of weight machines and a total of three treadmills. I didn't like going there, so I didn't go often. I pledged to find a new gym, a motivating gym, a gym that would imbue me with the exercise ethic I wanted and currently lacked. I'd do that next week, or next month—soon enough. I wasn't in any rush. I was on my break. I needed and deserved it.

In March 1996, Sylvia and Harry had a girl, and they named her Leslie, after Mom. Another Leslie Bruni. Harry was working in Manhattan and living just outside the city, sort of halfway to Scarsdale, in Mount Vernon, so I saw a lot of little Leslie in her first weeks and months. I made a point of it. I couldn't get my fill of carrying her around and rocking her and trying to teach her words long before it was time for that.

"You're talking to her in both English *and* Spanish, right?" I asked Sylvia, who had grown up speaking Spanish, the language of her Cuban parents, at home.

"I think it's a little early for that," she answered, noting that Leslie hadn't yet mastered the art of holding her own head up or sitting. Verb conjugations were a ways away.

"But you *will* do that, won't you?" I pushed. I wanted Leslie to be bilingual. I wanted her to be anything that would make her stand out and give her an edge and increase the odds that happiness would be hers.

"Yes, *yes*," Sylvia said.

"Harry, you'll watch? You'll make sure?" I was crossing into obnoxiousness. So be it.

"You have to try this cab-merlot blend," Harry said, pouring me a glass of wine. He was becoming a wine geek. But his actions at this moment were more about changing the subject, getting me to let up.

Adelle and I read to little Leslie.
I'm seriously in love.

"*Cómo estás?*" I said to little Leslie, on her back on the family room carpet with her pudgy arms clawing at the air, her pudgy legs kicking it.

"Unbelievable," I heard Harry mutter from a dozen feet away, where he hurriedly poured the wine for me.

"Maybe," I said, "I should speak to her in Italian." I'd studied it for two and a half years in college and had a decent arsenal of sentences and phrases. "*Come va*, my little Peanut?" That was one of our nicknames for her.

The intensity of my response to her was more like a father's than an uncle's, and mixed into it somewhere and somehow was the thought of losing Mom. That was clear to me even then. When Harry and Sylvia asked me to be little Leslie's godfather, the high I felt easily beat any I'd ever gotten from a swimming victory, a long run or my Mexican speed.

Meanwhile Mark's wife, Lisa, had announced that she was pregnant. Due date: late November, another marker for Mom to shoot for. It was as if her children had entered into this reproductive tag-team conspiracy to keep her going, to make it impossible for her to leave. There would certainly be more grandchildren after these first two: Harry and Sylvia and Mark and Lisa had made clear that they weren't planning small families, and Adelle and Tom had yet to get into the act. Mom had to stick around to spoil all of these grandchildren. She had to stick around to feed them.

Because Lisa was going to be delivering right around Thanksgiving, Mom and Dad and the rest of our immediate family decided we'd spend Thanksgiving Day at her and Mark's house in the suburbs of Boston, either greeting their newborn or awaiting the baby's any-second-now arrival. Mom was no longer hosting Thanksgiving; Aunt Carolyn had taken it over when Mom and Dad moved to California, too far away to stay in the family-holiday-hosting rotation. So we made our apologies to her and Uncle Mario, letting them know we'd be back (and more numerous by one) the following year. And we made our arrangements to travel to Boston.

Mom was looking more fragile than ever. More than a year had passed since Adelle's wedding, and during that time she had confronted the boundaries of her stamina. All the chemotherapy—at least three times as much of it as doctors had ever expected she could withstand—had so battered her immune system and weakened her blood that she was receiving regular transfusions and was diagnosed with leukemia, a new cancer to keep company with the old one. She slept so fitfully that she spent most nights curled up on the family room couch, where she could turn on and off the lights or TV without bothering Dad. She was happiest whenever she found a *Law and Order* episode she'd already seen; that way, she didn't have to worry about dozing off before the verdict. As for her serial-killer books, which she was going through at a faster pace than ever, I noticed that she'd taken to reading the last twenty pages first. She told me she'd simply lost her appetite for surprises. I wondered if she'd lost her confidence that she'd get to the end.

She was shockingly, frighteningly moody, pivoting from laughter to tears without any explanation or provocation. And she was, for the first time, pessimistic. Shortly before Thanksgiving she asked me for an unsettling favor. Would I take the two cats, Sable and Boo, to the vet to be put to sleep?

For decades our family had alternated between cats and dogs, occasionally having one of each at the same time. But after the English setter was hit by a car, we gave up on dogs. Mom liked cats better, anyway. Sable and Boo were the last in a line of more than a half dozen of them since I'd been born.

Mom attributed to them personalities much more complicated and fascinating than they had, and claimed to be able to read into their squeaks and peeps and full-throated meows whole sentences and paragraphs of meaning. Dad just rolled his eyes. They were her cats, not his; he tolerated them solely for her sake. And now they were getting old and addled, often going to the bathroom near, instead of in, their litter box in the laundry room. At this stage of their lives, no one was going to adopt them, and Mom didn't want Dad to be saddled with them when she was gone. No, there was only one sensible course of action. She should say good-bye to them now.

But she wanted someone with them, holding and stroking them, when they were put down, and she couldn't bear to be the one. She elected me. Although I was the son who listened to the weepiest music and blubbered most copiously during *Terms of Endearment*, I was also the one she trusted to be the most hardheaded and strong-stomached about certain things. That was why I was the one she always reminded about her adamant opposition to any extraordinary life-prolonging measures.

As I walked through the Scarsdale house to round up the cats for their ride to the vet, I tried to make light of it, telling her, "I feel like I should be carrying a scythe or something."

"My grim reaper," she said with a smile and a tiny, forced laugh, then hugged me. On my neck I could feel that her eyes were wet.

Two days before Thanksgiving, Lisa gave birth to a boy and named him Frank, after Dad. Mom wanted to see him right away and Dad was tied up, so she packed up some pots, pans, spices and such to supplement whatever Mark and Lisa had in their house. She hauled them into a car. Then she drove the three and a half hours to Boston by herself. That evening, in Lisa's hospital room, she cradled her first grandson and delighted in his coloring: he had the pale skin, pale eyes and red hair of her Irish lineage. In her own dark-eyed, dark-haired children and in the Italian values and habits and appetites she had developed, Dad's blood trumped hers. But here was a seven-pound, ten-ounce reminder that she was in the mosaic, too, and that she would stay there.

Lisa's parents, Betty and Mike, arrived on a plane from Dallas the next day, but Mom nonetheless insisted on taking charge of Thanksgiving dinner, though it would be slightly more modest than usual, given that she was feeding a smaller group and doing so with limited energy.

She debriefed Lisa on the best food stores in the area and went out the day before Thanksgiving to do the shopping. Back at Mark and Lisa's house she started chopping what could be chopped in advance and cooking what could be cooked ahead of time, including a turkey breast that didn't need to be served warm, since it was designated for extra meat for the evening sandwiches that traditionally followed the midday meal. She educated Betty on the importance of the extra breast.

"Without it you just never have enough white meat," explained Mom, still an evangelist for excess. She moved through the kitchen sluggishly, becoming palpably winded at times. She waved off suggestions from Betty and Mike that she let them take over. She had no choice, though, but to accept their offers of help.

On Thanksgiving morning she woke up at four a.m. so she could put the whole turkey in the oven and start making the rest of the meal.

For several hours she had the kitchen to herself. That was precisely how she wanted it.

Mark and Lisa returned home from the hospital with their son at about noon, in time for shrimp and quiche, because Mom had of course made quiche. She had also peeled scores of clementines and stacked them high in the shape of a pyramid. They were just a little something to be put on the table right after the dishes for the main meal were cleared and before the real dessert arrived.

We had that meal at two p.m. As soon as it was over, Mom excused herself and apologized: she needed to take a nap. She negotiated the stairs up to the second-floor bedrooms one slow, careful step at a time. She didn't come back down until three and a half hours later.

At the end of the Thanksgiving weekend she and Dad drove together back to Scarsdale, and at about five thirty a.m. Monday the phone in my apartment in Manhattan rang. Dad was with her at the hospital, where he had taken her in the middle of the night because she was having trouble breathing.

Adelle and Tom drove into the city from their apartment in Hoboken, New Jersey, to pick me up. By eight a.m. the three of us were with Mom and Dad in her room at White Plains Hospital. Soon Harry and Sylvia showed up, bringing little Leslie with them, and soon after that Mark arrived, too, having driven three and a half hours straight from Boston, where Lisa remained only because she had a five-day-old infant to care for.

Dad and all four of his and Mom's children were around her, encircling her, as her breathing became increasingly labored and her eyes darted this way and that, wild with confusion or maybe fury. We couldn't tell, and she wasn't able to tell us.

As she struggled ever harder for breath, her body began to thrash.

"You've got to help her," I told a nurse, who upped the amount of morphine going into Mom through an intravenous drip.

I told the nurse the same thing ten minutes later, when Mom's thrashing hadn't ceased. And the same thing again five minutes after that.

Dad balled his fists tighter and tighter, walked in circles, asked me if I was sure. I said yes. I had to say yes. Those were my orders.

Whenever I stepped back from the side of Mom's bed, I found myself plucking little Leslie, eight months old and unaware of what was happening, from Harry's or Sylvia's arms. I pressed my lips against her forehead, her nose, her cheeks. Over and over again. I couldn't let go of her.

Years later, when her personality came into sharper focus and it was the personality of a competitive, stubborn and sometimes bossy spitfire, we all joked that it wasn't death that took place in that hospital room.

It was just the transfer of an indomitable spirit from an older vessel to a newer one.

The days, weeks and months that followed Mom's death were, in the truest sense possible, a blur. I couldn't concentrate the way I usually did, and I often couldn't clearly remember what had happened one day by the time the next arrived.

Did friends of the family drop off platters of food, casseroles and cakes at the Scarsdale house, the way people often do after someone dies? It's possible. Probable. I can't say.

Was there any sort of ceremonial meal to go along with the moment when Dad, Mark, Harry, Adelle and I carried Mom's ashes to the pond across the street from the Scarsdale house and scattered them there, in a setting that always delighted her and gave her a sense of peace? There might have been. There *must* have been. But it's lost to me.

I remember walking to a lectern in the same Scarsdale church where Adelle had been married to give the eulogy at Mom's funeral, and I remember walking away from that lectern. But if Mark hadn't saved a text of that eulogy—written with his, Harry's and Adelle's help—it would be lost to me, too.

I talked to the hundreds of people who'd come to pay their respects about Mom's cooking, and about the lasagna for Mark's college teammates, a tradition that lasted all four of his years at Amherst. "It's an amazing thing," I said, "when you think about it: that a college-age kid would actively encourage dozens and dozens of his friends to meet his mother, and that those friends would like her—and, I'll admit, her cooking—so much that year after year, they would forgo getting back to campus in time for the Saturday-evening parties just to pay her and her home another visit."

I also put into words something I'd always believed, deep down, even when Mom had signaled disappointment in me over a swimming practice missed, a race lost, a nearly straight-A report card marred by a B-plus or ten pesky pounds I couldn't lose. I said that I'd had the luxury of going through life knowing there was someone who would love and support me no matter what. "For me, at least, she was the safety net that made every risk manageable, every uncertainty endurable," I told the gathered mourners. "Now, for the first time, I guess I'll find out if I have any courage of my own. I didn't need it before, because I had my mother."

After nearly a week in Scarsdale with Dad and my siblings, I went back to my apartment and back to work. I wrote an article on something—on nothing—and realized that it was probably the first piece of mine in the *Times* that Mom wouldn't read. She had been faithful that way.

As I made coffee one morning I caught sight of a book above the stove that I hadn't noticed in a long time. It wasn't exactly a book, but a binder filled with sewing tips and cleaning tips and many blank ruled pages onto which whoever bought it was supposed to paste, scribble or staple favorite recipes for whoever was receiving it. Mom had pasted, scribbled and stapled dozens. The book's title: *Where's Mom Now That I Need Her?*

There were thousands of scenes I could have flashed back on, many of them more colorful or eventful than the one that kept popping up in my mind. It was from four years earlier, when Elli and I had been working on our book about the Catholic Church. At that time Elli lived in Miami and I lived in Detroit, but we wanted to be in the same place for at least six weeks of the writing, so we moved in with Mom and Dad in Scarsdale, each of us taking one of the spare bedrooms in their empty nest. In their finished basement, which they seldom used, we set up Command Central: two large card tables with our files and our laptops on them.

Mom, then winning her battle against cancer, had decided that her contribution to the book would be caloric. She kept us fed. And when, early in our stay, she noted how quickly and happily we ate some fresh turkey sandwiches she had made for us, she decided that fresh turkey sandwiches would always be available. Every few days she bought a new selection of breads and a new turkey or turkey breast, which she roasted and stuck in the refrigerator, where we could get at it and pick at it if and when she wasn't home to make us something different, something else.

And if she was indeed home and turkey sandwiches were what we wanted, she'd make them for us. Not because she was some meek, doting servant: Mom drew too much attention to her exertions and was too transparent in her bid for plaudits to be taken for meek, doting or servile. She made the sandwiches for us because she knew we wouldn't slice the turkey as strategically as she did, in narrow but meaty slivers. We wouldn't arrange those strategically sliced slivers on the bread so that each bite of the sandwich pulled out some but not all of the meat. We might not take the time to clean and dry a leaf of lettuce for the sandwich, and we might not remember to spread the mayonnaise on the meat, not the bread, because bread too readily sponged it up, lessening its rich, fatty say.

She made the sandwiches, in short, because she was better at it. But she also made them because doing that, and presenting them to us, was her shorthand for telling us that she was rooting for, and watching over, us. That she was rooting for, and watching over, me.

In the scene that kept popping into my head after her death, I heard her footsteps coming down the basement stairs. I smelled freshly roasted meat. I turned to see her walking toward me and Elli, a plate in each of her hands. And I fielded a question as rhetorical as any ever uttered.

"So," Mom asked, "can I interest anybody in a turkey sandwich?"

Twelve

"What brings you here today?" asked the avuncular internist in whose office I was sitting. After nearly two years in Manhattan, I'd finally gotten around to selecting and paying a visit to a doctor. I'd neglected it before because I always avoided doctors, whose poking and prodding and above all weighing of me amounted to a judgment I didn't want rendered. Doctors made you stand naked or half naked in front of them. In the sadism sweepstakes, they had dentists easily beat.

I rearranged myself in my chair, willing a nonchalant posture and nonchalant voice.

"Just routine stuff," I said. "Since I moved here from Detroit, I've been using refills for existing prescriptions, and some have run out." I told him I thought it was time to connect with a new, local doctor. I made it all sound very matter-of-fact.

"What medications do you take?" he asked.

"Mainly Propecia," I said, referring to the hair-loss drug. I'd been using it for nearly three years, in the hope that it would fill in an incipient bald spot and slow down a receding hairline.

"Any problems, side effects?" the doctor asked.

"No."

"Good." He scribbled, looked up. "Any other medications you're taking?"

"Um, yes," I said, as if the next one were an afterthought. "Prozac."

It wasn't true. But I'd always thought I should take it and many friends had told me I should. So had the one therapist to whom I'd paid about eight visits at one point back in Detroit. But I'd resisted, equating the drug with a failure of character, wondering if it weren't some sort of numbing, flattening, homogenizing agent straight out of *Brave New World*. I was also suspicious of how many people had so quickly embraced it. Was it a psychiatric breakthrough, or the pharmacological equivalent of leg warmers?

At this point, though, I wanted to give it a try. I had to. Day in and day out I felt sad and anxious, and the feeling seemed larger than Mom's death. It spread everywhere, turning every big assignment at work into something approaching a panic attack: What if my calls weren't returned? What if I froze when trying to write the lead paragraphs? What if I got a major fact wrong and the paper had to run a correction? I'd wake up at three a.m. on a day when a long story was being published and belatedly question the spelling of a person's name, the date of a historical event to which I'd referred, my entire understanding of what sources had told me. I'd spend the next fifteen to eighteen hours willing the phone at home and then the phone at work not to ring, because the call might be someone telling me I'd screwed up.

Maybe Prozac would help. And maybe, as a bonus, it would have a side effect of weight loss—I'd read that some people on Prozac experienced that. My size 36 pants were snug again, and these were the most generously apportioned, mercifully cut 36s I could find.

The doctor asked, "You've had a good response to Prozac?"

"Yes," I said blithely. Too blithely? I toned it down a few notches. "It seems to work for me."

I went straight from his office to the pharmacy and waited for the prescription to be filled, passing the time by walking up and down the aisles. I noticed the Metamucil on one shelf. Been there, done that. I was now on to something more responsible.

It took more than a week for the Prozac to kick in. Once it did, there was no mistaking it. I got assigned a breaking news story that required me to take a ninety-minute subway ride to a remote corner of Brooklyn, and instead of feeling daunted and exasperated by that, I dwelled on what an interesting mix of people there were in the subway car.

One weekend I had to schlep out to the Ikea store in New Jersey, and Elli, visiting the city from her house in the Catskills upstate, drove me in her car. We hit traffic, it took forever, the Jersey scenery along the way wasn't particularly pretty. None of this bothered me. She and I were having our usual lively conversation—we were never at a loss for conversation—and I couldn't see how it mattered whether that conversation took place on the couch in my apartment or over a delicious dinner in a favorite restaurant or right here in her dusty gray Toyota Camry at a standstill on the New Jersey Turnpike. It was a conversation all the same.

I was resigned and reasonable and calm like that. And sleepy. Very sleepy. Prozac hadn't given me the speedy buzz it gave some people. It had given me the opposite: a gauzy lethargy. I frequently went to bed by nine p.m., contemplating the fluffiness of my comforter instead of the fact that my day was ending so uneventfully. I didn't get up until eight a.m. And while I ate as much as usual, I exercised less than ever, too tired and sluggish to be bothered with it.

There were other problems with Prozac as well. While it diminished my sex drive only modestly, it pushed back its satiation much more substantially, so that I found myself going round and round the block without any sure sign that I'd ever get to pull into the garage. As often as not I just gave up and left my car idling at the foot of the driveway.

During this period that problem had an impact only on me, on the time I spent with myself. But maybe because Prozac had reacquainted me with optimism, I harbored some hope that there'd be company in the near future. I didn't want to be denied the full enjoyment of it.

So I ditched Prozac, enemy of pleasure, collaborator with hunger, author of a modern-day Rip Van Winkle story. I went back to wide awake.

Now what?

Despite my initial anxiety, I was actually doing well at the *Times*. I wasn't so great when it came to spot news and had little talent for investigative work, but I was a faster writer than some colleagues, and I was good at the sorts of illustrative details and anecdotes that editors called "color." I gave decent color. So on the Metro desk, which was my home for my first three years at the newspaper, I'd evolved into someone used less for short, breaking stories than for longer features: a chronicle of a shooting victim's winding, uncertain road to recovery; an excavation of the tortured past of the woman who was famously stalking David Letterman and repeatedly breaking into his house.

I wrote many profiles, including in-depth portraits of political figures like Ruth Messinger when she was running for mayor of New York and Charles E. Schumer when he was running for the U.S. Senate. For the Home section, I spent a long, hazy night at Hunter S. Thompson's ranch outside Aspen. For the Sunday magazine, I spent several days trailing Vanessa Redgrave around London.

That last one started out as a nail-biter. In the days leading up to my departure for London, Redgrave's publicist held firm: all I could have was one ninety-minute interview, and that interview couldn't take place in her home. I needed much more than that to make a magazine profile work. I was scheduled to see Redgrave in a production of Ibsen's *John Gabriel Borkman* on the night I arrived, and I successfully pleaded with the publicist at least to let me poke my head backstage after the play for a glimpse of Redgrave in her dressing room and a five-minute hello—no more. *Maybe,* I thought, *I'll be able to push those five minutes to ten or fifteen.*

Redgrave greeted me warmly and distractedly. She had the air of someone never fully oriented to the circumstances around her. After we'd chatted a few minutes and she'd escorted me to the dressing room of her friend and costar Eileen Atkins so I could meet her, too, she asked me how she and I were supposed to proceed from there.

I was confused. Hadn't my marching orders from the publicist really come from Redgrave herself? Weren't they Redgrave's terms? If not, hadn't the publicist told Redgrave what was what and counseled her to stick to a certain plan?

Whatever the case, I sensed an opportunity.

"Right now I'm going to buy you dinner," I said, as if that were part of an established schedule, "and we'll chat some. Then, over the next few days, we'll just keep getting together to chat until I have what I need for the story."

She nodded, and sought clarification on one point. This dinner and any subsequent ones—did my expense account cover them?

"Absolutely," I said.

Her eyes lit up. As I fast learned, Redgrave's generous donations to her beloved political causes left her without all that much money for herself. So if I wanted to tag along with her to a refugee center where she did volunteer work or accompany her anywhere else, I just had to offer to take care of the cab fares, emphasizing that I'd be reimbursed by the newspaper. I got to see the exterior and a little bit of the interior of her unremarkable apartment by arriving in a cab to fetch her for her day's chores, and thus I noticed that in the foyer, in place of a real lighting fixture, a single bare bulb dangled from an exposed cord. It was a perfect little symbol of how little value she placed in material things, and a perfect little suggestion of how eager she was for anyone crossing her threshold to note that about her.

The Redgrave profile and others caught the attention of editors in various departments of the newspaper, some of whom presented new assignments.

The editor of the National News desk asked me if I wanted to work for three months—and maybe even longer—in the newspaper's San Francisco bureau. I went, eager for the change of scenery and pace and curious to see if it might be the catalyst I needed to start exercising more, slim down some and go on a few dates. It wasn't.

Then the head of the Washington bureau asked if I wanted to move to D.C. and cover politics full-time. I went, once again with the hope that I would get the jolt I needed. I bought a narrow attached town house in Georgetown and a gold-colored Oldsmobile Alero with a sunroof that I never opened and an expensive stereo system that I used constantly. And I spent most of my first six months of work in Washington sprinting through the halls of Congress to chase down Congressional representatives or senators for comments about one fiercely contested piece of legislation or another.

"Senator Snowe! Senator Snowe!" I bellowed as I elbowed aside five other reporters and rushed toward the Senate elevator in which she was poised to make her escape. "How much pressure is Trent Lott putting on you to vote with other Republicans on gun control?"

"Representative DeLay! Representative DeLay!" I screeched at Tom DeLay, the House whip, as he tried to crawl into some shadowy den beyond reporters' reach. "How exactly does one parlay a pest extermination business into such awesome political power and shameless political corruption?"

I'm kidding about that last question, but not about the games of chase I was forced to play as one of the *Times* reporters assigned to cover Congress, which was basically this sprawling hunting ground across which you tracked your journalistic prey as if they were so many hapless, jittery impalas on the veldt. The task was more aerobic than cerebral, requiring fleetness and stamina and above all agility, inasmuch as you had to race past and maneuver around freshly minted Congressional aides so young they were almost larval and newspaper photographers with cameras hanging like cowbells around their necks and television crews staked out everywhere. The crews' dependable presence explained my favorite Congressional incongruity: self-consciously macho Red State legislators galumphing from meeting to meeting in full pancake makeup. Estée Lauder may well make more money on Capitol Hill than in Beverly Hills.

It was inevitable, given all my own galumphing, that one of those crews or one of those photographers would at some point catch me in the frame, and sure enough a colleague nudged me one day, told me to look at the photograph on page something or other of the *Times* or the *Washington Post* (I quickly repressed the memory) and pointed out that I was in it, on the fringes, one of the jackals swarming around a bill's besieged sponsor.

I didn't fully recognize myself. My head was turned sideways, and the path of flesh from my chin to my Adam's apple was a direct, diagonal one, not the two-leg trip, with a ninety-degree turn, that it should have been, that it once was. When had I developed a wattle? Me at thirty-three: half man, half turkey. Which, I guess, made all of those sandwiches Mom had once prepared for me props in a surreal drama of prophetic cannibalism.

I was surprised by the change. Something strange happens when you keep gaining weight that you don't want to be gaining and keep breaking your resolutions to lose it: a part of your brain—the part that keeps your disappointment in yourself at a manageable level, trading real self-disgust for more routine self-flagellation—shades the truth a little, and then a little more, and then a lot. It tells you that while the 38s you're now wearing almost all of the time certainly indicate a thicker waist, they don't necessarily mean that all of you looks thicker and heavier. It's an adaptive mechanism, getting you through the days. There's some evolutionary wisdom in self-delusion.

That newspaper photograph wasn't the only challenge to mine. A short time later I took a weeklong vacation in Cuba, where at least a half dozen of the Cubans I encountered, including a waiter who was bringing me a beer I didn't need and a ticket-taker at a museum devoted to anti-American propaganda, looked at my midsection as they rubbed their own and said, "*Gordo.*" I didn't know a lot of Spanish, but I knew that word. It meant "fat."

"How can they be so rude?" I asked Elli, my designated analyst of all matters Latin American, when I got back from the trip. She had spent serious time in almost every Spanish-speaking country in the Western Hemisphere, so she would have to answer for Havana's ill-mannered legions of waistline censors. Was Fidel really just Richard Simmons in revolutionary drag?

"They're not being rude," Elli explained. "To be well fed is a sign of wealth. Saying you're *gordo* is like saying, 'Ah, you do well for yourself.'"

"They should find a different way of saying it," I huffed. "They're never going to get us to lift the embargo with this approach."

I worked longer hours in Washington than I had in San Francisco or New York, filing many more stories on much stricter deadlines. To calm my nerves I'd alternate keystrokes with handfuls of SunChips or pretzel rods, going through whole bags of them in mere minutes. When I was stressed out, I ate. And in Washington, where dozens of print and television reporters competed with one another for stories small, medium and large, I was almost always stressed out.

I often didn't get home from work until ten p.m., and sometimes wasn't done with phone calls from editors until well after eleven. It was around then that the Chinese delivery might come, or that I'd walk two short blocks to pick up two or even three Philadelphia-style cheesesteak sandwiches, plus an order of hummus with toasted pita, from a nearby takeout joint that stayed open past midnight. At that late hour the final verdict on whatever story I'd been pursuing that day—the answer to the question of whether I'd done better than the competition—was unclear and out of my hands, and I'd be seized by a sense of powerlessness. But what I could control were the thirty minutes of primal contentment before bedtime as I worked my way through the lo mein or the cheesesteaks or whatever else I'd rounded up.

The downstairs of my town house had a living room with sliding glass doors onto a brick patio in the back, a dining room with windows onto a brick sidewalk in the front, and a galley kitchen between them, plus a half bath tucked under the staircase. Upstairs were two bedrooms and a full bath. It was on a futon in the smaller of these bedrooms—the one I used as a TV and computer room—that I would open the evening's food bag and unfurl the evening's feed. The futon was ratty, lumpy and stained with soy sauce; the room was the dingiest in the house. It felt right to do my eating here.

I did a lot of eating here. I ate to steady my nerves, to distract myself from my apprehensions, to dull my occasional loneliness, to quell my sporadic boredom. I ate because I didn't have any dates on the next week's calendar or any romantic prospects in my sights and could postpone a new diet and a new discipline by a day, a week. I ate because I was in the habit of eating, because eleven thirty p.m. was cheesesteak time and a switch would automatically flick in my brain. *Want cheesesteak. Get cheesesteak.*

After months of *Times* bylines from Washington made clear to anyone who read the newspaper and recognized my name that I was now based in D.C., I started hearing from friends from the past who lived nearby.

First it was Jane, who had been a classmate at Loomis, then Nancy, my Carolina apartment-mate for several years. Each figured out my e-mail or found my number in the book and suggested we meet to catch up. To each I said yes, absolutely, no question, we'd get together, I could hardly wait.

And to each I also said that the meeting would, regrettably, have to be put off for just a little while. The current month, I fibbed, was too busy. The next month, I lied, was full of traveling. I promised to be in touch the month after that, as soon as my life calmed down. What that meant was that I'd be in touch the minute I lost fifteen or, better yet, twenty pounds, when the half wattle was gone and the 38s were history. As soon as I was back to loose 36s or slightly tight 35s, I'd be all for—and all about—warm and fuzzy reunions.

I never followed up with either of them, reasoning that I had newer friends who couldn't and wouldn't betray any surprise at the extra pounds I was carrying, because they'd known me only with those extra pounds. Better to stick with them, and not to look back.

There was a third person from the past who got in touch with me during my first year in Washington.

"You probably won't even remember who I am," he said when he called.

I told him to give me a shot.

"This is Scott," he said. "From Chapel Hill."

I remembered. I remembered meeting him at that Carolina campus newspaper party and wearing that black Windbreaker through our whole first date. I remembered that he had seen me as a preppie all-American—he had told me that many times.

He wouldn't see me that way now.

"Scott!" I said. "Wow. What are you up to these days? Where are you living?"

"I'm in Dupont Circle," he said. That meant he could be as little as a mile and a half away. He caught me up on his life. He was a lawyer. He had a boyfriend—a partner—he'd been with for many years.

He proposed that we meet for coffee or a drink or a meal, saying it might be fun.

"It would be great," I said. Then I explained that this month was unusually busy, and that I had an unusually hectic travel schedule the next month. I'd be in touch—I assured him of that. I even believed it. Scott's reemergence would be the summons I needed to cut back on the cheesesteaks and start running more than once every week or two, which was the frequency I was down to.

But the twelve-hour days didn't let up. Neither did the binges at the end of them. Increasingly they came to seem automatic, inevitable, more reflex than choice. And I was less agent than audience, watching myself gather up the food, watching myself lay waste to it, watching myself expand, then turning my eyes away.

As badly as I wanted to lose weight and as often as I pledged to, I also discovered that there was a strange mercy in being fat, a peculiar sanctuary. Being fat absolved me, in a sense, of so many other flaws. It took the blame for a whole host of setbacks and disappointments. It was a handy, hefty scapegoat.

Not managing to strike up interesting conversations at a party?

That's because no one gravitates toward the fat guy.

Not getting invitations to many *other* parties?

No one fattens the crowd with a fat guy.

Not doing as well as other reporters in cultivating Congressional sources?

A fat guy doesn't cut as compelling a figure or project as much confidence.

Love life moribund?

A possible deficit of wit or shortfall of charm needn't be pondered. Fatness is so far ahead of them in line.

I was getting to be a practiced, accomplished celibate. During my three and a half years in Manhattan, after my move from Detroit, I'd been sexually involved with just two people on a total of three occasions. Those three occasions were the only ones when I'd so much as kissed someone else. And during my first nine months in Washington, I'd been sexual with just one person on all of two occasions. Five physically intimate moments across more than four years: I didn't need a Masters & Johnson study to tell me that this wasn't usual for a successful single man in his thirties, gay or straight.

I was in retreat, my weight a reason not to reach out or take risks. I'd deal with my love life once I got thinner. I'd be more aggressive in trying to find original stories on Capitol Hill and make more of a name for myself once I got thinner. Until I got thinner, I certainly couldn't model myself after reporters who broke news and then rode their prominent bylines onto political talk shows. I wasn't fit for TV.

Fatness simplified life and lessened the stakes. It put life on hiatus, making the present a larded limbo between a past normalcy and a future one. It argued against bold initiatives.

But while I wasn't trying to make things happen, they nonetheless happened to me. In the late summer of 1999, nine months after my relocation to Washington, the newspaper's bureau chief in D.C. gave me a new assignment. George W. Bush, the Texas governor, had just formally announced his candidacy for the presidency. And I was to begin shadowing him full-time, going to every speech he made and major event he attended, hanging out in Austin when he wasn't on the road, interviewing him whenever he allowed it, schmoozing with and getting to know his advisers.

It promised to be fascinating. But it would also be a magnification of much of what I disliked about covering Congress: the race against so many other journalists for the same stories; the media groupthink that I either had to fall into or rebel against; the relentless pace and deadlines; the smarmy entreaties from political operatives trying to promote their agendas.

And it was the kind of assignment that did damage to many reporters' health, mental and physical, as two campaign-trail veterans in the *Times* Washington bureau immediately cautioned me. As they painted a picture of the road ahead, they emphasized that I'd have little or no time for exercise; that I'd be surrounded by the most fattening kinds of food; that I'd drink too much at hotel bars with fellow reporters on the trail.

"Be really careful," one of these veterans said. "A lot of reporters gain ten to fifteen pounds."

I flinched, first off because I could tell that this wasn't a warning given to everyone. It was a warning for people who showed some evidence of having trouble managing their weight. But I also flinched at the threat of those ten to fifteen pounds. Then I laughed inside, because these bureau veterans didn't realize how lunatic the idea of another ten to fifteen pounds was. They'd known me only since I'd come to Washington and weren't clued in to my life years before. So they weren't aware that I was already more than ten to fifteen pounds over how I was really supposed to look and how I would look as soon as I found my way out of this current slump. They didn't account for the fact that I was at my absolute apogee.

The next months—August, September, October—hurtled by, a blur of Bush speeches in New Hampshire and Bush rallies in South Carolina and enormous buffets of food at many of them and chicken wings and cheeseburgers at midnight in Marriotts and Sheratons and Hiltons in a half dozen states.

In late October, during one of my rare breaks from the trail, when I was back in Washington, I found myself trudging to the Gap for new pants.

I usually bought work clothes that were slightly nicer, from stores somewhat pricier. But I went to the Gap for the same reason I'd gone to T.J. Maxx when my weight had ballooned in Detroit: I had to believe that this new, worse ballooning was another exceptional situation, and that the pants I was buying were the most temporary of measures, calling for the most modest of expenditures. Besides which, I didn't deserve pants any better, not when I was in this kind of shape.

I bought four pairs of pants in all: size 38 chinos in a light tan and a darker, green-hued tan, and size 40 chinos in the same colors. While the 40s fit better and were the real reason for my trip to the store, the 38s were truer to what I was telling myself: that I was going to turn the corner any day now and be the lesser of the two sizes. I chose the colors I did because they were neutral, disposable, another sort of assertion that I was in a brief holding pattern.

Over the next months, my waist-down wardrobe for my assignment covering a potential president for the most influential newspaper in the country was confined to two cheap pairs of chinos, size 40. For a while I packed the 38s, too—maybe I'd succeed in fasting for two or three days on the trail and all of a sudden they'd fit. Then I stopped hauling them around in my suitcase, because the fast never happened and the 40s themselves were increasingly tight.

I resorted to dry-cleaning the 40s rather than laundering them, so that they wouldn't shrink and I wouldn't have to consider moving up to an even larger size. The 40s were as high as it could go. On this point I was adamant.

New Year's Eve wasn't a holiday that my dad, my siblings and I necessarily spent together. After Christmas we'd often go our separate ways, return to our separate homes, save New Year's Eve for big parties and for friends. But for New Year's Eve 1999—the turning of the millennium—we agreed that we should celebrate with one another. A moment this big and symbolic needed to be spent with the immediate family.

Dad asked us to join him for a black-tie dinner at the Scarsdale Golf Club, where our family had been members for many years and where he, now retired, practically lived, sometimes playing thirty-six holes of golf a day. We'd be joining not just him but Dottie, a woman he had met about a year after Mom died and later married. It was odd to see them together—to see him with any woman other than Mom—and it was sometimes awkward, too, because she was such a stranger to the family's dynamics and traditions. But I was glad he wasn't as lonely as he'd obviously been during the first years after Mom's death.

Mark, a predictably big success at the high-powered consulting firm where he worked, owned his own tuxedo. So did Harry, who had unpredictably redirected the enthusiasm he had once trained on *Star Trek* and then lifeguarding toward investment banking, and was every bit as successful as Mark. But I had to rent a tuxedo, which meant letting some stranger lasso a tape around my waist and fiddle with the ends of it until he had an accurate inch count. I tried not to watch. I didn't want to see the numbers on that tape.

I chose a cummerbund instead of a vest, hoping it might function as a kind of man-girdle. And as I walked around the party letting Dad introduce me to his friends and obediently furnishing them with lively behind-the-scenes anecdotes about Governor Bush, I kept reaching down to pull on the cummerbund's clasps and bands, to cinch it ever tighter.

Me (upper right) *with Adelle* (lower right),
her husband (lower left) *and some family friends.*

Maybe this man-girdle, coupled with the darkness of the tuxedo jacket over it and the amusing stories I was spinning, would prevent anybody from noticing how enormous I was. Maybe I could sail into a new year, a potentially good year, as something less than a blimp.

Mark looked thinner than ever, thanks in part to his itty-bitty-bites approach to meals. Adelle looked good: whatever curves she had weren't necessarily liabilities. Harry looked good, too. The weight lifting during those lifeguard days in La Jolla had given way to long-distance running—he'd even done the Boston Marathon—and while fatherhood and work were increasingly cutting into any exercise time, he had the body equivalent of a lot of goodwill stored up.

But he struck me as maybe a bit too full of himself. Because he was my younger brother, I never shrank from the task of deflating him.

At the New Year's Eve party, the pinpricks I made concerned how much he liked to spend money. His salary went up and up, and he charted that progress in cars, wine, nice jewelry for Sylvia and extensive home renovations. He could be showy, and on this night, as I sloshed through a third martini, I called him on it. I asked him if he and Sylvia now owned four cars or three. I asked him how many pairs of cuff links he had amassed.

I didn't see the color rising in his face until it was too late.

"Well, Frank," he said, pausing for a loaded moment, "at least I'm not fat."

Sylvia, standing within arm's reach of us, looked away. Adelle, also nearby, studied her shoes. The words hung there, heavier than me, and the silence in their wake stretched on and on, surrounding us like some ghastly bubble, beyond which I could hear the muffled strains of the party's music and laughter.

I had to get away.

I turned, walked out of the club's main dining room and hustled down the first staircase I found. I had some vague knowledge from the past that there were little-used hallways and bathrooms and locker rooms below ground level: hiding places. I wanted to be somewhere no one could see me. I needed to be invisible, because what I felt right then was hideously and horribly exposed.

So: they'd noticed. The whole family had noticed. And there was something in the what-the-hell, screw-the-tact tone of Harry's insult that suggested that they'd also been marveling for some time at my deterioration, discussing it, probably even cautioning one another not to mention it to me, because they all knew how sensitive I could be when it came to my weight and weren't sure how to nudge me in a healthier direction without sending me into a tailspin. They were pitying me, and what I felt now, as my stomach cratered and my heart jackhammered, was pitiful.

I started crying. In a far corner of a back hallway in an unfamiliar basement, I pressed the heels of my hands against my eyes to try to stanch my tears and I pressed my lips together to try to muffle any sound. I couldn't control the violent rising and falling of my chest, the whistling intakes of breath. I thought about Mom—couldn't *stop* thinking about Mom. Although she more than anyone else in the family would have hated seeing me like this, I wanted her here, needed her here, needed someone unafraid to ask me what the hell was going on and tell me I was in trouble and be able to do both without breaking me. If she'd been around, would I have let myself go? If she'd been present, would the impulse to do so have been so strong in the first place?

After ten minutes I found a bathroom, splashed cold water on my face and stood at the mirror, waiting for the wildness in my eyes to dim, for my nose to stop running, for my breathing to even out. I recognized this drill from those college days when I answered binges with purges. Here I was, more than fifteen years further down the road, and still I hadn't found a steady way to navigate it. Still I was lurching and swerving and scraping the rails.

When I rejoined the party, I stayed away from Harry, because I owed him an apology and didn't want to give it, and because he owed me one and I didn't want to hear it. I wanted the whole incident forgotten. If we revisited it, even obliquely, we'd just be giving it staying power.

I knew that the surest way to lose the shame I was feeling was to lose some weight. But the hell of it was that I'd never been in circumstances that made that more difficult. By January 2000, the Bush campaign had entered the phase in which reporters no longer forged their own paths in following the candidate. Instead they lashed themselves to the candidate's entourage. That entourage assumed control of their lodging and their transport.

That entourage also assumed control of their feeding.

Thirteen

The advent of eating is the crack of dawn. That's when the first of the day's many meals comes along, and it's no off-the-cuff, on-the-go improvisation. It's an upsized, deconstructed Denny's Grand Slam, sausages in one steaming metal warming bin, bacon in another, a viscous ocean of scrambled eggs here, leaning towers of pancakes there. The bins fan out along the wall of a hotel banquet room, its air humid in a way that's particular to the presence of enough cholesterol for at least two hundred people. Those of us in the press pack shadowing the candidate number no more than seventy.

We descend on the room for "baggage call," the appointed hour for handing our luggage to campaign aides in time to have it loaded onto the campaign plane for the first flight of the day. The baggage-call deadline is as many as ninety minutes before we ourselves must board one of the buses for the airport, and during this interminable wait we rummage through newspapers and marinate ourselves in caffeine at round tables within perilous olfactory reach of those bins. We breathe in the heady, greasy, piggy perfume of an unhealthy breakfast for the taking. Is it any wonder that I take it? That I allow myself a few spoonfuls of eggs to settle my stomach from the martinis last night, and maybe one link of sausage because I adore sausage and maybe a second link because it's going to be another epic, agitating day of multiple time zones and mind-numbing dictation, and I need and deserve just a small dose of happiness, don't I? Just a soupçon? Aren't some rendered, cased, spiced pig parts my due?

The second meal comes on the plane, no more than forty-five minutes after the end of the first. It's more eggs, more sausage, some cornflakes, a banana, white toast, a blueberry muffin, butter, jam. All of this is compressed onto one awesomely engineered tray, a geometric marvel of calories per square inch, delivered by a flight attendant who's fleet and insistent and above all sneaky, because she shimmies the tray into a nook of space beside my laptop before I notice her and wave her away. I was going to wave her away, I really was. But now the tray and food are right here, right under my nose and my chins, ready and waiting for me to get distracted or curious. It happens. And . . . wow, these sausages are possibly better—meatier, fattier, oilier—than the ones back at the hotel. I'll need another taste for a proper determination.

The third meal comes around eleven thirty a.m. It's the first of two lunches, and it's in yet another hotel banquet room, this one in the new city to which we've flown for the morning speech on tax cuts or educational standards or the privatization of Social Security. The speech is done, we're typing up our notes or stories, we may need nourishment. We're in a Southwestern state, so we've been given a Southwestern spread: enchiladas, quesadillas, guacamole. I suppose there are people who can pass up free guacamole, but they're either allergic to avocado or too joyless to live.

Wheels up. Back in the air. And back to eating: The flight attendants are passing out Lunch No. 2, which is Meal No. 4. It's a modest sandwich deal, the least tempting spread of the day so far, but the attendants pass out, for dessert, these Dove chocolate-covered ice cream bars, and they pass them out in a manner so persuasive I'm wondering if they moonlight

218 · FRANK BRUNI

as Hollywood recruiters for the Church of Scientology. The ice cream bars look delicious. Since I skipped the sandwich, I don't skip this.

Another landing. Another city. Another speech. Another hotel banquet or meeting room in which to set up our laptops and hunker down to work. No food this time around, because it's past lunchtime and well before dinnertime and the schedule is especially hurried during this later phase of the day. I have seventy minutes to write a daily story on what Governor Bush stated or didn't state or misstated—his malapropisms are legendary, and never go out of style—and must spend the first fifty minutes transcribing the tape. So it's a panting, praying, slam-bang, slapdash type-type-type deadline situation, and by the time I'm back on the plane yet again, being shepherded yet again toward the grubby seat stained by all the greedy eating I've done in it, I'm all nerves. Praise the lord and pass the Gouda: the charter company has laid out a cheese tray! With crackers. And chicken fingers and fried jalapeño poppers and of course beer or wine, take your pick. It's a happy hour's worth of fried bar snacks for an hour that didn't start out so happy. If we count this as a meal, and I think we must, it's No. 5.

No. 6 is served to us in our seats as we fly at night to be in place for the event tomorrow morning, when we'll wake somewhat later than usual, since we'll already be in place and won't have to begin the day by traveling. We can choose chicken or steak, salad dressing A or B: your basic airplane routine, only the portions are bigger and the food better, in fact just better enough to seduce a weary, besieged political reporter whose happy hour cheese consumption was compromised by calls from editors about a little nugget of information heard on CNN and about a big thought that someone high on the paper's masthead wanted to see reflected in the day's story—and, if it's not too much trouble, could I help one colleague by getting a quote from the Bush campaign about the capital gains tax and another colleague by getting a quote about doping in professional sports and another colleague, this one in the

Style department, about whether Laura Bush has a favorite handbag? On the campaign plane we're allowed to use our cell phones all the way through takeoff, and the calls don't stop coming until the plane rises too high in the air for my phone to maintain its connection, at which point pausing to eat just a bit of that chicken or steak isn't an act of unconscionable overindulgence. It's a hard-earned, meditative turn away from the pressures of the day. It's akin to a moment of prayer.

A seventh meal is still to come. Two senior Bush strategists have agreed to a long off-the-record conversation over food and drinks with me and an ABC News producer with whom I work closely, and that means we're buying them a big dinner in a decent steakhouse, because a big dinner in a decent steakhouse is the best way to make sure they'll agree to another long off-the-record conversation down the road. We all meet at about eight p.m., and what follows is the whole works: the martinis, the iceberg wedges with blue cheese, the porterhouses, the potatoes, the red wine. All stomachs having limits, even mine doesn't permit the kind of consumption that would be possible if I had steered clear of food since lunches No. 1 and No. 2. But it makes a valiant effort in the spirit of not dragging down the table's mood or distracting the strategists from the scuttlebutt they're giving up. It holds up through the cheesecake. It finally gets its reprieve at ten forty-five p.m.

At the bar on the ground floor of the hotel where the campaign is staying for the night, several of the best reporters assigned to the campaign are gathered, as are several of the workers in the press department of the campaign itself. There's only one responsible thing to do: join them. The reporters will be tossing around what they deem to be their most incisive observations and thus divulging what they know and what they plan to report. The campaign workers may get a little loose-lipped. So it's another few glasses of wine before midnight, and maybe, while drinking them, some peanuts grabbed absentmindedly from a bowl, but not so many peanuts that they constitute what would be Meal No. 8. The count stands at seven.

That wasn't an utterly typical day on the campaign trail. But it wasn't wholly atypical, either.

From the campaign's perspective, a well-fed press corps was an upbeat, docile press corps, so campaign officials made whatever arrangements necessary to ensure that we'd be fattened like Angus steers. Meanwhile the charter company that ran the planes had to justify the astronomical sums it was charging all of our news organizations for our passage, so it laid on the canapés, desserts and snacks. And the hotels that filled the banquet halls or meeting rooms with buffets for us knew that they were serving the traveling news media, so they saw every steroidal spare rib or cheese-mummified nacho they laid out as a marketing and publicity effort.

Not all the reporters got fat. For every one who gained weight there was another who found some way—often eccentric, sometimes extreme—to keep it off. One young female television producer was so appalled at the ten to fifteen pounds she put on in the first months of the campaign that she stopped eating altogether, and by the last months of the campaign her hair had started falling out.

A wire service reporter trying to wring some order from this chaotic food universe decided to eat only foods of a given color on a given day, an approach that sounded relatively straightforward until it was put into play. Was a banana yellow (the peel) or white (the edible fruit)? Was an egg white (the shell) or yellow (the yolk, as well as the results of scrambling)? Toward such weighty philosophical questions our worlds turned. A reporter could devote only so much thought, and so much conversation, to the pros and cons of lowering the capital gains tax.

I needed my own special strategy, something accommodated by the kinds of food typically available on the plane and on the ground, a regimen that would leave me with plenty to eat while limiting my calories enough to create the possibility of weight loss.

"Starting today," I told John Berman, the ABC News producer, and Kevin Flower, a producer for CNN, "I'm a fruitarian."

I didn't know if the word even existed, but I liked the sound of it. I liked saying it. So as I commenced the transition into my new self—pear-focused rather than pear-shaped—I talked as much about it as possible. I resolved to turn deprivation into shtick. What I was giving up in protein and fat I would gain in self-amusement.

John was eating some scrambled eggs for breakfast.

"I always preferred my eggs over medium, or as an omelet, to scrambled," I told him. "But that was before I became a fruitarian."

Hours later, as I assembled a vivid hillock of pineapple slices and strawberries from one of the fruit plates that always seemed to accompany the sandwich spreads in hotel meeting rooms, Kevin asked me, "What life changes have you noticed since you became a fruitarian?"

"I'm definitely more alert as a fruitarian," I told him. "I have more mental clarity. And as a fruitarian I have more energy."

"Can you have coffee," John asked me, "as a fruitarian?" We were all having some fun with this new script of mine.

"Yes," I said, "and diet drinks."

"Alcohol?" Kevin wondered.

I hadn't thought about that. I didn't want to give up alcohol.

I didn't *have* to give up to alcohol!

"Wine!" I exulted. "I can have wine, because it's just grapes. I have to steer clear of vodka, bourbon, beer. A fruitarian never drinks those."

My first day as a fruitarian was going swimmingly. I had gambled correctly: there were bananas on the plane for breakfast, so I ate three of those. At lunch there was the pineapple, the strawberries. During our airborne happy hour, I laid claim to a disproportionate number of the apple slices and grapes skirting the cheese. Fruit was around. Fruit was plentiful. And no one was going to out-fruit me.

Having no fat but loads of fiber in me made me feel instantly lighter of step and flatter of stomach, and I all but floated up to my hotel room that night. Then it hit me: the effects of such a sudden increase in fiber. I writhed in gastrointestinal distress. Sprinted frequently from bed. Slept maybe two hours in all. And used all of that as an excuse the next morning to do what I'd wanted to for all of the previous day, my testimonials of fruitarian bliss notwithstanding. I ate something other than fruit. I ate lots of somethings other than fruit.

I needed exercise, and there was rarely any time. If you wanted to run in the morning, you had to do it as early as five a.m., and you had to hope the city or country streets around whatever hotel you were inhabiting were suited for running, and you had to make peace with tightly sealed bags of sweaty clothes crowding your suitcase for days on end, because the campaign moved around too quickly for laundry to be left with any of the hotel laundry services. If you wanted to run at night, you might have to wait until ten p.m., because the days often ended that late. As for the gyms in our hotels, they were dreary and tiny, with maybe two StairMasters and one treadmill, always being used by others. The gyms were useless.

I'd have my occasional days of sudden and severe self-denial, when I imagined I could repair in twenty-four hours what I'd mucked up over months. But at the ends of many of those days, at one a.m., I'd find myself sitting on the floor in front of the hotel room minibar, famished and frenzied, reaching first for the Famous Amos chocolate chip cookies, then for the Snickers bar, then for the roasted cashews in the miniature Mason jar, then for the squat miniature can of Pringles. There were nights when I went through every single item other than beverages in the minibar, to the tune of close to a hundred dollars. The *Times*, as a matter of policy, didn't reimburse minibar expenses, so I didn't file mine. They cost me close to two thousand dollars over the course of the campaign.

But the financial impact paled next to the sartorial one. Before the midpoint of the year, I had to reconfigure the clothing in my suitcase yet again. I got rid of one of the two pairs of 40s. And to the remaining pair I added two new pairs of chinos from the Gap, size 42.

And then there was the matter of my jacket.

There were almost always a few things in my closet to which I had strong, superstitious attachments, and I was almost always attached to them because I thought they made me look thinner. At Carolina I'd worshipped this collared short-sleeved shirt with eighth-of-an-inch vertical stripes in gray and black: their darkness and verticality convinced me that the shirt was more effective than a month of protein shakes. I wore it every time I went to the gay bar in Durham, where I must have been known as the Striped Crusader, or maybe Umpire Guy.

When I attended Columbia and then when I worked for the *Post*, I favored this black overcoat that didn't fit me closely enough to show any unwanted curves but hung straight enough along my sides that it didn't create any impression of extra body mass that didn't exist. The material, a dyed, brushed denim, was matte, which was preferable to shiny if you were trying to deflect visual attention. The coat reached almost all the way to my ankles—I supposed that made me look taller. It wasn't thick and warm enough for cold weather, but I ignored any of my shivering or teeth chattering as I donned it instead of a puffy down jacket or parka even in December and January, when winter winds would make it billow up behind me. It was a sort of coat-cape hybrid, making me look one part Johnny Cash, two parts Vampire Lestat.

And in Washington, even before the campaign and all the pounds that came with it, I bought and clung to a gigantic hooded gray sweatshirt, treating it the way toddlers treat their favorite bedtime blankets, taking it with me everywhere. Its virtue wasn't just its folds and folds of figure-obscuring cotton but, even better, the big pouch in the front created by adjacent, front-facing pockets in which you could bury your hands. Since the pouch made anyone who wore the sweatshirt look like he had a belly, it made no one who wore it look like he had a belly. I loved that pouch and I wore that sweatshirt as often as I could. This was the era of Marsupial Frank.

The campaign trail brought about Frank the Human Tent, courtesy of a shapeless, floppy pale green Army-issue Windbreaker from the Timberland outlet in Hilton Head. At first I imagined that it made me look dashing, on account of its splashes of turquoise trim and all its flaps and zippers, which popped up in surprising places and at surprising angles. Beneath those flaps and zippers were pockets upon pockets: in the front, on the sides, down by the hips. It hung well below the hips, which was one of its best features.

All in all it looked like the kind of jacket worn by news photographers, who needed many baggy pockets for their lenses and film and backup cameras. So I could get away with it, sort of. It wasn't an entirely ridiculous coat, at least not until the weather turned hot, and then it was. Still I didn't ditch it.

"Aren't you boiling in that?" was a question I frequently got as we reporters stood outside for some campaign speech far south of the Mason-Dixon Line in July or August. Other reporters wore polo shirts, T-shirts: as little as they could get away with while on the job. I wore my shapeless Timberland.

"It's deceptively light," I'd say as I tried to blow upward inconspicuously and dislodge the bead of sweat on my nose.

"But you really seem to be hot," a colleague would counter, perhaps noticing that I had streaks of sweat just in front of my sideburns, that the skin above my upper lip was more than a little dewy and that even my palms were wet.

"I'm *warm*, sure," I'd concede. "But this coat is really convenient. It has all this space for notebooks and pens and tape recorder batteries. I like to have all of that handy."

I wore my Timberland when the temperature was eighty degrees

In my Timberland jacket, on the campaign trail.

and when it was ninety and sometimes even when it was a hundred. I wore it on the campaign plane and on campaign buses. I wore it over a dress shirt and tie, if for some reason I had to wear a dress shirt and tie, even though it nullified the effect of them. It nullified everything. That was the point of it. And so I continued to wear it even as it became mottled with dark blue stains from broken pens, even as zippers jammed and the insides of pockets tore. When my Timberland was on, nobody could see just how big I was. I could hide inside of it.

I was hiding in so many ways. Sexually, I had shut down more completely than ever, and what drove that home hardest wasn't the celibacy itself, which was now complete—I'd gone the length of the campaign without any intimate contact of any kind with anyone. It was the way my colleagues and friends on the campaign trail interacted with me.

The campaign trail is famous for the furtive hookups, tortured affairs and budding relationships it encourages; being on the road, far from home, sends people into one another's arms. While covering Bush, I watched that happen and I listened to colleagues' confessions. I was a good, reliable audience. And as colleague after colleague confided in me, I realized that one reason I seemed a safe storehouse for their confidences was that I existed apart from it all, a placid and neutral territory, a sexual Switzerland. I realized that none of these people ever asked me if I had anything going on. It was assumed I didn't, and the assumption was correct.

I increasingly wondered if, free of my Timberland and my embarrassment, I might be enjoying this whole chapter of my life on a whole different level. How much better would I be able to focus on the exhilarations of covering a presidential campaign for the *Times*? On this close-up view of something most people saw only from a distance?

I had a great job and a great house in a beautiful neighborhood. I had an expanding, adorable brood of nieces and nephews: Harry's children Leslie, Erica and Harrison; Mark's children Frank, Sarah and little Mark; Adelle's son, Gavin, just born. But I was increasingly haunted by all that I was letting pass me by and slip away from me. Those failures dogged and dulled everything else.

When the campaign ended I resettled in my house and made a deal with my editors. I'd agree to their wishes and cover the White House for six to nine months; they'd agree to mine and, after that point, let me work as a Washington-based staff writer for the newspaper's Sunday magazine.

It would be a job with less travel, less chaos, less competition, less frequent deadlines. I figured it might help me get some of my weight off, and some of my life back.

A few months after the campaign ended, I went to my Washington doctor. I'd gone to him only once or twice before, and he'd told me that I needed to lose weight. He told me that again on this visit. I stifled the impulse to ask him about his own plans for a diet. He was easily thirty to thirty-five pounds too heavy, by my amateur's estimate, and I dwelled on that rather than on what he was telling me. Who was he to be lecturing me?

"When was your last physical?" he asked me.

I said I couldn't remember, and reminded him that I was there only because I had some sinus congestion that wouldn't go away. Couldn't we just settle on the right antibiotics and move on?

"I'm going to take some blood," he said, and started gathering the necessary medical paraphernalia before I could mount an effective protest. "At your age, we should be watching your cholesterol." In went the needle.

He listened to my lungs and took my blood pressure, and the next thing I knew he was shoving me onto a scale.

"Just don't tell me the number," I instructed him as I stood on the scale. "I'm serious. Don't tell me."

"OK," he said.

I stepped off and was about to thank him when he announced: "You weigh 268 pounds." Just like that. Defiant. Staring at me. Saying without saying: you can't be allowed to run away from 268 pounds.

268 pounds?

It was worse than anything I'd feared. In my mind I batted the number away, but it kept coming back, a measure somehow blunter and more irrefutable than the size 42 pants, a final contradiction of something I'd always assumed about myself without ever quite articulating to myself. I was someone who let things get a little out of hand, not a lot—or so I'd believed. I'd done that with bulimia at the start of college, with my Mexican speed at the end of college. I done that with my Tyson chicken in Detroit, and later, with Greg, I'd caught myself and righted myself after our trip to T.J. Maxx. I always pulled back before things went too far.

But 268 pounds was too far. I heard Harry's voice—*at least I'm not*

*Interviewing President Bush on Air Force One
during his first months in office.*

fat—and thought for the first time that he'd actually been kind. He could have gotten away with "obese."

I wanted better bearings than I had. I was 268 pounds compared to *what* in the past? All I knew was that at certain points in my late teens and early twenties, I'd been under 190. So the 268 meant that I'd gained at least 78 pounds since then.

I was appalled at myself.

And yet.

I was now saddled with covering a new presidential administration, and while my travel load had lightened, my workload hadn't. Nor had the stress. The late-night eating went on.

Then there was the number itself—*268!*—and what it said about how much self-denial was in store if I was going to get back to where I wanted to be. The magnitude of the journey, once revealed, made it all the harder to begin. It was one thing to stare down a fifteen- to twenty-five-pound challenge. It was another to be looking at seventy-five or more.

And so, yet again, I faltered, beginning a diet and exercise program on a Monday only to stop it on a Wednesday, because I'd slip up and decide that I should wait until the following Monday and the blank slate of a new week to begin again. Then I'd treat Thursday through Sunday as a free pass, a last-hurrah opportunity to get all my cravings out of my system.

I'd order pork lo mein and cashew chicken and barbecued spare ribs from my go-to Chinese. I'd wonder as I ate my way through this food if I should have addressed a pizza craving instead, and I'd call Domino's, asking for a large sausage pizza and adding some buffalo wings with blue cheese to the order just before hanging up. Since I was never going to eat this way again—since I could never *allow* myself to eat this way again—I'd give final vent to all of my gluttony on this one night.

The delivery would come, I'd make my way through all of it, and then I'd think: *dessert*. How can I resist the temptation of dessert during my forthcoming diet if I don't treat myself to some right now?

There was an all-night 7-Eleven about six blocks away, and I'd *drive* to it, because it would be one a.m. at this point and I'd need to wrap up all of this eating and get to bed. I'd buy a pint of Ben & Jerry's and a chocolate-covered ice cream bar and some Nutter Butter cookies to boot. Each was something I relished, and the smart thing to do on a night like this was to have everything I relished and be done with it.

These last-hurrah meals happened as often as once a week. They'd undo whatever progress I'd made since my *last* last-hurrah meal. And they put me in a laughable bind with a ludicrous solution.

Fourteen

Shortly after the election I signed a contract to do a book for HarperCollins that would mine all the time I'd spent watching and interacting with Bush. It was to be an anecdotal, impressionistic portrait not so much of Bush the governor or of Bush the novice commander in chief as of Bush the guy, a sometime stumblebum with an informal nature seemingly at odds with the lofty office of the presidency.

I worked furiously on the book from January through June 2001, taking only one five-week break from my White House duties for the *Times* and otherwise staying up late or sacrificing any weekend fun in order to sit at my computer in that dingiest of rooms in my Georgetown house. The book was like a whole second job, stress piled on stress, and by the time I finished a full draft, I hadn't lost any weight.

But I was due, already, to have my book jacket photograph taken.

That was my bind. I couldn't let an accurate image of me get out there and let all the old acquaintances I'd been avoiding see me this way.

So I called my friend Barbara, a former photojournalist living in

Among friends, fat but not happy.

Austin, and asked her if she could hook me up with someone adept at using special poses or crafty angles or smoke and mirrors—whatever it took—to transform the round into the oblong, chubby into chiseled, gone-to-seed into come-to-Papa. I told Barbara that it wasn't really a photographer we were looking for; it was an illusionist. Fit for Diane Arbus, I needed David Copperfield.

She sent me to someone in Austin, which I still occasionally passed through for work. Although she had already prepped him on the challenge at hand, I wasn't taking any chances, so I prepped him anew.

"The goal is thin," I said.

"Uh-huh," he replied.

"Emaciated, even," I said. I figured you should always set the bar high, so that in falling short, you still ended up somewhere satisfactory.

"Got it," he answered, with a bit of an edge.

He had me turn my face to the left and to the right. He had me tilt my head a few degrees forward, then a few degrees more, then a few degrees beyond that. I could see that my shoelaces had come untied.

He repositioned the lights he was using, swapped one camera lens for another. He took pictures from three feet away and six feet away. He kept stepping farther and farther back, stopping only when he hit the wall.

"Is it working?" I asked.

No answer. Good, good: he was too focused on the task to respond. I needed him to be focused.

A few days later the head shots came to me as e-mail attachments.

They were an improvement on what was in the mirror. But they weren't improvement enough.

"We're not done," Barbara said.

She sent the digital images to a friend of hers who was an expert at photo manipulation. Her friend stretched the images vertically, treating my face as if it were Silly Putty, making it longer. She e-mailed me a sample to see if I approved.

My face was significantly less round than in the prior batch of images, but it wasn't anywhere close to angular. I'd been fantasizing about angular.

"Do you think," I asked Barbara, "we can stretch the images a little more? Just a little."

"When's the last time anyone at the publishing house saw you?" she said.

"The people I'm dealing with there have never met me," I said. "They've just talked to me on the phone. And by the time they *do* meet me, I'll in fact be much thinner. This jacket photo just snuck up on me. I'm planning on some serious dieting."

"Then we can get away with a little more," Barbara said.

We stretched the image a little more.

I printed out several of the altered images and happened to have them with me one day as I walked to my seat in the press section of Air Force One.

When one of my colleagues asked me how my book was coming, I reflexively hauled out the pictures.

"I'm considering one of these for my jacket photo," I said. "What do you think?"

As she stared at them she looked baffled. "When were these taken?" she asked. "Five years ago?"

"No!" I answered. "They're more recent than *that*." I snatched the pictures from her and hurried to my seat, a few rows from hers, before she could ask any more questions.

And I went ahead and sent the pictures to HarperCollins, because they weren't really lies, just forecasts of the physical improvements I'd effect by the time the book tour came along.

The publication date was initially set for the fall of 2001, but after the terrorist attacks of September 11, HarperCollins pushed the date back to March 2002 so we could make changes to the book, too light-hearted in the context of what had happened. We ditched the planned title, *Bushed*, and the planned cover, a photo of the president that made it look as if he were hurtling sideways through space. The new image we chose showed him striding across a red carpet in the White House. The new title was *Ambling into History: The Unlikely Odyssey of George W. Bush*.

Around the turn of the year, with March approaching, I confronted the fact that I'd be booked on a morning television show or two and many political talk shows and that people I'd avoided for years might now catch a glimpse of me. And I couldn't photo-manipulate my way into presentable shape.

My self-styled diet of choice this time around: salmon fillets and skinless chicken breast halves—which I could buy in bulk at Costco and cook on my slanted, fat-reducing George Foreman grill—punctuated with Balance nutrition bars. It was sort of Atkins, sort of not, built yet again on the notion that I could still permit myself a significant quantity of food by focusing on foods with particular qualities. The salmon and chicken steered me clear of carbohydrates. And the Balance bars, well, they promised at least to be *balanced*—that was their point, their packaging. Besides, each one was only about 200 calories. Never mind that I sometimes ate three in a row.

Since I'd left the White House beat and started writing instead for the *Times*'s Sunday magazine, I was working frequently at home and had more control over my hours, so I could not only cook myself lunch and dinner on that grill but also carve out more time for exercise. This exercise wasn't as regular as it needed to be. But I increased the frequency and the distance of my runs. I mapped out two- and three- and four-mile routes along the Potomac or through Georgetown, and I did one or another of them at least twice a week.

By late February, the 42s were history, and the 40s were loose. So with a hope I hadn't experienced in years, and with a confidence I hadn't fully earned but yearned to feel, I went to buy a new suit. I chose Brooks Brothers because I knew its clothes were generously cut, but I willfully discounted that as I tried on different suit pants, intent on being reassured by what I could fit into. I managed 38s. And they weren't even all that tight!

I stepped in front of a mirror. The person staring back at me wasn't as thin as I had imagined he would be, but maybe it was the mirror. Or maybe my self-critical bent. I couldn't be sure. I didn't want to be sure. I wanted only to dwell on the fact that I'd put those 42s behind me. And while there had been a time in my life when 38s were a cataclysm, I reminded myself that I'd been younger then, and I supposed that bodies changed as they aged, getting more solid and squarer. I supposed that the 38s I was wearing in the Brooks Brothers store might be the equivalent of a younger man's 36s. And for all I knew Brooks Brothers had in recent months begun tailoring their clothes less forgivingly than they once had.

I studied the mirror again. I squinted, cocked my head, shifted my stance. I didn't look so bad. In fact, if the lighting in the dressing room hadn't been so harsh, and if I had shaved that morning, and if I had a tidier haircut, which I resolved to get, I'd look better still. I'd look like a man with no need whatsoever to fear a TV camera.

Midway through my book tour, I sat one night in a greenroom at the CNN studios in New York, waiting to be interviewed. I was pumped up by all the radio and TV interviews I'd already made it through, by an Amazon ranking in the low double digits. I was pumped up even more by my new suit, which was a bit looser than when I'd purchased it just two weeks earlier. The adrenaline of the tour had somehow quieted my appetite, and facing TV cameras day after day had kept my worst impulses in check.

A dark-haired, doe-eyed man in his midtwenties came into the room to say hello. He introduced himself as a junior correspondent for CNN and said we'd met once during the Bush campaign. We talked about the campaign, the book, politics. More than ten minutes went by and he made no motion to leave.

Was he flirting with me?

It was a question I hadn't asked about any handsome man—about *any* man—in years. But was it really such a crazy thought? Maybe not anymore, considering my slimming dark blue suit and the winnowed me inside it and my briskly selling book. Maybe I had a whole new currency.

I was pretty sure he was gay: he'd made a few references that suggested as much. And the intensity and duration of the attention he was showing me certainly seemed to go beyond friendliness.

I made a point of mentioning that I'd be in New York for a few more days. He asked me if I'd be up for a drink.

The next night we met in the bar on the ground floor of my hotel. It took me one martini to get to talking, another to hold his gaze for more than a few seconds, and a third to do what I really wanted to.

I asked him if we should have one last drink in my room.

He didn't respond at first, just blushed and laughed awkwardly. He looked away. And then he noted how late it was, saying he could stay with me in the bar for a few more minutes, but then had to get going.

"That's actually better, I've got an early morning, too," I said, too emphatically.

I searched for the waiter. I signaled for the check. I signaled a second time just fifteen seconds later. I wanted to get out of there.

The next morning I called a friend to recount my humiliation.

"It's not you," she said, telling me what friends almost always do. I was great, I was a catch, I shouldn't think about it, he probably had a boyfriend.

"It's his loss," said another friend, going through the same stock litany.

Then, back in Washington, I recounted the story to my friend Maureen, who did something more honest—and, really, kinder. After listening to me, nodding sympathetically and shaking her head on cue, she pulled out her checkbook. She grabbed a pen. And she began writing out a check.

"What are you doing?" I asked.

"I'm buying you two sessions with my trainer," she said, and she wrote down his name and phone number as well.

That's how I met Aaron. And that's when I really turned the corner, accepting that if I wanted to do more than merely whittle at the edges of my excesses, I had to put real energy into the effort. I had to be methodical about it, and it had to hurt.

For the first fifteen minutes of my first fifty-five-minute session with Aaron, we only talked.

"What do you want to get out of this?" he asked.

"Isn't it obvious?" I said. "I need to lose weight."

"Here's the deal," he said. "We can only do so much in fifty-five minutes. They're going to be an intense fifty-five minutes. But before or after—you choose—you owe me thirty minutes on one of those StairMasters."

He pointed to two machines right inside the door of his exercise studio. "You can come early to use them," he said. "You can stay late. But you've got to give me those thirty minutes. And on the days when you don't come in here, you've got to be doing cardio on your own. StairMaster, running, I don't care. Not biking—I don't want you sitting when you're exercising. Not walking—I want your heart rate up. No easy stuff."

He told me that if I was going to use him and stick with him, he wanted to see me twice a week. And he told me to be prepared for several months of twice-a-week sessions, plus good behavior in between them, if I wanted serious results.

I used the two sessions Maureen had bought for me. I bought myself ten more, and then another ten after that. They were seventy dollars a pop, an expense that definitely added up, but the payment I'd received for my book meant that I had extra money, and I couldn't think of any better way to spend it.

Aaron's exercise studio spread out over several floors of a yellow brick town house in the Adams Morgan section of D.C. It wasn't a conventional gym: you had to be working with Aaron or with one of about a half dozen other private trainers in his employ to use it, and during any given hour no more than four clients and four trainers would be present. Sometimes there'd be only two trainers and clients. That created a sense of privacy that helped me. I had often talked myself out of visiting a gym in Georgetown that I'd joined a year and a half earlier by deciding that I had to lose some weight before I went, lest I be embarrassed in the midst of so many less flabby exercisers. At Aaron's studio I could jiggle in something closer to solitude.

Aaron had a barrel chest, a tiny waist and not an ounce of fat on him. Although he was twenty-nine, he had an oversize mane of overlong, overfluffy hair that sometimes made him seem five to ten years younger and that belonged in a 1970s time capsule. I jokingly told him that he looked like the lost Cassidy brother, an amalgam of Shawn and David, ready for a seat in the front of the Partridge Family bus. He told me to shut up and do another bench press.

During our fifty-five-minute sessions, he never let me rest. We rushed without pause from one Cybex or Body Masters weight machine to another or we used free weights or he plunked me down on a section of padded floor.

"Here!" he bellowed as he raced ahead of me to our next location, our next station, our next grueling exercise. Then it was on to the next: "Here!" I felt alternately like a cowed spaniel in obedience school or like a misshapen, misbegotten recruit in basic training, the John Candy character in *Stripes*. For his part Aaron was a combination of drill sergeant and garden-variety sadist: the Marquis de Sweat.

We did crunches, about twice as many as I ever would have gotten through on my own. We did squats, but with a heavy bar of as many as sixty pounds balanced on my shoulders. We did curls, and we did them until my arms quivered like the strings of a clunky cello. If I stopped before Aaron thought I humanly had to, he kept me pressed in place and made me resume.

I would pout and sneer and wail and sometimes even scream at him. It was part of this whole comedy routine we developed, a way of making the torture go down easier and the minutes go by faster.

"I'm getting dizzy!" I'd shriek.

"Good," he'd say.

"I'm going to pass out!" I'd warn.

"I'll make sure you don't hit your head on anything too hard."

"I'm going to throw up!"

"Great. It'll mean you're really working."

"I'm going to throw up on *you!*"

"Not if you know what's good for you."

The other trainers tended to move their clients to a floor of the town house that Aaron and I weren't using. They found us too disruptive, and a few of their clients were put off by my tendency to shout out curse words to cope with my fatigue and pain.

I frequently told Aaron my body wouldn't twist in the manner he was prescribing. He'd twist it for me as I sputtered, "Ouch! Ouch! Ouch!"

I'd seek his congratulations for a set of exercises well done. He'd counter that it was proof of what a superior trainer he was.

"A modest one, too," I'd say.

"Save your words for writing," he'd snap.

One day he didn't have a trainee after me and, as I climbed onto one of the StairMasters, he left the gym to go to the post office.

"Thirty minutes," he reminded me. "You owe me thirty minutes."

After ten minutes I was exhausted, and I climbed down. What were the chances he'd return in the next twenty?

By the time I arrived home, there was a message on my voice mail.

"Quitter!" Aaron was shouting. "Wimp!"

If I showed up for one of my twice-weekly sessions looking no slimmer than I had at the last one, he said so, asked me what I'd eaten the day before, told me it had been too much and suggested I give him thirty-five minutes on the StairMaster instead of thirty.

If I tried to hold on to the StairMaster's rails while I pumped my legs up and down, he raced over and swatted my arms back to my sides.

Then, as punishment, he increased the tension on the machine by another level. And glared at me, for good measure.

I despised him and adored him and knew either way he was my best hope. Not just because of the paces he put me through when I was with him but because of the extra conscience he provided for me, the mirror I couldn't hurry past. He was my yardstick, my checkup, my one-man Weight Watchers. With Aaron I couldn't lie or stall or drape myself in something baggy. He saw me twice every week, and he saw me in a T-shirt and shorts. He could tell whether I was behaving, and he was never shy about telling me what he saw.

And I behaved, partly because the rhythm of my twice-weekly appointments with him allowed me to stop thinking in such big, daunting, long-range terms, and to start thinking in increments. The goal was simply to be good for another three days, until the next session. The goal was to shut him up.

But I also behaved because I finally had the ability to keep to a schedule and no longer had excuses not to. Working for the magazine meant that my deadlines came along only every few weeks and I had flexibility in planning interviews and establishing the structure of my days. I could decide to take three five-mile runs in a given week and, if I found the energy and will for them, also find the time.

I was lucky in another way, too: my many years of competitive swimming had taught me what serious exercise was, giving me a sort of body memory of it. I knew how to work out, or rather knew that working out wasn't fifteen minutes of moderate walking on an inclined treadmill while reading the latest issue of the *Economist*.

I also knew that I had to try to find some joy and reward in the exercise itself. As my running routes along the Potomac grew longer, I made certain that they were the prettiest ones I could trace, with water views, bridges and grass-lined paths.

The more weight I felt myself losing, the more determined I was to keep losing it. The adage was true: nothing succeeds like success. And I was exhilarated by my success. I was addicted to it.

I still ate a lot. Although I didn't count calories closely, I had many days when I consumed more than three thousand and possibly as many as four thousand. It seemed to me that by not trying to push the calorie count too low and by trusting that this sustained and sometimes furious exercise would pay off, I avoided those anxious binges, the ones that sprung so readily from the valley of low blood sugar and profound hunger, and I avoided sleep-eating and the compulsive counting of the days until whatever diet I was on was done. I wasn't so focused on an end point, and thus wasn't consumed with the idea that everything leading up to it was an act of barely endurable asceticism.

On some nights I'd nonetheless be tempted to stage one of my all-out feasts, but I'd think about my upcoming visit to Aaron or the next run I was going to take and about how mad I'd be for not feeling any lighter and for having wasted the last training session or most recent run. I'd been stuck for too long, and this liberation from that feeling was infinitely more rewarding than anything I could eat.

Every two weeks or so I made a point of going out and buying some new article of clothing I wouldn't have been able to fit into on my previous shopping trip, and I also made a point of rummaging through my closets and throwing out something that had become too loose. I set it up so that if I gained weight again, I didn't have old clothing to return to and would instead have to go out and buy replacements for it, spending money I didn't want to. That became another threat that helped to keep me in line.

I began to experience familiar routines in unfamiliar ways. There was a diner of sorts around the corner from where I lived; I had often gone there in the late morning to get a toasted bagel with a fried egg, a sausage patty and cheese on it. I still did this, because I needed fuel before or after a run or a session with Aaron. But in the past I'd

With a cousin, Mark (second from right) *and Lisa*
as I work my way back to fitness.

thrown on a pair of loose sweatpants and my hooded sweatshirt and even
a baseball cap to walk to the diner, and while waiting for my breakfast
sandwich, I had tried not to make eye contact with the server, and I'd
willed the people around me not to notice me, a man too heavy to be
eating this way. Now I found myself entering the diner without a cap,
in the T-shirt and shorts in which I was about to exercise or in which I
had just exercised. And I occasionally struck up a conversation with the
server.

Two months after I'd started with Aaron I was even able to fit—
snugly—into some size 36s that didn't come from Brooks Brothers.

It had taken years for me to get as big as I'd gotten; it took much less time to get smaller again. Maybe that was another bit of luck, or maybe a testament to how fiercely I wanted this.

On so many fronts I was calmer and more content, and that included work. I preferred my magazine job to my previous jobs in Congress, on the campaign trail and at the White House. Not only were the hours saner, but I liked being able to dwell on a topic and to take the time to fret over the structure of each piece, even each paragraph.

I landed the first long interview that Gary Condit, the Congressman then under suspicion in the disappearance of a female intern, gave after a disastrous TV interrogation by Connie Chung. And I got an unusually generous amount of time—hours and hours—with Hillary Clinton, who was early in her first term as a New York senator. The editors at the magazine had the clever idea of a joint profile of her and of Chuck Schumer, the senior senator from the state; it was smart because each senator had to worry that the other would try to hog my attention, so neither could be stingy with the access I was allowed.

At one point I had dinner with both of them, and Schumer, trying to get over a cold, ordered tea. Clinton asked me what I was going to drink. I sensed that she was looking for permission, and I said I might like some wine. She instantly echoed that, her smile widening, and went on to drink two glasses. Up close, she was a good deal less stiff than she had ever seemed from a distance.

About six months into the job, as my editors and I pondered who else in Washington to profile, I was presented with a much different opportunity. The position of Rome correspondent for the *Times* had suddenly become open, and the newspaper needed to fill it with someone who didn't have a web of personal commitments and could relocate right away. I qualified. On top of that I had some exposure to Italian culture, had studied Italian for a few years in college and—because of the book on priest abusers—had some knowledge of the workings of the Catholic Church. The newspaper's foreign editor asked me if I might be interested in the position.

Absolutely. It was a chance not only to live and work abroad, but to do it in Italy, which wasn't exactly a hardship. It was a position with clout but without huge responsibility: the most serious European news was covered out of Paris, London and Berlin, the capitals of countries that mattered more to the United States, both economically and diplomatically. The newspaper's Rome correspondent typically spent more time on colorful features than on straightforward news stories. That suited me.

And the timing was ideal. As much as I loved hearing Washington friends and acquaintances marvel at how much weight I had lost, their comments were a constant reminder that in Washington I wasn't simply fit: I was the fat guy who'd *become* fit. People there saw me through the prism of my weight, and every compliment was a retroactive gibe.

I wanted to be seen as who I now was, or was quickly becoming: a normal guy, neither trim nor tubby, whose size didn't warrant particular notice, positive or negative. In Italy I could be that guy, so long as the absence of Aaron didn't trigger a backslide.

I certainly feared a backslide, but I also knew that I couldn't lean on Aaron forever or let worries about regaining weight hold me back from the sorts of adventures that were the best part of life. I had withdrawn from the world during my fattest years. I wanted to throw myself back into it now. I wanted to know what it would be like to walk through Piazza Navona on my way to work, to hear the music of the Italian language every day, on every street corner. I wanted gelato. No, I'd have to go easy on the gelato, to give myself a better chance at an Italian romance, which I wanted, too.

So when the *Times* formally offered me the Rome job in late May 2002, I took it, agreeing to land in Italy by the middle of July. Then I signed up for a crash course in Italian, put my house on the market and sold my car.

Shortly before I left, I went to Scarsdale to visit Dad. I hadn't seen him or any of my siblings in months. Mark was also visiting, with his wife, Lisa, and their kids, and at one point we all went to the Scarsdale Golf Club to use the pool. I splashed around with the kids, and when I climbed out of the water and stretched out on a lounge chair, I didn't bother to put on a T-shirt.

Lisa looked me up and down, smiled and uttered just two words, as powerful in their way as Harry's remark at that New Year's Eve party.

"Nicely done," she said, and I knew exactly what she meant.

Nicely done. I kept hearing the words, basking in them. *Nicely done. Nicely done.* They were musical. They were the two happiest words I could think of.

·FOUR·

Critical Eating

Fifteen

hink of Italy and you think of food. You think of *prosciutto*, *pancetta*, *guanciale* and all the ways that enterprising Italians have devised for butchering, curing, smoking and ingesting a pig. You think of veal, or at least you should, because Italians are nearly as calf-adept as they are pig-obsessed, and I'm not talking veal *piccata* (too austerely lemony) but rather veal *saltimbocca* (the pig joins the calf!) and *osso buco* (a fatty cut of shank, with a cavity of marrow to boot) and *vitello tonnato*, northern Italy's nonpareil contribution to surf and turf. For the uninitiated, it's a quasi carpaccio of thinly sliced meat smothered in a paste of tuna and capers and anchovies—but just faint traces of the anchovies, for an extra-salty edge—and olive oil. Imagine the richest, most *liquid* tuna salad you could possibly whip up. Now imagine pouring it without particular restraint on the pinkest, most delicate ribbon of baby beef you could find. That's *vitello tonnato* at its best, and that's reason alone to fly round-trip to Italy, no matter how awful the euro-to-dollar exchange rate, no matter how much the airlines have started charging for an extra suitcase.

Beyond the meat there are Italian cheeses, matched in quality and variety only by those of France, certainly, and maybe Spain. I suppose there's an argument for Britain, too. But that's it. And none of those countries have anything exactly like Parmesan, intensely salty and at once gritty and milky, or like Italy's *mozzarella di bufala*, made with milk from water buffalos, which gives it a vague, pleasant sourness that rescues it from any blandness, a taste crucially racier than the cheese's texture.

And the pasta. I haven't gone into the pasta. There are more kinds of pasta than most non-Italians ever realize: quadruple the number, quintuple, as if the historical purpose and defining mission of this boot-shaped peninsula—at least once it moved past aqueducts, plumbing and all those other basics-of-civilization advancements—were to curl, straighten, flatten, thicken, elongate, abbreviate, coil, spiral and otherwise sculpt noodles until any and every conceivable shape had been achieved. There's a pasta to evoke butterflies, for which it's named: *farfalle*. There's a pasta mimicking little worms, for which it's named: *vermicelli*.

Does a cuisine need *bucatini* as well as spaghetti in addition to linguine and on top of tagliatelle? All are long, relatively thin strands, but an Italian will tell you that no two types of strand hold sauce quite the same way, so different dishes call for different varieties. There's no fudging or approximating or compromising when it comes to pasta. A given dish, meal or appetite needs what it needs, and there should be a noodle to meet those exact criteria. Italians are picky that way.

So why aren't they fatter? That was a question—asked not only about Italians but also about French people and some other Europeans—that I frequently encountered in articles in American newspapers and magazines, perennially intent on explaining our own country's plumper populace. And when I moved to Italy, it was a question with special resonance for me.

If I could just figure out how Italians staved off second chins and love handles, maybe I could do it, too. The answer might give me some sort of meaningful protection—not just another new, doomed trick—as

I romped across a landscape more delicious than any I'd previously inhabited.

The answer wasn't exercise. My experience trying to find and use a proper gym—somewhere with a full complement of weights, an attractive array of cardiovascular machines for rainy or cold days, and a setting that blunted the potential drudgery of it all—made that immediately clear.

In the center of Rome, where the *Times* office was located, there was nothing like a spacious, gleaming Equinox. What passed for legitimate fitness centers were the sorts of perfunctory setups you found in hotels: a few rooms with meager scatterings of equipment. They were depressing. They weren't going to motivate me to visit often or linger for more than a few minutes at a time.

But in a slightly less central location, along one edge of the Villa Borghese park, was the Roman Sport Forum, or *La Roman,* as people in the know called it, speaking of it as they might La Loren or La Jolie. Romans saw it as an ostentatiously endowed diva of a gym, even though it was little larger or better outfitted than the kind of health club you find in any strip mall in any American exurb. It had a modest pool, a weight room with scores of machines, a glass-walled exercise studio for calisthenics, and perhaps two dozen treadmills, StairMasters, recumbent bikes and the like. It was darker than any American gym I knew, making me wonder if Italians considered mood lighting a catalyst for working out. I was thinking along the wrong lines. Working out wasn't really the point of La Roman.

In fact the managers of La Roman seemed intent on *preventing* it. For starters, there was the signed doctor's note they insisted I get in order not just to join the gym but even to venture as far as the locker room during an initial visit. I produced a note, paid for a six-month membership, changed into my workout clothes and found an available treadmill. I had been on it less than five minutes when I noticed one of the gym attendants standing at my side, flapping his arms and yelling at me.

"*È vietato!*" he was saying, and I would soon realize that whether you were speaking to an attendant at La Roman or reading one of the many signs posted on the walls, that phrase was the most prevalent one, a kind of motto for the gym. *È vietato! È vietato!* Translation: it's forbidden. But precisely *what* about my activity on the treadmill was *vietato? Running?* All the Italians on the treadmills around mine were walking, and they were walking rather slowly at that, nary a pinprick of perspiration smudging their fashionable exercise outfits. My own T-shirt was already mottled and wet. Maybe sweating was *vietato*.

The attendant explained that while the note from my doctor entitled me to use the gym's pool, weight machines, locker room and of course snack bar, it didn't entitle me to use any cardiovascular equipment. For that I needed to submit to an independent examination, including a stress test with heart monitors taped to my chest, by the gym's own physician. It would cost me a hundred dollars. And an appointment wasn't available until a week from then.

I bided my time, paid my money, passed the stress test and returned to the treadmill without incident, using my gym visits to run three or so miles on a treadmill and spend thirty to forty minutes lifting weights. In the weight rooms were signs spelling out, for unexplained reasons, that it was *vietato* to chew gum. It was *vietato* to leave free weights lying around, a transgression that might require one of the half dozen attendants to do something other than gossip with one another, harangue unauthorized treadmill users and unwind in the snack bar, which was a nearly full-scale trattoria, with seating for dozens and a menu that included *bucatini all'amatriciana* and *prosciutto e melone*. My path to and from the locker room skirted its tables, at which I'd sometimes spot, on my way out of the gym, the same La Roman staffers and members I'd spotted on my way in.

It apparently wasn't *vietato* for a member of La Roman to lean against or straddle a weight machine for twenty uninterrupted minutes, monopolizing it without attempting anything more physical than the arching of an eyebrow. La Roman members did this all the time, provided that the weight machine in question afforded them a good view of other patrons and vice versa. Although most of them were thin and no small number of them were gorgeous, their time at La Roman deserved little credit for that.

I was marveling one evening at their languorous, even phobic relationship with physical exertion when, yet again, a flapping, yelling gym attendant materialized at my side. He spoke in such rushed, histrionic Italian that I had to implore him a half dozen times to slow down, back up, repeat himself, maybe use fewer polysyllabic words. What exactly was *il problema*?

He pointed to my gym shorts, then grabbed my arm and tugged me toward a sign I hadn't noticed before. It explained that it was *vietato* to wear shorts that didn't adhere tightly to your legs. My shorts didn't, and were thus *vietato*.

Trust me on this: the shorts I was wearing were as unremarkable and unobjectionable as athletic shorts could be. They were precisely the type of shorts—ribbed waist, drawstring, thick cotton, material reaching more than halfway down the thigh—that every college since the dawn of academia has printed its logo on and sold in the student store. They weren't flamboyant shorts. They weren't tattered shorts. They weren't skimpy shorts. They were archetypal, boring athletic shorts.

Why did it matter whether they adhered to my legs?

I told the attendant, in my flawed but functional Italian, that for my next visit to the gym, I would get and wear shorts that were adherent or adhesive or whatever they were supposed to be. Then I turned away from him and headed to the next weight machine I planned to use. I felt a tug on my arm. He wouldn't let me go.

He held up an index finger—the international signal for "wait a second"—and bolted away. Within less than a minute he was back.

With two thick blue rubber bands.

I'd seen rubber bands like these before: they were the kind often wrapped around the base of a head of broccoli. Maybe that's where they'd been at some point. But as he handed them to me, I understood that where they were supposed to be now was wrapped around each too-floppy leg of my too-floppy cotton gym shorts.

I fingered them. Looked strangely at them. Looked strangely at *him*, trying to work some self-pity and pleading into my expression and get a pass. He didn't waver. And so I bent to his will, or rather *snapped* to it, and spent the next forty-five minutes stalking La Roman like a human broccoli, each thigh banded in blue.

A few days later I ran into one of my few acquaintances at the gym and asked him if he could shed some light on this floppy-shorts policy.

"You can't wear floppy shorts," he explained, "because if you did, other people could see up your legs, to your crotch."

"But all they'd see is my underwear," I said.

"You don't understand," he said. "The problem the gym was having was that some people were wearing short, loose-legged shorts and *not* wearing underwear." He paused, then added: "Deliberately."

Now I understood. What was actually *vietato* was flashing your fellow gym users, and what many La Roman regulars most wanted to do wasn't shoulder presses and a full half hour on the elliptical. They wanted to pose (hence the mood lighting), preen (hence the avoidance of perspiration) and give their fellow fitness enthusiasts a gander at the family jewels. That last impulse explained not only the policy on floppy shorts but also a sign posted in the men's locker room.

It stressed that it was *vietato* to shower with the door in front of your individual stall open.

So what was it then? Why was the typical Italian I met so much narrower than the typical American?

Were Italians walking more? I kept an eye out, and what I noticed wasn't a pedestrian utopia. What I noticed were *motorini* (the Italian term for small motorcycles or mopeds) snaking between cars, skittering down cobbled alleyways, threatening to mow down anyone who stepped in front of them and blocking the doorways to stores and apartment buildings, which had been turned into unauthorized *motorini* parking lots. Romans were indeed less reliant on cars than Americans, but that wasn't because they were doing anything as potentially attire-wrinkling and brow-dampening as traveling across the city on their own two legs.

What about smoking? Was nicotine restraining the Roman appetite and accelerating the Roman metabolism? While Romans did, as a rule, smoke more than New Yorkers, that was becoming less true all the time. During my first months in Rome I noticed the NO SMOKING signs (*è vietato!*) proliferate, and that trend continued until I left nearly two years later. I met more Romans who didn't smoke than Romans who did. And there wasn't a noticeable difference in the relative slimness of one camp versus the other.

Another slender-Italians hypothesis that I heard all the time was that Italians didn't have Americans' taste for sweets. But walk into any coffee bar, which is where seemingly every Italian man has his breakfast, and what's he eating? A *cornetto*, which is the kind of pastry—often loaded with sugar, sometimes filled with custard—that's designed to accompany his sugary cappuccino. If you spot him twelve hours later, shortly after he's finished his dinner, he may well have a cup of gelato in his hand.

Sure, he's not drinking vats of Coca-Cola or Dr Pepper, but his day is bookended by sweets.

By my observation the Italian secret wasn't aerobic activity or cigarettes or an avoidance of sugar or even lighter drinking, though most Romans indeed chose wine over hard liquor and stopped at two glasses, three tops. It was this: they didn't supersize anything.

The 7-Eleven Big Gulp? Neither it nor any Italian analogue existed here. The Starbucks Venti-size cappuccino? Romans drank their cappuccinos from squat, old-fashioned coffee cups, and where Starbucks was concerned, Italy had sealed its borders tighter than North Korea's. The all-you-can-eat buffet? That was, technically speaking, what the antipasti tables in some Italian restaurants amounted to, but no Italian would ever describe them that way, with an implied exhortation to test the limits of a stomach, with an emphasis on quantity over quality. Quality was what mattered to them, and it was most aptly savored in modest portions.

That morning *cornetto* and that cappuccino were often the whole of an Italian man's breakfast, sugary but too modest, in volume, to do much caloric damage. That nighttime gelato was usually the equivalent of one large scoop or two small ones.

In Italy pasta came on plates, not in troughs, and the amount might not be more than a dozen forkfuls. A roasted chicken was more likely to serve four or even six people than two. As for snacking between and before meals, Italians limited that, if they did it at all. I seldom saw them tunneling idly into bags of chips or hauling in nuts by the fistful. On Italian bars the bowls of peanuts weren't more than three inches in diameter and an inch and a quarter deep, and you plumbed them not with your fingers but with the kind of itsy-bitsy spoon also used to stir espresso. The spoon was there primarily as a hygienic measure, but its size was an indication of the restraint with which Italians parceled out their epicurean pleasures.

In the end, Italians were generally slimmer than Americans for the plainest, most obvious reason of all.

They ate less.

The meals at the first dinner parties I attended and at the first Roman restaurants I visited were revelations, because I had erroneously equated Italian food with bounty, with superabundance, the defining characteristic of a Bruni family feast, in which food remained a badge of affluence and generosity long after anyone had anything to prove, in which the approach to special-occasion eating had its roots in a particular kind of Italian soil: southern, rural, peasant. Superabundance had also been a selling point of many of the red-sauce Italian restaurants that were the only, or at least the main, Italian restaurants in America when I was young. A bottomless bowl of pasta: *now that's Italian!* Or so we were all led to believe, and I didn't pay enough attention during my first spin through Italy in my early twenties to be disabused of that myth. I was too busy consuming nothing but bread and beer for days on end.

This time I took note. I went to a fancy event in a Roman socialite's sprawling apartment beside the Quirinale, the building where the Italian president lives, and watched white-gloved servers ferry silver platters. There was beef carpaccio in thinly sliced ribbons, and each of the guests around me took just one. I had been contemplating four or five. We were given clean larger plates for a subsequent course of fettucine with cream and mushrooms, and I figured the size and emptiness of this new canvas were signals to fill it up. But no: the modest hillocks of pasta that my tablemates gathered onto their plates had circumferences little bigger than a baseball's. When the rack of lamb came, each guest took just one tiny chop. I'd allotted three per person on a few occasions when I'd cooked rack of lamb for company in D.C.

In a Roman restaurant I'd order a *primo piatto*, or first plate, of ravioli, and there'd be just three or four round envelopes of pasta, each smaller than the base of a wineglass. The *secondo piatto* would come: maybe six ounces of filleted *orata* (sea bream) or *rombo* (turbot). Dessert would be modest and would be followed by an espresso that went down in only a few sips, continuing to make the point: the fineness of the sensations you experienced trumped the number or the duration of them.

I was getting a reeducation in what constituted indulgence: not second and third helpings but a leisurely, prolonged time at the table, during which the virtue of a four-course meal—*antipasto, primo, secondo* (with *contorno,* or side), *dolce*—was the rhythm it established, along with the variety it permitted.

Italians weren't wasteful like Americans, who have an ethic of boundlessness woven into our national character. Instead they were particular, convinced they had cracked some epicurean code and were following some epicurean master script. They cared about having the right things at the right times: cappuccino in the morning, for instance, but never, ever after dinner, the theory being that consuming milk in the wake of consuming wine would foil proper digestion, which would be assisted by the bitter acids of coffee only if they were unencumbered by milk. They cared about having *superior* things: prosciutto as it was prescribed around the city of Parma; *mozzarella di bufala* as it was perfected in the countryside near Naples.

At lunchtime, if I was working in Rome and not traveling somewhere for a story, I'd often walk just a few minutes from the office to a cheese shop in a tiny alley off a back corner of Campo de' Fiori, one of Rome's beautiful piazzas, which hosted a sprawling outdoor market every morning. Sometimes I'd get *ovoline,* or "little eggs," of mozzarella, which was always stored in milky water, so that it remained as silken and creamy as possible.

Or sometimes I'd get *ricotta fresca di pecora,* sheep's milk ricotta, which had a different kind of creaminess, vaguely chalky instead of silky, less luscious but heartier. There would be an enormous cake of it, round and tall and pure white, behind the counter, and one of the shopkeepers would place a long, flat knife just above its surface, then slowly move the knife sideways, measuring the size of the piece you wanted.

"*Di più?*" she'd ask ("More?"), and drag her knife farther along the surface of the cake.

"*Di meno?*" she'd ask ("Less?"), and then move the knife backward.

When the knife was precisely where you wanted it, you'd say, "*Basta così.*" ("That'll do.") She'd cut the slice, then wrap it in thick, patterned paper, folded so carefully and crisply it almost qualified as origami. That was the Italian genius: finding opportunities for art and for prettiness in even the smallest gestures and most basic chores; filling life with beauty and ritual.

My ritual was to go from the cheese shop to a brick-oven bakery and buy some *pizza bianca*, essentially naked, undressed pizza, just the cooked, crunchy, golden brown dough, sometimes with a sheen of olive oil on top of it, sometimes with just a rumor of herbs. Somewhere along the way I'd pick up a plastic knife. I'd walk to Piazza Farnese, a quieter, more elegant piazza between Campo de' Fiori and the Tiber. I'd take a seat on one of the stone benches that were essentially part of the front of Palazzo Farnese, a sixteenth-century palace whose design and construction reflected input from Michelangelo himself.

Staring out at one of the two regal stone fountains on opposite ends of the piazza, I'd put the ricotta in my lap, unfold the patterned paper around it. Then I'd use my plastic knife to spread it onto one square of my *pizza bianca*, then onto another and then—sometimes—onto a third. I'd eat slowly, listening to the splash of the fountain, hearing the hum and buzz of unseen *motorini* nearby. Maybe I'd turn off my cell phone, even though I was usually loath to: the Pope might die; another Italian government might tumble. So be it. A fifteen-minute delay wouldn't put me too far behind, and a man deserved a moment's communion with his ricotta. Italy was teaching me that.

This wasn't the lightest of lunches, but it wasn't gluttonous. It wasn't about the act and thrill of simply filling my stomach. Whether at lunchtime, dinnertime or points in between, I fixated on which store I'd go to for my *Parmigiano Reggiano*, which for a *porchetta* sandwich. A sense of adventure and discovery replaced the abandon of overeating, which came to seem some violation of the whole Italian ethos. I didn't feel the urge to eat so much because what I had to eat was so excellent.

And I also had Louis.

I met him in Athens, on a reporting trip: the geographic purview of the newspaper's Rome bureau extended to Greece, which had plenty of stories to check out. It was going to be the host for the 2004 Olympics, and international Olympics officials were in a constant, justified panic about its state of preparedness. It was a European Union newcomer, and thus a prism through which to assess the dynamics of power and disbursements of money within the EU.

Louis was an American who had been living and working in Athens for several years, and he knew people who knew me, so when he saw that I was the new *Times* correspondent in charge of Greece, he got in touch and suggested we share a meal when I found myself in Athens. We had that dinner in a seafood restaurant near the peak of a steep street in the city's fashionable Kolonaki neighborhood.

We'd been talking for an hour and a half—about European politics, European gyms, his weakness for black musical divas, mine for dubiously poetic white female singer-songwriters—when it hit me how much I liked this man. I wanted the conversation and the evening to last another hour and a half, and then another hour and a half after that. Well educated, well traveled, well acquainted with high culture and low culture and all culture in between, Louis could talk. He could talk more and faster and better than I could, and I was a talker. I finished sentences he had begun; he revised and refined sentences I'd thrown out too hurriedly and sloppily. The space between us was crowded with words.

I usually went for more strapping, darker types, and Louis had pale skin, freckles, blue eyes and light brown hair that had obviously once been blond. He was shorter and much slighter than I was. Younger, too, by a few years. But there was an energy in his eyes and he had oversize lips that I suspected would be fun to kiss. I hadn't kissed anyone in years.

We began flirting by text message and by e-mail within minutes of parting and continued that flirtation over the days to follow, when I was back in Rome. The boldness of the compliments we gave each other and of the questions we asked each other grew, to the point where I suggested he use an upcoming three-day weekend to fly to Rome and stay with me. He agreed to.

My apartment had two big bedrooms, each with its own private bath. As I imagined his arrival in a few days, I sweated over whether I should carry his suitcase to the spare guest bedroom, just to show that I wasn't making any assumptions. Or would that cause *him* to assume I actually wanted him in a separate bed, which I certainly didn't? Was "assumptions" even a word that should be in play? Although we hadn't even kissed, he was flying two hours for a second (or, depending on how you counted, first) date. Was there really any ambiguity in that?

I made dinner reservations. I plotted walking routes. I plotted espresso stops. I bought flowers and put them in vases that usually went empty. I visited La Roman on Tuesday, and again on Wednesday, and again on Thursday, careful each time to wear something acceptable, which in my case was my typical cotton gym shorts *over* a pair of clingy, adherent, longer-legged bicycle shorts. This way I conformed to gym rules without letting anyone see me in something so formfitting that all the flaws in my form—and there were plenty left—were immediately evident.

To start the weekend on a warm note, I arranged for the driver who sometimes sped me around Italy for *Times* work to pick Louis up at the airport when he was due to arrive on Friday evening, at an hour when I was going to be tied up at the office. I bought a gift bag to be put in the backseat of the car so that it was waiting for Louis when he got in. Into the bag I tucked a tall bottle of water and a small box of hazelnut-filled Italian chocolates. I stuffed the bag with purple tissue paper, and within the paper's folds I placed two compact discs, along with a note: "One of these you will like, and one of these you *should* like." The former was a compilation of Whitney Houston's greatest hits; the latter was the newest release by Tori Amos, titled *Scarlet's Walk*.

Louis had the gift bag in his hands when I opened and let him through my front door. As we headed toward the kitchen to get some wine, I left his suitcase where he had set it down on the foyer floor. I didn't volunteer to carry it to, or suggest that he put it in, either bedroom. A few hours later, I put it in mine.

I went to see him in Athens about two weeks after that. From that point forward we managed a visit about every three weeks, usually in Rome or Athens, sometimes in some other European city where we both wanted to spend a long weekend. After about four months of these visits and of nightly phone calls, he decided, with my encouragement, to put in for a leave of absence from work and, as soon as that took effect, move in with me in Rome. Before we'd known each other for even a year, we were living together.

If the Italian attitude toward food was one big reason I didn't regain weight in Italy, Louis was the other. My relationship with him was completely unlike my relationship with Greg, whom I had come to take for granted. My *attitude* was different: more grateful and more fearful. Maybe because Louis followed so many years of nothingness, maybe because he wasn't given to sweeping declarations of ardor, I worried all the time: that he'd wake up one morning and decide he'd made a mistake; that the inevitably fading intensity of our physical interactions would leave us with too little too soon; that I'd gain five pounds and tip the scales against me. I treaded lightly around Louis, and that meant eating sensibly and supplementing my time on the treadmill at La Roman with runs through the Villa Borghese park and along the Tiber river; along the Arno if work took me to Florence; along the Seine or Danube when Louis and I traveled. I was motivated by more than just holding on to him. I was motivated by how I wanted to feel when we were holding each other, by my determination to enjoy that and my desire for only a third of my brain, as opposed to all of it, to be conscious of what he might notice—too much flab, too much softness.

I was motivated by my movements through the world beyond Louis, too. During the Washington years and even during some previous periods, my thoughts before meeting someone for the first time, whether in a social or professional setting, whirled around the questions of how heavy they'd deem me, what they would read into that, how much it might lower their estimation of me, whether it would make me seem coarse or sloppy or just plain sad. As I fretted over whether I was saying the right things or asking the right questions, I would fret even more over how I looked. Now it was different. I could concentrate better on something other than my physical shape.

I wasn't yet pleased with it, and guessed I'd never be. In Rome I wore size 36 pants that were somewhat loose and size 35 jeans that were somewhat tight, and I could feel myself moving up and down within perhaps a five-pound range. At one point I even got on a scale. Of course I didn't own one, but I spotted one on the bathroom floor of a hotel room I was staying in. Curiosity got the better of me, especially because the scale was in kilograms and I knew that would mean a lower number.

The scale said 92. My weight was 92! I went to my laptop, went online, found the conversion. It equaled just under 203 pounds. That was still more than I should be, more than I wanted to be. But 203 was 65 pounds less than the last time I'd known what I weighed.

It was a weight I could live with and sometimes even forget about, which was the main thing, the best thing. I felt lighter in spirit, and I preferred life this way, enough to stop myself before I rounded up too much food when shopping for groceries and to catch myself when I was about to order the biggest dessert on the menu.

I was having an adventure. I was having a blast. One week I'd find myself plying the canals of Venice in a floating police cruiser for a story about a crackdown on boaters breaking the maritime speed limit; another week I'd find myself on the slopes of Mount Vesuvius interviewing stubborn residents who refused to relocate somewhere beyond the threat of lava.

I spent weeks in Turkey monitoring its government's response to the American invasion of Iraq, and even traveled close to the border between Iraq and Turkey, to watch for any signs that Turkish troops were taking advantage of the war to move into Kurdish strongholds on the other side. I spent weeks in Israel pitching in with reporting there at times when Israeli–Palestinian tensions spiked even higher than usual.

Wherever Pope John Paul II went, I went: to Guatemala, Croatia, Poland. Poland was something else. As a gesture of respect for the Pope, any city or town he visited there went dry, at least officially, for the duration of his stay. But veterans in the Vatican press corps found ways around this temporary prohibition. They packed their own flasks of whiskey and vodka, and if you were nice enough to them, they shared. Or they sweet-talked waiters into serving them alcoholic drinks that didn't look like alcoholic drinks. On a papal trip to Poland, the screwdriver suddenly became every reporter's cocktail of choice. To the naked eye, at least, it was just a glass of orange juice.

And in every country, in every city, I sized up the food. The logical coda to a long day of reporting—and a good way to get acquainted with a new place—was to go out and find something special to eat. So I tracked down the juiciest lamb in Diyarbakir, Turkey; the fluffiest falafel in Hebron and Jerusalem; the richest veal-stuffed *agnolotti* in Turin; the most vibrant pumpkin-stuffed ravioli in Parma. But it wasn't food as a compulsion; it was food as an investigation, an education, a discovery. I found I could enjoy it without overdoing it. In fact I could enjoy it more, because it wasn't tinged with anticipatory guilt or incipient panic over how much tighter my pants might feel the next day.

At home in Rome, Louis would be waiting, in our rambling, oddly situated apartment. It was on the top floor of a six-story building in which the first five floors belonged to a middlebrow hotel, with which it shared an entrance and elevator. The hotel desk clerks were our de facto doormen, cranky Donatella and affable Stefano and gorgeous Giacomo, who always flirted, simply because he enjoyed the effect. If I ran out of coffee and was too lazy to go out for it in the morning, he let me walk downstairs to the breakfast room in the basement and pretend I was one of the hotel guests. He winked at me as I went.

Like Greg, Louis cooked, but he didn't cook like Greg. He cooked more like Grandma, in a frenzy of motion, pots clanging, crumbs scattering, liquid splattering. The kitchen was the smallest, saddest room in our otherwise spacious, light-filled apartment; within minutes of the beginning of a meal's preparation, Louis would have every square inch of it covered in excess syrup, fugitive grease, discarded peelings and spilled powder. I'd look in on him and think how I should get a drop cloth, put it under him, maybe even line all the cabinet faces and countertops with plastic.

And I'd wait and wait for the results, as the hour grew late even for dinner in Europe.

"Forty-five minutes out!" Louis would shout at about nine fifteen, the first of a series of curiously timed progress reports.

At ten he'd announce: "We're only a half hour out!" He made it sound like a positive update. Like a happy surprise.

At ten twenty-five: "Just twenty more minutes, sweetie! Is the table set?" The table had been set since eight forty-five.

And at ten forty-five: "About seven minutes, maybe eight!" That meant fifteen, so I'd wait another ten to light the candles.

Cleanup was a nightmare, but I felt obliged to do at least half of it, since he was doing the cooking, and since he'd done all the shopping. With his days free, he scoured Rome for ingredients, and it took him forever, because he wanted to make and eat food at home that we couldn't easily find in Rome's restaurants and that wasn't typically stocked in Rome's stores—Thai food, Indian food, that sort of thing. He was going through this whole Asian phase.

We ate out as often as we ate in, and made a vigorous tour of Roman restaurants, finding unheralded ones, developing favorites. For its lavish antipasti spread, delivered to each table as soon as the diners sat down at it, we loved Santopadre, just a half block from our apartment, where the mistress of the house, Dina, would greet us with kisses and wonder why we hadn't stopped by in so long, even if we'd been there just a week earlier. She reminded me of Grandma.

For its savory Parmesan and Gorgonzola and zucchini-flavored custards we loved Trattoria Monti, about two miles from our place, where the female chef's two handsome sons, Enrico and Daniele, recited the entire menu in perfectly enunciated Italian, punctuating the mention of each dish with the phrase *e poi abbiamo*, which meant "and then we have," before naming the next option. We would order several courses, always concluding with the pistachio *semifreddo* in bittersweet chocolate sauce. Then Enrico or Daniele would put bottles of *amaro*, *limoncello* and *grappa* on the table, so we could help ourselves, free of charge, to however much of whichever we wanted. That was the way Italian restaurants treated cherished regulars, which we'd become. We often left Trattoria

Monti more than three hours after we had arrived, and were usually the last customers to go.

Before long Italian friends who had lived in Rome much longer than I had were asking *me* where to eat. Somehow, I'd segued from restaurant enthusiast to restaurant savant, and without gaining any appreciable weight.

Sixteen

You're not going to believe this," I told Louis when I walked into our apartment one night in January 2004.

He had to turn off the food processor, in which he was whipping up some Asian concoction. He had to turn down the volume on Mary J. Blige.

"I got a call today," I said, then filled him in on a chain of events to which I hadn't attributed much meaning before then.

Weeks earlier Barbara Graustark, an editor at the *Times* whose purview included the Dining section, had sent out an e-mail to the staff announcing that the current restaurant critic, William Grimes, was leaving the job. I knew Barbara a little—I'd written some stories unrelated to food for her in the past—so I took the opportunity of her e-mail to write back and say a chatty hello.

"I hope you've got a lot of extra space on your desk," I said in my e-mail, "because you're about to be deluged with résumés and appeals."

She replied: "Will one of them be yours?"

I didn't take the question seriously. "It would be a dream job," I wrote back, and on a conscious level, at least, I meant that literally. It was a job I'd have, and be able to do, in my dreams, in some fantasy realm where my suitability and aptitude didn't matter, and where I didn't have my warped history with food.

But she didn't interpret my response that way. She sensed, maybe correctly, some curiosity on my part. Now she was circling back to tell me that in the meetings of editors mulling the question of who should be the newspaper's next restaurant critic, my name had come up. And she had told those editors that I might just be interested.

On the phone she explained that editors at the *Times* were looking at the situation two ways. They had drawn up a list of food mavens who had already written extensively about dining out, but they were also considering writers newer to the subject matter, with potentially fresher perspectives. Apparently I fell into the latter category.

To the thinking of Barbara and several editors above her, I had plunged into political reporting without considerable buildup or past experience. The same went for foreign reporting. So why not restaurant criticism? Especially when I was a known restaurant fan? Many of the paper's senior editors were aware of that because they'd eaten with me. They also knew that years earlier I'd been a movie critic for the *Free Press*, so criticism wasn't alien to me.

I assumed the chances of being chosen were slim, but it was harmless fun to contemplate it. So I told Barbara that if *Times* editors were willing to consider it, I was, too. In a few weeks, I thought, this diversion would end with the appointment of someone else.

I didn't hesitate to share all of this with Louis, who was hardly bound to Rome or invested in my continuation as the newspaper's correspondent there. His leave of absence from work was finite and he had already begun wondering aloud about what we were going to do and how we were going to stay together, given the lack of any work for him in

Italy. So I expected him to be intrigued by the prospect—no matter how fantastic—of my returning to New York, a much easier city for him to navigate professionally.

I also expected him to find the idea of my becoming a restaurant critic absurd.

To my surprise, he didn't.

He noted that almost nothing pleased me more than a great meal—it was why he loved cooking for me—and that almost nothing disappointed me more than a bad one. He reminded me that in Rome, in Athens, in so many other European cities and in Vietnam, where we'd taken a long trip together just weeks earlier, I was always on the prowl for interesting restaurants and I always put dining at the top of my agenda.

"You've eaten in more countries than most other people," he said. "You've eaten in more kinds of restaurants."

It was true, I supposed. For some reason I'd never before thought of my travels as eating expeditions, though many of them had turned into precisely that.

Did I actually have some legitimate qualifications for this job? Could I take a credible stab at it? Possibly. What I didn't know I could make a point of learning. I was capable of that sort of diligence. I'd bring energy to the task, given the newness and challenge of it. I was opinionated: no problem there. And to the extent that I wasn't a dyed-in-the-wool foodie, well, what fraction of a restaurant review's readers were? Maybe I'd be a better proxy for consumers than someone more deeply immersed in the world of restaurants would be.

Then again, maybe not, and I didn't want to sign on to being a hack. I didn't want an assignment, especially one that meant as much as this one did to many readers, that I was bound to fumble. And I didn't want to be plagued day in and day out by the worry that I was out of my depth.

Over the next weeks I carefully read perhaps three-quarters of the reviews that William Grimes—who went by the nickname Biff—had written, and half of those written by his predecessor, Ruth Reichl. I had conversations with Barbara and other editors, during which we discussed the ways in which restaurants were about much more than food—they were theaters, social laboratories, microcosms of their neighborhoods and their moments—and the ways in which a broad spectrum of journalistic experience might help a critic capture that.

Those editors made a request. So that I could get a sense of how comfortable I felt with this form of writing, and so that they could get a sense of that as well, they asked me to do what other candidates for the job were also doing: visit a serious restaurant and write a pretend review of it. In my case, the restaurant would have to be in Rome.

I chose a relatively new, ambitious and expensive place named Hostaria dell'Orso and went there in a group of three, so we could order and taste a variety of dishes. Then I hammered out my appraisal, noting the blandly seasoned scallops, the gummy spaghetti carbonara and the way these and other dishes contradicted the restaurant's grand setting and ostentatious sense of ceremony. I concluded:

> So much elaborate show, so little actual event: maybe this is a restaurant tailored to today's Italy, in which confidence often trumps performance and surface sheen counts more than what lies beneath.
>
> Around the time I dined at Hostaria dell'Orso, the prime minister, Silvio Berlusconi, was admitting that the reason he had spent a solid month away from office, in hiding, was cosmetic surgery. His popularity seemed unaffected. Hostaria dell'Orso could be a huge hit.

I e-mailed the review to the editors, shook my head—what a bonkers, *bonkers* digression this whole episode would surely turn out to be—and went back to my usual routine. I combed Italian newspapers and magazines for a new batch of story ideas. I made a round of calls to Vatican sources, checking anew on the Pope's questionable health. I had a series of lunches with political sources, updating myself on the reliable turmoil of Italian government.

In late February, Barbara called again. She offered me the job.

And I accepted. In spite of what I'd told myself the day I sent in the review, I'd been hoping for her call and imagining it constantly over the weeks since.

There were many reasons I said yes. Although I had eighteen months to two years left before my stint in Rome was supposed to be over, I had no idea what I wanted to do next at the *Times*, and I'd seen too many former foreign correspondents at loose ends, too seasoned and too senior to be put in small jobs but not quite right for whichever bigger jobs happened to be open at the time. I worried that I'd wind up in that same situation, especially since I wasn't interested in another posting abroad and more time away from my father and my siblings and my expanding brood of nieces and nephews, nine of them now. The restaurant-critic job was an answer to all of those concerns. It would get me back home.

In addition, New York made some sense for Louis and me. His bosses wanted to send him to a post in Southeast Asia. If we were going to stay together, one of us would have to quit his job. But my job prospects in the country that he was potentially bound for were even worse than his in Rome. New York was somewhere we might both be able to do work we wanted to.

Also, there was this: when I'd bolted from political reporting, it was partly because I craved a less frenetic and healthier lifestyle, partly because I didn't enjoy pack journalism, partly because I simply needed a change. But in addition to all of that, I had come to dread the intense scrutiny and nasty second-guessing that went along with covering politics for a news organization as influential as the *Times*. I chafed at the skewering to which I and so many of my colleagues were routinely subjected in publications that justly turned the tables on other reporters, analyzing *them*. In my case the naysaying and nitpicking had exacerbated the full range of my insecurities, feeding the disgust I was already feeling over the mess I had made of my physical self.

I wasn't proud of how I'd bowed out of covering anything more than the first few months of the Bush presidency and then bolted to Rome. The restaurant-critic job would once again paint a target on my back, because it was a high-profile position with a glamorous aura and serious economic influence. I didn't want to shrink from that. In my personal life I had stopped hiding, stopped stalling; here was a way to do the same thing in my professional life. It was time.

Besides which, the very idea of the job was undeniably thrilling. When I'd gone into journalism, and then when I'd joined the *Times*, I'd relished the acquisition and upgrading of a passport into societies and experiences that I would never otherwise be part of. Here was another strange land to which this amazing passport would be granting me access. I wanted to travel there.

But what about the eating? What about the constant, compulsory eating? This was the most surreal aspect of what I was signing up for, and it did scare me.

But in Italy I'd given more than a little thought to where I'd always gone wrong and why I'd always had such troubles with food. I'd been foiled time and again by the kinds of behaviors and thinking I wouldn't be able to give in to in this new job: the fad diets that I'd prepare for or answer with outrageous binges; the fraudulent, self-styled science of permitted foods and forbidden foods and foods eaten in bunches and foods eaten in specific combinations.

In this new job, I wouldn't be able to practice that black magic. I wouldn't be able to tell myself that I could be naughty today because I'd be extra virtuous tomorrow and the day after. So I'd have to watch my portions, as I'd learned to in Italy. I'd have to stick to regular exercise, as I'd done since Aaron. The postponements—the lies—couldn't be justified. I'd have to be steady, and I'd have to be sensible.

Before Biff started as restaurant critic, he was allowed some preparatory time in which to travel for the sole purpose of research, of eating in places whose cuisines he wanted to know better. Over many weeks he drove slowly through Italy and France.

Now the same extreme hardship was being visited upon me, and I needed a strategy and itinerary of my own. Italy I knew: whenever I had gone anywhere in the country for work or fun, I'd sampled the local restaurants. But I hadn't spent much time in France. So I planned a week in Paris, during which I'd hit a Michelin one-star restaurant, a Michelin two-star restaurant, a Michelin three-star restaurant (the highest rating). I also planned a week in Hong Kong, which served as a crossroads for many Asian cuisines, sometimes fused: Cantonese, Sichuan, Indian, Thai, Japanese.

But what I needed first and foremost was to reacquaint myself with New York. I hadn't eaten in some of the most important restaurants that had opened over the last five years, not to mention a few important restaurants that had opened earlier than that. So I scheduled three weeks there, during which I'd eat out for dinner every day and for lunch, too, on many days. New York would be the first stop on my grand gastronomic tour.

I wanted to hit all five of the restaurants that had ratings of four stars—which signaled an "extraordinary" experience and was the highest number of stars on the *Times* scale—from either Biff or Ruth Reichl, so I made reservations at Daniel, Jean Georges, Bouley, Alain Ducasse and Le Bernardin.

It seemed just as important to have variety in my survey, to dine in one-star ("good"), two-star ("very good") and three-star ("excellent") restaurants with more casual settings, so I reserved at Pastis, a boisterous Downtown brasserie run by the star restaurateur Keith McNally, and at the Red Cat, a much beloved, unfussy American bistro on a western edge of Chelsea that was slowly attracting restaurants. I reserved at Spice Market (supertrendy Asian), Bolo (moderately trendy Spanish), Strip House (quasi-trendy steak), WD-50 (untrendy avant-garde) and about a dozen other places.

My schedule set, I headed alone to the Rome airport—Louis was going to join me a few days later—to catch my flight to New York. The date, fittingly enough, was April 1. In the plane I was surrounded by a group of American tourists who had been doing some amateur musical performances in Europe, from what I overheard of their conversations. Most of them wore loose-fitting, elastic-waisted warm-up suits.

The group members conferred with one another about the treats they had rounded up for the long trip. Someone produced a large bag of mustard-flavored pretzels; someone else hauled out a box of sugar cookies; yet another person unveiled individually wrapped chocolate cubes. About ten minutes into the flight, they started passing the food around and eating it in what struck me as a mindless, time-passing manner that I knew all too well. Although I felt my stomach gurgle, I thought: *That's what I can't be lured into anymore. That's a luxury I can't afford.*

I arrived in Newark in the midafternoon and met Barbara Graustark at Daniel around nine p.m. We stayed until midnight, savoring a meal that included curried cauliflower soup, mustard-crusted lamb and wasabi-seasoned tuna so luscious I half-wondered if a big fat bluefin could be hand-raised, if this one had been coddled in some gargantuan aquarium in an enormous mansion where it was massaged hourly.

"It's not always going to be like this," Barbara told me.

I nodded. I knew that. "I'm sure there are going to be more bad meals than good ones in the years ahead," I concurred.

"Oh, yes, that," she said. "But I mean you're not always going to be this anonymous, not at a restaurant like this. They'll be on the lookout for you. We haven't announced your appointment yet, because we wanted you to have these weeks in New York in peace. Once we do, Daniel Boulud and Bobby Flay and the rest of them will be rounding up any pictures of you that they can find and studying them. They'll be watching for you at the door. You'll become a marked man."

And so I did, about two-thirds of the way through my Manhattan eat-a-thon, when a *New York Daily News* gossip columnist called the *Times* for comment on a leak that I had been chosen as the next restaurant critic. The *Times* quickly distributed a news release announcing my appointment, after first making sure that my employee photograph had been taken down from the paper's Web site. There wasn't any way to purge my *Ambling* author photograph—once a lie, now not far from the truth—or other snapshots of me from the Internet, which was making life easier for the restaurateurs who wanted to spot critics and harder for the critics who didn't want to be spotted.

On one of my last nights in New York, I ate with Louis, Biff and his wife at the restaurant BLT Steak in Midtown. As I was telling Biff about my meal the night before at Alain Ducasse's restaurant, he became distracted by the arrival of a pair of well-dressed, distinguished-looking men with French accents at the table adjacent to ours. I blathered on, segueing from commentary on the Ducasse dinner to an exegesis on dinner a week earlier at Jean Georges. Biff kept glancing toward the two men, making odd motions toward them with his head and widening his eyes at me.

Finally he whispered: "You know that restaurant you were just talking about?"

"Jean Georges?" I asked.

"No," he said. "Before that."

"Alain Ducasse?" I asked. At this point I was whispering, too, a matter of blind conformity.

Biff nodded, widened his eyes again and motioned with his head once more. And then I got it, or at least I was pretty sure I got it. Alain Ducasse was one of the men—no doubt, the older of the two—who had been seated right beside us. What were the chances?

I sneaked another peek at him and noticed he was staring at me. I chalked it up at first to the fact that he no doubt knew what Biff looked like, and was simply checking to see if he happened to be acquainted with any of the other people at Biff's table.

Then he asked me a question: "You are coming from Italy, yes?"

"Yes, I've lived there a while," I said, responding automatically, not yet processing the situation clearly and cogently enough to be vague or to hold anything back. I assumed that Ducasse had simply overheard some comment I'd made about Italy to Biff, and was trading meaningless banter with a stranger.

"In Rome, yes?" he pressed, and only then did I think: *He knows the answer already. He knows me already. I haven't written a single review, not even a syllable of a review, and I'm on his radar. Incredible.*

I was trying to come up with something clever to say when he remarked, "I'm opening a restaurant in Italy."

I'd read about it. And his mention of it gave me an opportunity to show that I'd done some homework, too.

"At a country inn in Tuscany," I said.

"Yes," he answered.

"In La Maremma, to be exact," I specified, referring to a coastal area of southern Tuscany.

"Yes," he nodded.

He smiled coyly.

I smiled coyly back.

Although the flight from Rome to Paris a few weeks later was a short, nonstop one, the airline nonetheless managed to lose my luggage, and I was due to dine that first night at Pierre Gagnaire, one of the half dozen most acclaimed restaurants in the city, with three Michelin stars. The only clothes I had with me were the ones I had on: a short-sleeved blue sport shirt from Armani Exchange that was so frayed I was planning to throw it away before I returned to Rome, a pair of gray-green Dockers chinos, Nike running sneakers.

Of course the airline wasn't willing to give me money to buy replacement clothing before at least twenty-four hours had passed; what it gave me was an emergency toiletry kit that included not just toothpaste and a tiny, makeshift toothbrush but also a condom. Bereft of clean underwear, confined to one outfit, estranged from my usual grooming supplies, I was nonetheless expected to be contemplating intercourse with an unfamiliar partner? I was going to miss Europe.

I called Daphne, the administrator of the Paris bureau of the *Times*. She had made the Pierre Gagnaire reservation for me, and because she had had some difficulty getting me in, she'd used my real name and cited my *Times* affiliation in order to pry loose a table. That was something I would never do in New York, but it was permissible in these circumstances, on the opposite side of the Atlantic, in a restaurant I wasn't actually reviewing. On the phone with Daphne from the airport, I said she'd have to move my dinner to a subsequent night. I explained that I didn't have the proper attire and wasn't willing to buy it: I'd spent $150 on new shoes for that dinner at Daniel in New York, because Continental had briefly lost my luggage, and a few months before that I'd spent $400 on emergency clothing in Ankara, Turkey, after Turkish Airlines had misplaced my bags for an entire week. I'd had enough.

"I bet it's OK for you to go as you are," Daphne said.

"You haven't seen me," I told her, then described myself. "Please, please, try to move the reservation."

She called me back five minutes later to say that the restaurant had insisted that I come that night anyway, and had done so even after she specified how I was dressed. The restaurant assured her that many of its customers these days dined in jeans and the like.

Hours later, I pulled up to Pierre Gagnaire in a cab. The restaurant's doorman gave me a once-over—focusing not on my face but on my outfit—and blurted: "Mr. Bruni!" Apparently word on my attire had gone out, and apparently no one else really could be expected to show up at Pierre Gagnaire looking like I did.

"I'm so sorry," I sputtered. "I'm so embarrassed. I just flew in from Rome, and my suitcase didn't follow me."

He put a hand on my shoulder and nodded sympathetically.

"What can you expect?" he said, his voice dismissive as he went on to mention Italy's principal airline. "Alitalia."

And I laughed, not at the recognition of unreliable Italian service but at the confirmation of French arrogance. I had flown in on Air France.

But the French knew how to cook, and how to stage an elaborate meal; there was no taking that away from them. At Pierre Gagnaire I had a dozen or so courses, some with a variety of dishes that celebrated and toyed with a single theme or ingredient: a crab consommé, for example, beside strands of pulled crabmeat beside a crab mousse. The meal spanned three and a half hours. I wondered how I'd possibly show up to lunch the next day with any kind of appetite.

But show up for lunch I must, because I had a reservation at a Michelin *two*-star restaurant, which is no meager number of stars: any Michelin stars at all are a sign of distinction. Still stuck with the same outfit I'd worn for Pierre Gagnaire, I had Daphne call ahead once again to make apologies, which was how this restaurant, at the Hôtel Le Meurice, also came to be told exactly who I was. As the lunch ended, the chef appeared at my table to ask me, in a visibly nervous fashion, how I liked the potato-crusted cod, and if I thought the mustard-flavored ice cream in the gazpacho was a success. Inside my head I responded: *You're going by me? Not so long ago I was sitting on a stained futon at two in the morning watching* Law & Order *reruns with a large pizza and a box of chicken wings in my lap.*

Back then, no one had been watching me eat. I couldn't get over how closely people were watching me now, a reality that hit home even harder a few months later, when I visited the French Laundry, in California's Napa Valley.

By that point I had settled back in New York, and I was paying regular visits to, and getting ready to review, Per Se, a multimillion-dollar project on the fourth floor of the new Time Warner Center and arguably the most significant restaurant, in terms of its culinary ambitions, to open in New York in a decade. Its significance stemmed from the worldwide acclaim that its guiding chef, Thomas Keller, had earned at the French Laundry, which regularly made almost every list of the world's top twenty-five or even top ten restaurants. The French Laundry was America's most celebrated temple of haute cuisine. And my editors and I agreed: to see Per Se clearly, I should intersperse my visits there with a meal at the French Laundry.

It was an extravagant decision, so I booked the trip to last little more than twenty-four hours: JetBlue from New York to San Jose one afternoon; dinner that night; JetBlue back the next day. I asked Harry and Sylvia, who had moved a few years earlier from New York to Los Angeles, to join me. Harry had by this point become an even greater success; flying round-trip from L.A. to the Napa Valley for dinner wasn't any hardship for him.

The three of us showed up at the restaurant around nine. We gave the made-up name we'd used for the reservation to a hostess, took seats in the outdoor garden, had some Champagne and waited to be brought to our table.

Once we were at the table, a waiter presented us with menus but said that we had another option beyond the menu: we could just turn ourselves over to "Chef Keller" and let him cook a multicourse meal of his choosing for us. For one or two "VIP" tables a night, a restaurant like the French Laundry or Per Se would make this offer, and the diners who received it almost never said no. They'd be fools to. So as Harry and Sylvia looked to me for guidance, I said yes, we'd let Keller cook for us, because there was no way to know for certain why the offer was being made—maybe there simply hadn't been any "real" VIP tables that night and we'd drawn some lucky number—and because even if I'd been recognized, which seemed unlikely, it made practical sense for me to be exposed to, and aware of, the very best that Keller could do.

Our waiter smiled and exhaled too loudly; his delight that we'd made that choice was so obvious it was suspicious. Why should he care so much?

Over the next few minutes I noticed that servers who had nothing to do with our table slowed down as they walked by it and took long, curious looks at us, especially at me.

And then the courses began to come, and they didn't stop coming, and for most of them Keller sent out not three servings of one dish but three different dishes, so that I had something different from Harry, who had something different from Sylvia, who couldn't stop giggling.

"Oh my God, oh my God, oh my God," she said when the ninth course came, sounding at once exhilarated and overwhelmed. Five courses later: "This is crazy! Unbelievable! I've never, ever eaten like this."

We had something like twenty courses, representing something like fifty dishes. It was a show of virtuoso skill so ostentatious it verged on caricature.

"They know," I said to Harry and Sylvia. I shook my head. "In New York, that wouldn't surprise me, but out here? How do they know?"

I learned later, through food-world back channels, that the restaurant's manager, Laura Cunningham, who regularly shuttled between New York and the Napa Valley, had looked out into the garden, seen me and recognized me instantly from a visit to Per Se, where she had in turn recognized me somewhat less instantly from my *Ambling* photograph. Once she spotted me in the garden, the French Laundry went on full alert, and my meal became the primary concern of Keller and everyone on the staff.

It was an epic meal, an endless meal, and my stomach was so swollen with such rich food that I couldn't sleep that night. Me, the champion binger. Harry told me the next morning that he hadn't been able to sleep, either.

"How many nights a week do you do this?" he asked.

"This?" I said. "Almost never. It usually isn't anything like this."

"I know," he said. "But how many nights do you eat out?"

"Well, seven," I said, because that was the truth so far. "On a couple of nights I've even eaten two dinners in a row, and I could see that happening again from time to time."

I broke it down for him: I was supposed to review one restaurant every week, and I was supposed to visit every restaurant I reviewed at least three or, better yet, four times. Meanwhile, I was supposed to acquaint or reacquaint myself with restaurants integral to understanding the ones being reviewed, and I was *also* supposed to try restaurants that might, after one or even two visits, prove too inconsequential to be written about. With only seven nights in a week, I pretty much had to use all of them for dinners out in order to make the math work. On some weeks I could throw a lunch or two into the equation, but the vast majority of restaurants really weren't best judged at lunchtime. Lunch wasn't the answer.

"How many years does someone usually do this job?" Harry asked.

I told him that no recent critic had done it for less than four.

He refined the question: "How many years do you think *you* can do this job?"

I wondered what, if anything, was behind the "can." Did it refer to the possibilities of exhaustion and boredom? Or to the threat, and then maybe the reality, of regaining an unhealthy, misery-making amount of weight?

I told Harry the truth. I had absolutely no idea how long I'd manage this.

Seventeen

ere's what I did before that twenty-odd-course dinner at the French Laundry: went to the fitness room at the Marriott where I was staying, commandeered a treadmill and didn't budge. For forty-five minutes. The treadmill measured my run as nearly six miles long, and as I built up to that distance, pushing past the three-mile and then four-mile and then five-mile mark, I told myself, *Foie gras.* I told myself, *Coddled eggs. Lamb. Petits fours.* In a few hours this and more would probably be coming at me, and I could eat it with a stab of terror about the way I'd feel in my clothes afterward, or I could earn it—could subtract hundreds of calories now so I could add these hundreds of calories later—and thus enjoy it. Stride after stride, mile after mile, I earned it. Or at least some of it, as much of it as I could reasonably manage on a treadmill in a Marriott with only an hour's free time and a thirty-nine-year-old body that hadn't always been maintained with care.

And here's what I did back in New York, not the first day back, because my flight arrived too late, but the second day: laced up my sneakers and set out for Central Park. I ran the whole six-mile road that traces an ellipse just inside the park's rectangular outline, ending at the point where I'd begun and not taking any shortcuts, even though I was desperate to stop halfway through. I had to keep going. There were too many dinners ahead, dinners lined up all week long, some in restaurants where the norm was four courses and the food was relentlessly heavy. I couldn't afford to let up. I needed to get this exercise done now, and it had to be sustained, serious exercise. I inhaled deeply and pumped my legs some more.

From the moment I signed up for the new job, I'd been more virtuous than ever. More virtuous even than with Aaron. It started right away, with the family's annual Hilton Head vacation, which fell just before my April eat-a-thon in New York. On the island I ran daily, never less than four miles.

It continued over the weeks and months that followed. In Paris I took runs in the Luxembourg Gardens, anywhere from three to five miles a pop. Between lunch and dinner in Hong Kong, I would spend ninety minutes in the hotel gym: thirty on the treadmill, thirty doing mat work or lifting weights, thirty on the StairMaster.

In fact I was so faithful that by mid-May, when I landed back in New York for good, I was pretty sure I'd actually *lost* some weight. The first time I visited the studios of WQXR, a *Times*-owned radio station to which the restaurant critic contributed a short daily broadcast, the station manager looked at me and said, "Not *another* ectomorph!" She was referring to the beanpole thinness of Biff, who had seemed genetically incapable of gaining so much as an ounce. He certainly *was* an ectomorph, that slimmest of body types on the scale from ecto- to endo-. I definitely wasn't. That she had tried to cast me as one, even half-jokingly, kept me smiling for hours.

I bought an apartment on the Upper West Side, near Central Park, drawn there largely by the park's alluring running routes. I joined the Reebok club, one of the city's tonier gyms, on the theory that the better-looking and better-equipped the workout areas, the more likely I'd be to frequent them.

I tried to seize opportunities for exercise where they weren't immediately apparent. As a bit of a stunt for one of my early reviews, I ate two dinners in one night, the first at the restaurant under consideration, Wolfgang's Steakhouse, and the second at the historic restaurant that had sired it, Peter Luger. Although Wolfgang's was in the East Thirties in Manhattan and Peter Luger in Williamsburg, Brooklyn, I walked from one to the other, covering more than four miles. It was good copy, sure, but it was also smart weight management.

And after several months in the job, even though all was going well and I'd survived the one dinner at the French Laundry and six at Per Se without any noticeable expansion, I purchased myself an extra level of insurance, both physical and psychological. I called Aaron.

He said he had heard about my new job, and asked, "How fat are you?"

I was slimmer than he'd ever seen me, I told him, and I was determined to stay that way. To that end, I said, I wanted to set up a weekly appointment. Actually, two weekly appointments, one right after the other: contiguous hours. My idea was that I'd take the train down to D.C. on Wednesday mornings, do back-to-back sessions with him—or one with him and one with another trainer at his studio—and then take the train back.

"You're really going to do that?" he asked.

"I really am," I answered.

And I did, catching the eight a.m. Acela, arriving in Washington just before eleven, eating a moderate lunch (tuna salad sandwich, fruit cup) in Union Station, working out with Aaron from noon to one p.m., working out with a colleague of his named Chris from one to two p.m., catching the three p.m. Acela back to Penn Station in New York, arriving just before six o'clock and heading off to dinner at seven thirty or eight.

At a party back in New York, and staying in shape.

Every Wednesday. Week after week.

It was an expensive habit, especially for a newspaperman paying a mortgage on a two-bedroom apartment in a prime Manhattan neighborhood, but that was the point. The roughly $280 round-trip train ride, on top of the $160 for the two back-to-back sessions, was a statement about my priorities, made by me, to me. It was also a method of taunting myself: How could I possibly spend this kind of money and then go ahead and gain weight? How much of a fool would that make me?

The weekly twofer was less about what happened on that Wednesday than about what happened on the six other days of the week. I'd once again turned Aaron into my Weight Watchers check-in. And it was not only useful but comforting to have him harangue me about doing another repetition, to listen to him berate me about abbreviating the intended range of motion on a shoulder press. It served as a reminder of a time when working out had been a more desperate measure.

I kept the Wednesday ritual secret. I didn't tell my editors, who were accustomed to having me work from home and could still get me on my cell phone on the train. I worried that if I made them aware of my vigilance against any weight gain, they might start looking for it to happen, checking on my waistline, making *me* check on my waistline more than I already did. I needed to stay sane.

I didn't tell Adelle or Mark or Harry or Dad, because I knew that they were all scared on some level about my decision to take this job, and I didn't want them to think that the only thing separating the fit me from the old me was a regimen this extreme, or that I was having to struggle with all my might to hold back a tide of flesh. I was working hard at it, yes. But my visits to Aaron were preventive, not remedial. They were born of caution, not urgency.

I would surely have told Louis, if he had followed me to New York. But in the end he hadn't.

He hadn't really wanted to quit his job. He had long wanted to live in Southeast Asia, an opportunity now available to him. And his time in Rome, without work or a wide network of his own friends, had been tough on him. It had convinced him: he wasn't comfortable signing on to someone else's journey and deferring to someone else's agenda. I could certainly understand that.

But I was stunned, now, by how lonely I felt, given how thoroughly on my own and isolated I'd been for years before he came along, how practiced I was at it. This new loneliness was nothing like what I'd felt after Greg. It wasn't tinged with relief or overshadowed by the ugliness of the disentanglement. Louis and I hadn't picked at each other as we parted. We'd shed a few tears and shaken our heads: Why did it have to be so complicated for two people who love each other to *be* with each other? Why couldn't we have met in easier circumstances or had career paths that converged?

O ver the next months the sadness subsided, mainly because there wasn't much time or space for it among all the new challenges I was facing, and because the exhilarating unfamiliarity of what I was doing filled the cracks in my life.

As a restaurant critic, I discovered, I needed skills beyond those of a typical journalist, and I needed to be more than just a gourmand. I had to become a concierge, a cruise director, a counselor, a covert operations agent.

I should explain a bit about how it all worked—especially about the intricate scheduling and elaborate arithmetic of the job. In a city as mammoth, as addicted to novel experiences and as filled with modest and immodest dreamers as New York, many hundreds of new restaurants opened every year. From their ranks and from the ranks of restaurants that had gone unexamined too long, I picked a weekly target for review, sometimes combining two targets in one week. I operated pretty much as I'd been told that my predecessors had, considering a new restaurant fair game for a published appraisal around its two-month mark; in its very first weeks, the thinking went, it might demonstrate a shakiness—or, conversely, a focus—that wasn't a reliable indication of what was to come. I planned most visits to a new restaurant during its second month and tried to separate each visit by at least a week.

For every visit to a restaurant I used a fake name and typically reserved a table for four. I needed three companions to order different dishes and help me cover as much of the restaurant's menu as possible. If I was making my first visit, I usually laid down only one rule for my tablemates: no duplicate orders. Four different appetizers. Four different entrées. Four different desserts. If I was making my second or third visit, I'd call out the dishes that had been previously tried and shouldn't be ordered this time around.

290 · FRANK BRUNI

How to try a bit of everyone's food? There wasn't really any good way to avoid drawing a server's attention to the aggressive food sharing at the table and arousing suspicion that a critic was in the house. My companions and I could use bread plates to ferry food to and from one another, but some companions were less adept than others at making sure that the sample of salmon they provided was glossed with the sauce and accompanied by the ramps that the kitchen had included with it.

I preferred to have everyone rotate the plates, lazy Susan–style, even though it was just as attention-getting. At three- or five- or seven-minute intervals, determined by how quickly the fastest eaters at the table were going through their food, I'd chirp, "Let's pass!" At least I'd try to chirp this, in an upbeat fashion, to avoid seeming and feeling as much like a petty culinary dictator as I was. I'd decree a clockwise or counterclockwise motion for the plate passing, usually in accordance with whether I was most eager to try the dish to my left or the one to my right. And I discovered that people in midconversation and mid-Chardonnay tend not to have the best sense of direction. Two people would pass their plates one way and two would pass the other way, the plates knocking against each other, arms entangling. What had been intended as a stealthy, fleet and efficient transfer devolved into a tabletop version of Twister.

How to remember what I ate and liked? At first I kept tiny pages of notepaper, along with a pen, in one of my pockets and paid frequent visits to the bathroom in order to scribble on the pages. Then I realized I could use my phone to send text messages to myself. Or I could step into the bathroom to call myself and essentially give dictation to my voice mailbox. Later that night or the next day, I'd transcribe the dictation into a computer file.

So that I didn't have to carry around hundreds of dollars of cash or pay at the end of a meal with a credit card with my name, I had many pseudonymous cards, acquired via a special arrangement between the

Times and American Express. I got more than one, and changed an old batch for a new batch every so often, because I'd been warned that restaurants that had figured me out might write down any and all details about my visit—including the name on the fake card—and pass them along to other restaurants.

In the very beginning, a few times, I used my own card when I was sure the restaurant was on to me, reasoning that the jig was up and I should at least safeguard the fake cards. But I stopped doing this when I realized how easily it could be misinterpreted.

That realization came after one of my first visits to Per Se, when a server offered me and my tablemates a tour of the kitchen. This was before the French Laundry visit, and I wasn't at all sure that the restaurant's staff had detected me, so I accepted the offer, as most diners would—I figured that turning it down would be the more suspicious response. In the kitchen, it turned out, Thomas Keller stood ready to greet us and shake our hands. When he introduced himself, I was the only one in my group who said hello without saying my name.

A few days later I got a call from a gossip columnist checking out a rumor: Was it true that I'd divulged my identity at Per Se by brazenly marching into the kitchen to meet and chat with Keller? Rather than go into the whole chain of events and spell out my thinking, I said no, it wasn't true, because it hadn't gone down that way—it wasn't at all like that. The columnist never published an item on the incident. But it taught me that I should never do anything, no matter how justified or innocent, that an uninformed onlooker might regard as a reckless surrender of anonymity. That ruled out paying with my own credit card, even if it was abundantly clear that the restaurant knew who was paying.

What I'd do, instead, was surreptitiously give one of the fake cards to a companion, hoping the restaurant would assume that the card actually belonged to him or her. It was a flawed ruse, because no matter how well the companion understood the game being played, he or she almost always did this: held the card up high, stared at it long and hard, squinted and said, too loudly, "Who am I? Joseph Mazzone? Is that what it says? How did you come up with that name?"

Mazzone was Grandma's maiden name, Joseph just Joseph. For my first batch of five fake cards, I made the mistake of choosing only male names. This presented a problem if I dined with three women, none of whom could pass convincingly for Joseph or Joe or Gavin. For subsequent batches of cards, I threw some gender-neutral names into the mix. I had a card that said "Pat Reynolds," a card that said "J. T. Martinson," a card that said "Robin Parker." This solved one problem but not others. The fictive Pat or Robin or J. T. still held that damned card up and stared at it and then, after signing the check, handed the card and receipt back to me, at the table, rather than waiting until everyone was outside on the sidewalk, beyond the view of restaurant managers and servers.

There was a reason most people didn't go into the spying business. They had no aptitude for it.

And my own aptitude? It came and went, waxed and waned, serving me well with certain of my covert operations, less well with others. And it was attended, always, by the feeling that I was living a surreal life, which I found alternately exhilarating, exasperating, nifty and just plain silly. Not silly because it was unimportant: the job seemed to me very important, in terms of how seriously so many New Yorkers regarded restaurants, in terms of how seriously I myself regarded them. Silly because, by a quirk of fate and in a matter of weeks, I'd gone from political analyst and papal chronicler to gastronomic double agent.

I adjusted immediately to the reality of caller ID, making sure my number was blocked whenever I contacted a restaurant from home or from my cell phone. I adjusted immediately to the need, when the restaurant asked for a callback number, to blurt out a plausible but imagined sequence of digits, so that there'd be no actual phone number that might be recognized as one I'd used before or that could be traced back to me or a known acquaintance. I tried hard to do everything possible to prevent restaurants from knowing in advance that I was going to show up.

I usually remembered to call the restaurant and to confirm my reservation before the restaurant tried to, because if the restaurant dialed the imagined sequence of digits I'd given them and got a nonworking number, a red flag might be raised. But sometimes a restaurant beat me to the punch, and when I contacted it the day before or the day of my reservation, the person on the other end would say, "What's your number? Because the one we tried wasn't right and we had trouble reaching you."

I was ready for this. I'd look in my schedule, where I'd written down the imagined sequence of numbers as soon as I'd imagined it. And if the sequence was 874-2576, I'd say, "874-2567." The person on the other end of the line would say, "Oh, we mixed up those last two digits!" Situational dyslexia would take the blame for the restaurant's unsuccessful call to me, and my cover wouldn't be blown.

But the tricky part for me, the part I kept screwing up, was coming up with the fake reservation name. It had to be a different fake name almost every time, because if a restaurant *did* spot me, it might put the name under which I had reserved on a list—for future reference and for other restaurateurs—of "tells" that I might be coming. For that same reason I could use the name and number of any friend who was a regular dining companion only once or twice. And I couldn't use one of the pseudonyms on my American Express cards, in case the restaurant had taken note and passed along those names, too.

But I could be Greg Jones or Bill Jones, Tom Johnson or David

Johnson, Michael Smith or John Smith, as long as I wasn't using those names over and over again. I could be Maladupa S. Dupamaladis if I so desired, though I'd be drawing more attention to my reservation than I'd ideally want to with a combination of letters like that. The point was that I had a boundless world of possibilities open to me, yet I repeatedly, by virtue of some odd and persistent tic, failed to decide on a fake name beforehand, then froze and went blank while on the phone.

I didn't do this every time I called a restaurant, because each episode of freezing and going blank would remind me, for the next three or four restaurants, to settle on a name in advance. But then I'd relapse. A voice on the other end of the line would ask me for my name, I'd realize I hadn't come up with one, and I'd panic, glancing frantically around me.

I was usually at a desk when this happened, and desks usually had reference books, so I dined out in these early days as Mr. Webster and Mr. Roget, Mr. Fodor and Mr. Frommer, Mr. Strunk and Mr. White. There were sometimes novels lying nearby: I dined out as Mr. Wharton and Mr. Eliot, Mr. Didion and Mr. Turow, though never as Mr. Naipaul, because I didn't want to present a face at odds with the ethnic suggestion of the name.

If there weren't books nearby, there were periodicals, so I dined out as Mr. Libby, with a first name other than Scooter, and as Mr. Manning, with a first name other than Eli or Peyton. There were movies in my head, so I dined out as Mr. Pitt, as Mr. Crowe and as Mr. Stiller, though I really screwed up on that last one. When the reservationist asked me for a first name, I blurted out what instantly came to mind, and what instantly came to mind was Ben.

What a way to avoid a red flag on a reservation! Go out to eat under a famous actor's name! But because I often ended up hearing restaurant-world gossip about me, I later found out that this Ben Stiller gambit actually *did* throw the restaurant off my scent. Although the host and servers thought the man who showed up for the reservation looked an awful lot like me, they assumed it couldn't be, because a restaurant critic would never reserve a table in a movie star's name.

For one week I happened to make most of my planned reservations using the Italian surname Gentile, pronounced jen-TEEL-ay, and I simply changed first names from one reservation to the next: Paul, Marc, Anthony. One of these reservations was for the restaurant Solo in Midtown Manhattan. It serves haute kosher cuisine and is, for the most part, run and patronized by observant Jews. Because I was thinking of the surname in terms of its correct Italian pronunciation, and because I said the surname that way on the phone, I didn't realize how it might look and read to a third party noticing it in the reservation book. So I was unprepared for the Solo hostess's tone of voice, at once skeptical and withering, when I showed up, mentioned a reservation for four people at eight p.m., and heard her fill in the remaining information by asking: "Oh, are you the *gentile* party?" Oy.

On occasion I lost track of things, what with all the different reservations and all the different names.

One Saturday night I walked into the Red Cat to meet three friends for dinner. Although Biff had reviewed the restaurant right after its opening years earlier and had given it a single star ("good"), I liked it more than that—thought it might deserve an upgrade to two stars ("very good")—and went there periodically with that possibility in mind. On this night I approached the host station, smiled at the woman standing there, opened my mouth . . . and froze. As I'd rushed out of the house on my way to the restaurant, I'd forgotten to look at the dining schedule in my computer and refresh my memory of the name under which I'd made the reservation.

I combed my brain, feeling like an idiot. I had some vague recollection that the reservation name might be Carlisle. I knew I had a reservation at *some* restaurant I was due to visit in this span of days under

Carlisle. Maybe it was this reservation. Without any other alternative, I gave the name a try.

"Carlisle party of four at nine forty-five," I said. That I had reserved for four and for nine forty-five was definitely the case.

"That's so funny," the hostess said, "because someone else checked in under Carlisle"—she motioned toward the bar—"but we don't have any Carlisle in the book." I looked in the direction she'd indicated and saw my friend Charles there. I'd apparently given him this same reservation name to use, and I'd apparently been as wrong then as I was now.

The hostess asked, "Which other names should I look for?" She obviously assumed that if I ticked off the people in my party, we'd trip across the right name. She assumed wrong. The reservation wasn't in the real name of anyone in this group of regular dining companions.

What now?

"Well," I said cheerily, sidestepping her question, "it must just be whichever party of four is in your book for nine forty-five!"

"Like Langston?" she asked, glancing at her reservation book.

"Yes!" I said, not because I was trying to pull a fast one but because, as it happened, Langston sounded like a name I would use—or, in this situation, *had* used. It was the last name of a good friend's husband: that's no doubt where I'd gotten it.

"Langston," I repeated to the hostess. "That's me!"

She looked at her reservation book more closely.

"Mrs. *Zoe* Langston?" she said, noting the first name on the reservation.

I could have told her that I'd meant to say I was part of Zoe Langston's *party*, but, unfortunately, all my companions that night were men. So instead I stood in front of the hostess silently and glanced around idly, trying to buy time, hoping a hole might open up below me and swallow me. When I looked back at her, she shrugged her shoulders, laughed and just went ahead and led Charles, me and our other two friends, who had shown up by that point, to a table.

I made other blunders, too.

In an Italian restaurant on the Upper East Side, I put, on the table, in full view of our server, a bag of prescription medicine with a label stapled to the outside. I didn't notice how clearly the label spelled out Frank Bruni for a good long while. In an Asian restaurant in the East Village, I left behind an issue of *The New Yorker* with the subscription information, including my name, on the cover. A server gave it back to me while I stood in the vestibule, zipping up my coat. He looked at me closely and smirked just a little.

A few months after I resettled in New York, I heard again from Scott: Scott, my first-ever boyfriend from Carolina, the one who'd found me when I was living in Washington. Back then I'd told him I was too busy for the two of us to catch up, when really I was just too fat. This time, when he told me that he and his partner had relocated to New York and that he'd love to see me, I said yes. I invited the two of them to join me for dinner. We had an effortlessly chatty, comfortable time, and soon afterward I made plans to meet Scott and a friend of his for drinks.

On the night in question, he gave me the time and place: nine thirty at Therapy, a gay bar in Hell's Kitchen.

I hadn't been in a gay bar in nearly a decade. In New York in my early thirties and then in Washington, I'd avoided gay bars on purpose, not wanting to subject myself to any visual assessments by men who might be looking for someone to date, men who might look right past me. But I wasn't so afraid now. Besides, I was heading out to Therapy at a relatively early hour on a weeknight. The atmosphere wouldn't be sexually charged.

At the bar Scott, his friend and I ran into two men that Scott knew, and the five of us grabbed beers and found an open table in a lounge area. The man I was seated next to, Paul, focused his attention on me, but I assumed that it was just a logistical thing, a matter of my being physically closest to him.

When I got up to leave around ten forty-five, he got up, too, saying it was time for him to head home as well.

As I set out on foot for the short-term rental nearby where I was living until the purchase of my apartment went through, he tagged along, talking all the time but never saying a word about what he was doing, where he was heading.

I wondered if his place was also just blocks from Therapy—if he didn't need to hail a cab or hop on the subway—and was in the same general direction as mine.

I wondered if he was some strangely gallant guy exercising an atavistic impulse to escort me.

Finally I accepted the most likely possibility. He was wordlessly hitting on me.

I went with it, letting him accompany me into the building, letting him through the door of my apartment, and never really pausing at all to ask myself what I was doing, or whether it was something I wanted to be doing with this man. I was too caught up in the excitement—in the relief—that I *could* do it.

I'd gone from romantic exile in that dingy upstairs bedroom in Georgetown directly to Louis, who had seemed to me like some sudden and random gift from nowhere, and quite possibly a fluke. Apart from him, there had been almost no dates and no kisses for the vast majority of my thirties. Now here I was, on the edge of forty, aware of my imminent slide into middle age, angry about how much of my youth I'd squandered. Could I make up for it now? Before it was too late?

There were months during my first years back in New York when

I went out to a gay bar as often as once a week, a frequency unusual for some other men but extraordinary for me. Even in Detroit, before Greg, I hadn't found myself in a gay bar more than once a month.

But in my current state of mind and need, I liked the terms and dynamics of a gay bar—liked knowing that the men who approached me or invited my approach did so without any knowledge of my job, which was considered unusually interesting by many people. These men were attracted by the way I looked. And for me that was an affirmation more powerful than it was for many others.

During the long period when I'd been sure nobody could possibly want me, I hadn't consciously asked myself: What if I never climb out of this? What if these size 40 pants are as good as it will ever again get? What if I can't lose more than 15 of the 268 pounds I've somehow managed to put on?

But I realized now that on some level, I had pondered and dreaded all of that, because my behavior and elation on the far side of fatness were those of someone living in a country he never thought he'd see, with privileges he never thought he'd have. And I saw that there might be something harder to repair than the physical damage Aaron and I had gone to work on a few years before.

Eighteen

A fter about six months in the job, a friend e-mailed me one day.

"Had an excellent lunch at V Steakhouse," he wrote, "and I had a great meal at Bar Tonno, where the owner reports you have been spotted twice."

I shook my head, amazed. "It's very interesting," I responded, "that the owner of Bar Tonno says he's spotted me twice there. I've never been!"

The friend explained that he had asked the owner if many reviews of the restaurant had come out yet, and the owner said he was anxiously awaiting mine. "He said he wasn't there when you came in, but that 'everyone' spotted you instantly," my friend reported. "I love that! You are like a ghost!"

I wished.

With each passing month I got more of an education into just how much of a premium restaurants put on identifying me when I was there and just how much energy they put into being able to do that.

I turned one day to the Web site Eater, a gossipy report on restaurant news and restaurant-world personalities, and saw an item headlined: "To Catch a Critic: The Case of the Kitchen Flyer."

It presented a snapshot and description of a piece of paper that apparently hung in many a restaurant kitchen and was meant to help the staff recognize me when I was dining there. At the top of the flyer was a fuzzy copy of the *Ambling* book jacket photograph. Below that was a list of six aliases and two fake phone numbers I'd been known to use. It was precisely the sort of compendium I'd been warned about, and I assumed it would be considerably longer if I weren't taking all the precautions I was.

And below *that* were some descriptions of me intended to be helpful to any restaurateur wondering if I was in his or her midst.

"He looks very young," said the first line of the description, and—I'll admit it—I paused happily after reading it, then read it a second time.

"His guests are very often female," the description continued. "He is extremely polite with staff." Here I paused again, this time for Mom. She'd always been adamant about proper etiquette. She would have been thrilled.

The flyer finished: "Questions about food are asked in a very casual, unassuming manner." This was true, and this was on purpose. For all that I messed up, I wasn't about to press servers for the specifics of a dish's cooking or ingredients in a rapt way that tipped my hand. I wasn't *that* clueless.

The flyer was only a part of it.

At Le Bernardin, I'd been told, the chef Eric Ripert insisted that his staff do more than merely round up whatever pictures of me existed on the Internet. A staff member also researched where I'd appeared on television during my political-reporting years, then went to those networks and acquired footage, so the workers could get a sense of my facial expressions and body language.

Sometimes I'd be sitting at a table near the front of a restaurant and

I'd notice someone walk in the door, huddle with a server or manager, look in the direction of my table, then loiter in the vestibule or bar area for just a few minutes, stealing second and third and fourth looks my way. Minutes later the person would leave, without having had so much as a glass of water. And days later I'd see that person again—standing at the host station of a new restaurant that critics, like me, were in the process of visiting. I was just starting to make sense of this when a friend in the restaurant industry explained it for me outright: managers at restaurants that had spotted me would instantly send word out to peers in nearby establishments so they could hustle over and see me in the flesh.

When it came to identifying critics, restaurants weren't in competition with one another; they were in cahoots. One night I stopped by a Midtown restaurant for a glass of wine with my brother Mark, who was visiting from Boston on business, before the two of us joined two friends of mine elsewhere. A manager at the restaurant recognized me and heard me say, as I paid the check, that I was off to dinner. She assumed for some reason that I was on foot and destined to eat somewhere nearby. So she called several prominent restaurants within a five-block radius to warn them that I might be walking through the door at any minute. They waited for me in vain. I was in a taxi headed to an Upper East Side restaurant some twenty-five blocks uptown.

The staff at Bar Tonno weren't the only twitchy, overeager bird-watchers convinced they'd happened upon their quarry even when they hadn't. The restaurateur John McDonald e-mailed me one day in regard to one of the places he ran, writing that he had noticed me in the restaurant the previous night and that I'd left behind a notebook. He said he'd sealed it tight in an envelope and was eager to send it back to me, calling it a "Pandora's Box that I prefer not to possess." When I sent him a response, I told him he should feel free to make like Pandora and let the mischievous creatures out to play. They didn't belong to me. I hadn't visited the restaurant in many weeks.

Eater posted the following communication from one of its readers, who apparently demanded certain redactions:

I just went to [redacted] for lunch and had a long conversation with [chef]. He told me a juicy Bruni tidbit. On one of his two visits to [restaurant], Bruni rode in on a scooter. Not a Vespa—a scooter. He was also wearing running shorts and a fanny pack. Is Frank just a sartorially weird scooter enthusiast, or was this an attempt at disguise? Note: if you decide to publish the scooter bit, [chef] doesn't want you to mention him or [restaurant]. Bruni still hasn't reviewed the restaurant and [chef] doesn't want to incur his ill will.

I hadn't been on a scooter since Europe in 1986. And someone who's worried that his ass, like his love handles, might be too big doesn't wear a fanny pack.

When I was legitimately spotted, I usually knew it. The table's server became awkwardly stiff or entirely spastic, while other servers did what those at the French Laundry had: drew close to the table for no good reason and studied me, no doubt because management had told them to take a good look so they could assist in my detection on any future visits.

If I was spotted ten or twenty minutes into a meal, the restaurant might swap out a less experienced server for a more experienced one. Or it might swap out a moderately attractive woman for the most attractive man on hand. The restaurant had done its homework. It wasn't going to leave any trick untried.

I was a magnet, when recognized, for extraordinary courtesy and extreme solicitousness. If it was raining out and I'd arrived at the restaurant unprepared for that, the manager, host or hostess would try to shove a complimentary umbrella on me. On my way out of many restaurants, there'd be as many as a half dozen workers of various altitudes lined up like flight attendants to say "good-bye," "have a good night," "hope you enjoyed your evening," "good having you," "*great* having you," "*so great* having you," or "we look forward to seeing you again." I never believed that last line. It was contradicted by the audible gust of relief I'd hear as the door closed behind me.

At L'Atelier de Joël Robuchon, in the Four Seasons Hotel, the staff went into a panic when I clumsily spilled some red tomato sauce on my white shirt and I began trying to undo the damage with a wet napkin.

Suddenly a manager was at the table.

"One of the advantages of being in a hotel," he said, "is that we have laundry services on the premises. We can launder that for you right now."

I declined, mainly because I didn't want to accept special treatment, but also because I wasn't about to sit in my white V-neck Banana Republic undershirt in the middle of a restaurant that served entrées between thirty and fifty dollars.

Toward the end of my fourth and final meal at Nobu 57, an Uptown successor to the Downtown standard-bearer, I returned from the bathroom with a dark splotch on the front of my tan shirt. Embarrassed, I explained to my companions that I had been klutzy with the soap dispenser.

A few minutes later, when our eavesdropping waitress brought the check, she announced that two glasses of white wine weren't on it. They'd been removed as an apology for the way the bathroom soap dispenser malfunctioned.

"But it didn't malfunction," I assured her. "I malfunctioned. I banged way too hard on it and was leaning too close to it."

"Well," she said, "you have our sincere apologies."

Not wanting to prolong the awkwardness, I didn't insist that the wine be added back and instead covered its cost with an extra-large tip. I got up to leave.

As I walked toward the door, a manager intercepted me.

"Sir," he said, "I want to apologize about our soap dispenser."

"What about it?" I asked, though I knew what was coming.

"Didn't it malfunction?" he said.

I corrected him. Exonerated him. Told him he really, really needn't worry.

He handed me his card. "Even so," he said, "if you have trouble getting the shirt clean, please contact me. We can pay for dry cleaning or for a new shirt."

At this point I felt the need to draw attention to a crucial detail that suggested that the splotch would come out rather easily.

"It's *soap*," I said.

To which the manager added, with audible pride: "And it is *Kiehl's*."

Being recognized meant that my experiences were—obviously—different from other diners', but there wasn't any good way around it, especially as I logged more and more time in restaurants. Managers and servers who'd figured me out over the course of four visits to one establishment sometimes wound up at another just a few months down the line, and they'd nab me there on my first or second visit. Like my pseudonyms and fake phone numbers, surreptitiously taken cell phone photographs of me circulated among restaurants—one of them even got posted on Eater—and gave them a less dated image of me than the *Ambling* picture or old TV footage.

But being recognized didn't mean that I (or the many other

frequently recognized critics) couldn't see a restaurant accurately and evaluate it skeptically, noticing its flaws. Most of those flaws couldn't be hidden at the last minute. A restaurant couldn't reinvent its menu or find a new purveyor of better ingredients just because a critic showed up. It couldn't retrain the kitchen staff: I got undercooked fish and overcooked pasta in places that knew full well I was there.

What it could do was deploy extra waitstaff to my table or have the manager keep a closer eye on me and my companions. So I took that into account and made adjustments for it. I never automatically assumed that the pampering I was receiving—or that the nervousness-induced flubs by servers dealing with me—extended to other tables. I looked around to see what was happening elsewhere in the restaurant.

And I kept a distance, as best I could, from the restaurateurs and chefs in my sights. Part of what had made me attractive to my bosses at the *Times* as a reviewer was my independence: I hadn't forged any relationships or crossed paths with prominent figures in the New York restaurant world. I didn't have friends I might not want to insult or people I owed any favors or special consideration. When invitations to restaurant-related parties came my way, I declined them. I didn't go to awards ceremonies. I didn't go to food festivals.

But that didn't stop chefs, restaurateurs and their emissaries from trying to influence me. No one ever tried to bribe me, something Biff told me he'd encountered when a restaurateur pleading with him to drop by for a visit kept repeating that it would be "worth your while." But publicists e-mailed me rhapsodic accounts of meals just eaten in clients' phantasmagorical new restaurants, swearing that the praise was untainted by any professional connection. If I went on to write negative reviews of some of these restaurants, the same publicists would e-mail anew, as if they hadn't done so before, to tell me I was absolutely right and that they had given their clients unheeded warnings about the precise failings I'd pointed out.

Before one review appeared, a woman who identified herself as the mother of the restaurant's chef e-mailed me to fill me in on the life of hardship he'd overcome. "Sorry if I compromise you in your profession," she wrote, then went on to tell me about the recent grave illness of the chef's father, about his own health problems, about his fierce work ethic and about how little he slept. A day later the chef e-mailed me and I heard about his father's health problems again. Both e-mails arrived after I'd already written my review, which was mostly positive, and decided on a rating—two stars. I didn't know if that was a star less or more than the chef and his mother were hoping for. I tried not to think about it.

In one fancy restaurant, as my companions and I waited for our desserts, the owner walked right up to our table to talk to me. At first it wasn't clear that he owned the place, but it became obvious in the course of what he said.

"These are my four stars," he began as he held his iPhone toward me to show me images of children, presumably his.

Four *stars*? Was he making a reference to reviews, acknowledging what I did for work and what I was doing—and deciding—right then and there, in his restaurant?

He kept scrolling through the images, talking not only about how much the kids meant to him but also about how much he'd risked by pouring his money into the restaurant. He detailed the work that had gone into the restoration of the space the restaurant inhabited. He looked around the dining room, which was mostly empty, and bad-mouthed his publicist, who he said was doing a lousy job.

"No one even knows the place is open yet," he groused.

Then, eliminating any doubt that he was trying to lobby me, to emotionally manipulate me, to *guilt-trip* me into praising the restaurant, he said, "We're really hoping for a positive review."

"Anyway," he concluded, "I hope you had a good time tonight."

We hadn't, not particularly. The steak had been sauced too sweetly and lavishly. The pork chop hadn't been any juicier than a dog's chew toy. I winced inwardly, because I knew that I'd have to reflect that in whatever I wrote and that while he was likely aiming for three stars, I was about to give the restaurant one. My main obligation was to be honest with readers.

But at times like this I wasn't eager to be. At times like this the job made me feel a little sick.

Only occasionally did I hear from chefs or restaurateurs after a review appeared. Bobby Flay was the classiest, reacting to a review in which I demoted Mesa Grill to one star from two by leaving me a voice mail that thanked me for at least taking the time to visit the restaurant and assured me he wanted to fix whatever was wrong with it. Mario Batali, too, had a jolly way of rolling with the punches, even when I could tell he was ticked.

Another Italian-American chef, Cesare Casella, sent me a gift of sorts after I wrote a short appraisal, not a full review, of his restaurant Salumeria Rosi. In the article, which was a mixed bag of positive and negative remarks, I noted Mr. Casella's trademark habit of keeping a decorative clump of rosemary in his shirt pocket, and I observed that the clump had "mutated from the few sprigs he used to sport to a bundle of branches—to a shrub, almost. If he stays on this trajectory, he'll be clumping around his next restaurant with an entire tree slung over his shoulder." What arrived on my desk a few days later, with a card from him, was a large rosemary bush.

Few review targets complained, no doubt because the damage was done and they didn't want to risk alienating me—I might review that restaurant, or another with which they were connected, down the line.

But there were exceptions. One restaurateur wrote an actual letter, as opposed to an e-mail, to tell me that on the morning when his restaurant received two stars instead of the three he was shooting for, he'd been unable to get out of bed. Keith McNally, who owned the famed

Downtown brasserie Balthazar, publicly attributed my one-star rating of Morandi, an Italian restaurant he opened in Greenwich Village, to its employment of a female head chef and to my clear sexism.

And then there was Jeffrey Chodorow.

In the 1980s and 1990s Chodorow had opened a string of hit restaurants, including China Grill and Asia de Cuba, both of which continued to flourish. They weren't exactly critical darlings, but they'd never received the kinds of drubbings meted out to some of his subsequent efforts, which also didn't do as well commercially.

Chodorow had suffered two particularly big failures right before I became the *Times*'s restaurant critic. One was a collaboration with Alain Ducasse called Mix; it survived just two years. Another was a collaboration with the chef Rocco DiSpirito called Rocco's on Twenty-second Street. It wasn't so much a restaurant as a stage set for a reality TV show, *The Restaurant*. And it died an even faster death than Mix had, though it lived on in a miasma of civil litigation between its principal players, including Chodorow.

So he wasn't riding high when I came along, and my responses to the restaurants he opened on my watch didn't make things any better. To his tricked-out Japanese restaurant Ono, in the Meatpacking District, I gave just one star. Then I gave a no-star rating to his Italian collaboration with the chef Todd English, goofily named English Is Italian.

I didn't formally review his next restaurant, the even more goofily named Brasserio Caviar & Banana, a Brazilian befuddlement. But in a brief write-up I warned diners that the décor evoked a third-grade arts and crafts project and that the thicket of long skewers on which grilled meats were served made the whole experience rather pointy and frightening, like dining with Edward Scissorhands.

Chodorow churned out new restaurants at a brisk clip, and not too long after Brasserio came Kobe Club, named for an area of Japan where special *wagyu* cattle, known for their fat-marbled flesh, are raised. Kobe Club's conceit was to serve, and let diners compare, *wagyu* beef from Japan, Australia and America. The restaurant was an apt, colorful illustration of not only how popular steakhouses had once again become but also how the glut of them was prodding restaurateurs to fashion novel takes on the genre. So it warranted attention. I scheduled—and made—my customary series of visits.

In the review I subsequently wrote, I referred to Chodorow as a "gimmick maestro," noting that Kobe Club served no fewer than four kinds of mashed potatoes and thirteen kinds of sauces for the steaks, which came with little toothpick flags planted in them, to designate which of the aforementioned countries the beef had come from. The décor included more than two thousand samurai swords hanging upside down from the ceiling, a menacing canopy that prompted a server to tell my friend and me that they were properly anchored and that we shouldn't be scared. (What *was* it with Chodorow and pointy objects?) The décor also featured rippling screens formed by hundreds of shoelace-narrow strips of leather. "If Akira Kurosawa hired the Marquis de Sade as an interior decorator," I wrote, "he might end up with a gloomy rec room like this."

I took exception in the review to the thirty-two-dollar price of a chicken entrée, to a rubbery pork chop, to limp iceberg lettuce, and to a clam with an alarming metallic taste. The review concluded:

> On the night when the server assured me of my safety, as I put my coat back on and headed toward the door, I suddenly found that I couldn't leave. Something was pulling me back, but what?
>
> A delayed appreciation for the restaurant's triple-decker crab cake? A yearning to retrieve a toothpick flag? A need to make peace

with the check, which had come pinned to a wooden board by a dagger?

No, it was one of those leather strings, which had wrapped like a tentacle around me. Scary indeed.

The review, admittedly, was snarky. My feeling was that a negative appraisal might as well be lively, since its readers weren't going to use it as a road map for the restaurant. And the rating surely displeased Chodorow. I gave no stars to Kobe Club.

A few weeks later, he sent a letter to the *Times*.

Not to me, and not just any old letter. It was addressed to Pete Wells, the editor of the Dining section, but written for the general public, a fact made clear by something else Chodorow reportedly did: paid a premium of forty thousand dollars for the letter to appear as a full-page advertisement in the *Times* in the spot of his choosing, opposite my weekly column.

I was shown the letter just a few days before it was published. In it Chodorow claimed that my review of Kobe Club was off base, mean-spirited and one in a series of "personal attacks" by me and a few other critics, motivated by the messy debacle of *The Restaurant*. And he maintained that the issue wasn't just my Kobe Club review but all of my reviews, and that I was flatly unqualified for the job.

It definitely rattled me, the thought that so many people might see his rant and that it might yield chatter—in blogs, maybe even in published articles—about how well or not I was doing my job. I was rattled, too, by the reminder that what I wrote often wounded people, and I asked myself questions I already asked myself plenty: How could I ever be 100 percent sure I'd given a restaurant a fair shake? How could I know I'd experienced and assessed it in the most accurate light?

Maybe, I told myself, his letter wouldn't draw much notice.

It did. There were articles about it by the Associated Press, the *Washington Post* and *The New Yorker*, among others. To my enormous relief most of them portrayed Chodorow as a hothead and took little or no exception to my review of Kobe Club or my performance as a critic. But I was nonetheless left with a problem.

During the many interviews Chodorow was giving to journalists and bloggers, he said that the next time I was seen in one of his restaurants, he would have me thrown out. He said he was even offering a free vacation to any employee who ousted me. And yet he was about to open a new place, Wild Salmon, in the old English Is Italian location. Wild Salmon was a project splashy enough to call for a review; if I didn't write one, it might seem that I was running away from him—that his pledge to foil me had successfully spared his newest restaurant an assessment. That wouldn't be a good precedent. I didn't want to let it happen.

So I had to figure out how to dine repeatedly in a restaurant from which I had been officially barred.

"Sit still, darling," John said to me, putting a hand on my shoulder and pushing down, trying to fix me to the bottom of the chair. "You have got to sit still."

I couldn't. Without meaning to, I kept swiveling my head to survey his salon and check whether the other clients were gaping at me. I kept squirming. I hated the way the wig that he had affixed to my head felt: itchy, sweaty, furry and wild, as if somebody had scraped a dead squirrel off a patch of hot pavement and slapped it onto my scalp. The wig sort of looked that way, too. I was on the leading edge of a whole new trend: roadkill chic.

"This is ridiculous," I told John. "Nobody's going to buy this."

"They will when I'm done," he said, his voice curt, as if I'd insulted him. I supposed I had. I told myself: Calm down. Lighten up. If you get

In the Bergdorf salon, I meet the wig I'll wear to Wild Salmon.

thrown out of Wild Salmon, you get thrown out of Wild Salmon. It'll be mortifying when it happens; a badge of honor by the next day. And the important part is that you'll have tried. If the story gets around, that's what it will prove. That'll be the takeaway. You tried.

The unruly mass of synthetic light brown strands was much thicker than my own hair, covering up my faint bald spot and receding hairline. John pushed it a few millimeters forward, then a few millimeters back. He rotated it slightly to the left, then to the right. And he snipped and snipped, cutting it as carefully as he would the real thing. I'd had no idea that wigs got customized this way. I'd had no idea they got styled.

Some of the clients in nearby chairs and some of the stylists attending to those clients indeed stared at John and me, no doubt because we presented a mystery: Why were we taking such pains to put me *into* this wig when I looked infinitely better *out* of it?

"He's an actor," John said to everyone and to no one, answering a question that hadn't actually been articulated. "He's doing a small walk-on part tomorrow." That's how careful he and I were being. On the chance that someone in the salon might be connected to someone in the restaurant industry, we were guarding who I was and what I was doing there. I'd even checked into the salon under the name Frank Browning.

Before Wild Salmon, I had used disguises only twice, during my first months as a reviewer, and had concluded they were too unsettling and not effective enough, at least if they were anything less than seriously expert. And seriously expert disguises took too much time; they certainly weren't nightly options. Restaurant critics who touted their proficiency with disguises usually didn't mention that a night in costume was the exception, not the rule, and they either disregarded or truly didn't know that restaurateurs often recognized them anyway but were careful not to show it. Restaurateurs didn't want to spoil the disguised critic's fun.

My first attempt at a disguise was for my third visit to V Steakhouse, the short-lived Jean-Georges Vongerichten restaurant that the friend who had e-mailed me about Bar Tonno had also mentioned. I had sensed that I was recognized on my second visit to V Steakhouse and I wanted to recapture my anonymity. So I didn't shave for a few days. I used a shiny gel to slick my hair straight back; usually I wore it parted on the side, without any product. I put on little granny glasses. Did it work? I wasn't sure. But I felt awkward, my companions kept giggling at me and I had to struggle to stay focused on the meal.

My next attempt was at Per Se. For my third visit there, about a week after my trip to the French Laundry, I slicked back my hair. I sported a minor beard, the product of a full week without shaving. And I put on a bulky, flashy pair of purple-rimmed eyeglasses with clear lenses, which

I'd purchased solely to be used as camouflage. My companions couldn't decide whether I looked like a young Bob Evans, an over-the-hill porn star or the deranged subject of a forthcoming book by Oliver Sacks. Our waiter took one look at me and, despite an obvious struggle not to, broke into an enormous, you've-got-to-be-kidding-me smile. He was the same waiter who had spent four hours catering to Harry, Sylvia and me at the French Laundry. Facial hair, styling gel and purple eyeglasses weren't going to fool him.

But for Wild Salmon, a restaurant focusing on the Pacific Northwest (with Chodorow, there was always a tidy theme), I had no choice. I had to try a disguise again, and it had to be better this time around.

So I contacted John, a friend who owned the salon atop Bergdorf Goodman in Midtown and had many associates in the theater business. If anyone could be entrusted with the job of disguising me, it was him. He called some makeup artists and costume designers he knew and had them send over a few wigs and fake mustaches. He gave me an appointment in the salon ninety minutes before my first Wild Salmon reservation, so I could go straight to the restaurant from there. I showed up for it dressed for the meal after, in a semiformal manner that was deliberately uncharacteristic: dark blue suit, light blue shirt, solid green tie. And again I wore little granny glasses.

John had one wig in a dark brown color that matched my hair and one in a lighter shade. After putting each on my head, he chose the lighter shade. Then he went about taming and sculpting it, spending forty-five minutes on that mission before leaving its completion to an assistant, Marco.

At some point I pressed one of the fake mustaches to my upper lip. It looked and felt like a dark centipede. I decided to skip it on this night and maybe use it for my second or third visit to Wild Salmon.

As Marco used a blow-dryer to finish styling the wig, I kept feeling it move, or imagining that it was moving—I couldn't tell. I was sure that during the coming dinner, I'd tilt my head forward to glance into my chowder and the squirrel would drop from my head to the bowl.

"Are you sure this won't fly off?" I asked Marco.

"Maybe in a hurricane," he said.

I studied my image in the mirror. My face was tiny beneath this grand mane, which was indeed becoming more realistic by the second but still struck me as much too poufy and wavy. I no longer had to wonder what sort of offspring Andy Warhol and Farrah Fawcett might have produced. I was looking at him.

Wild Salmon was on Third Avenue near Fortieth Street. I'd told my companions for the night, Patty, Jason and Michelle, to meet me about two blocks away, at the Capital Grille, so we could coordinate our stories and go over our script.

I'd chosen Patty because she'd dined with me only once before, at an out-of-the-way restaurant that certainly hadn't spotted me: there was no chance her face was associated with mine. I brought Jason and Michelle along because they, too, were infrequent dining companions. Even better, they were in their twenties—younger than most of my eating partners—so they gave our foursome a different demographic profile than that of my usual groups. I told them that they'd be posing as a couple and I told Patty that we would be, too. And I invented a story line to guide our conversation whenever servers were near: Jason and Michelle were about to be married; Patty and I were already married and were friends of Jason's family. We were giving the newlyweds-to-be marital advice.

"What do I do for a living?" Patty asked me at the Capital Grille, as I prepped everyone.

"You're a veterinarian," I said.

"And you?" she said.

"I'm a pharmaceutical sales representative." I liked the idea of having access to good prescription drugs.

"How long have we been married?" Patty said.

"Too long."

We walked to the restaurant. I made the three of them enter just ahead of me, an advance guard. I kept my head low, looked toward the floor, tried to be inconspicuous. At the table I took a seat that put my back to the open kitchen. Whenever the waiter approached, I buried my face in the menu.

"All this fish: it's just too much like work," said Patty, the pretend veterinarian, as she perused her menu.

"But you don't treat fish, sugarplum," I mumbled, face deep in my own menu.

"I'm training," she said. "I just need to get my scuba certification."

When the waiter took our order, Patty couldn't remember what I'd told her to get, and had to look to me for guidance. "What do you think I should eat, honey?" she asked me.

I told her she'd seemed interested in the cedar plank salmon, which she then ordered. As the waiter gathered our menus, I said to Jason and Michelle, "Half of what makes our marriage work is that I remember for her what she does and doesn't like to eat."

"The other half," Patty said, "is the sex." Fortunately, the waiter had disappeared before the end of her sentence.

Patty, Jason and Michelle passed me bites of their appetizers and entrées quickly, and furtively: there was no rotating of plates. At the end Jason paid the check with *his* real credit card, as I'd told him to in advance, promising him a check as soon as we reached the sidewalk.

And we got away with it. We actually got away with it. The staff at Wild Salmon hadn't known I was there. I was certain not just because I hadn't been ejected, but because no one in the restaurant had paid an iota of extra attention to us and because our server, without a trace of irony or self-awareness, had recommended certain dishes by saying that they'd been praised in early reviews of the restaurant. That comment and many of his others weren't the kind a server would ever make to a known critic.

For my second visit, I brought Joyce and Max, who were considerably older than my usual dining companions. I wore the same wig and, for variety's sake, the mustache, glued to the flesh between my nose and upper lip. I kept imagining that it was slipping and I couldn't stop poking at it to make sure it was still in place. Every time I did this Joyce frantically lifted a napkin to her mouth and swiped vigorously.

"Did I get it?" she'd say, thinking I'd been signaling to her that she had a smudge of food on her face.

I'd shake my head no and point emphatically to my fake mustache, and she'd interpret the gesture to mean she should swipe again—and even more vigorously.

"*Now* is it gone?" she'd ask.

My third time at Wild Salmon I had a different wig, darker and stippled with gray, purchased from a Manhattan wig wizard who often dealt with celebrities with cancer. I went to the restaurant in a group of four men of different ages and looks, all of us dressed in suits, the conceit being that we were colleagues fresh from work at the bank. Again the food sharing was done with special subtlety. And again the restaurant seemed not to notice us in any particular way.

I gave Wild Salmon one star. I took pains to say that the various kinds and preparations of salmon were appealing, but I couldn't ignore how uneven the rest of the food was, and I had to call Chodorow out on his stubborn penchant for gimmickry, which I flagged at the start of the review:

I wish I'd had Al Gore with me at Wild Salmon, where I stumbled across a new sign of climate change. It concerned dessert, and it might well have concerned him.

I ordered the baked Alaska, a frigid diorama in which the meringue is molded to resemble an igloo. And I noticed right away that something was extinct: a proud chocolate penguin, described in write-ups of the restaurant, that had once stood beside the frosty abode. In its place a few humble chocolate fish were adrift.

When I ordered the dish a second time, even they were gone, the ecosystem impoverished once more. The igloo looked smaller, and its ice cream interior was softer. A fluke? Maybe. But I wonder about global warming.

A week later Chodorow took out another ad in the Dining section. This one was small, squeezed into the corner of a page far from my column, and went largely unnoticed. It was also in the form of a letter, addressed this time to me.

"Dear Frank," it read. "The penguin has returned to the South Pole where it belongs. I'm contributing the money I would have spent on a larger ad to the fight against global warming. Really glad you loved the wild salmon at Wild Salmon. It is like no other salmon I've tasted. Regards, Jeff."

Nineteen

Through it all I ate, often with the people I'd eaten with from the start. I ate with Harry at the restaurant Blue Hill in Greenwich Village and with Dad and Dottie at its bucolic offshoot, Blue Hill at Stone Barns, in Westchester County. I ate with Mark and one of his business partners at Eleven Madison Park, on Madison Square Park in Manhattan, and I also ate there, separately, with Uncle Mario and Aunt Carolyn. I ate with Uncle Jim and Aunt Vicki at Alto, an Italian restaurant in Midtown. I ate with Adelle more often than with any other family member, because she was living just outside the city and traveled in and out most frequently. She saw the reviewing rigmarole as the very summit of all intrigue.

"Are they on to you yet?" she asked at the restaurant Jean Georges, where she, her friend Val and I sat down one night after ten for dinner. Adelle was always obsessed with the question of whether we were flying under the radar.

"I'm not sure," I said. Jean Georges was the kind of restaurant, like Le Bernardin, that was going to do whatever it took to make sure critics didn't go undetected. But I sensed that our late arrival at the restaurant, which was visibly winding down, had possibly thrown the servers off our scent, at least for the time being.

"What do *you* think, Val?" Adelle asked. "What's your read?" Adelle's tone was breathless, revved-up. She liked to whip up some drama, some suspense, whenever and wherever she could. At Princeton, acting had been one of her passions, and in a sense it still was. She'd merely moved her theatrical performances offstage.

"I just saw that waiter over there motion to a busboy to come over, and then the waiter leaned over to say something to the busboy!" Val whispered, as if she'd been let in on an important secret and was passing it along.

"Well," I said, draping my voice in sarcasm, "that settles it. The two of them can't possibly be talking about, I don't know, the need to clear the dishes from that table by the window."

"There should be more servers looking this way," Adelle sighed, knowing what usually happened when I was spotted. She sounded disappointed—defeated. "I don't think they *are* on to us. Damn!" She preferred it when they knew. She found the fawning hysterical, and when a particularly obsequious server would drift right out of earshot, she'd make jokes about the various errands or chores we might ask of him or her, charting a whole twelve-labors-of-Hercules agenda that included the retrieval of dry cleaning and maybe even some attic cleaning.

I also ate with old friends and new friends and even, on a few occasions, celebrities, because some of them were food lovers who thought *my* job was glamorous. The pathetically starstruck side of me couldn't resist the opportunity that that presented, so I found myself at the restaurant Artisanal one night with Matthew Broderick and Sarah Jessica Parker. She had a curious culinary pet peeve.

"Would you mind," she asked me, "if we asked the kitchen not to put any parsley in anything?"

I wasn't planning a full-fledged review of the restaurant, and I couldn't imagine that there'd be much parsley in many dishes to begin with, so I didn't mind at all. But I also wondered if she was pulling my leg, because I remembered a *Sex and the City* episode in which Carrie tells a server that she's flat-out allergic to parsley as a way of making absolutely sure no parsley wanders into or near any of her food.

I didn't ask her if she was allergic or just averse. But I tracked down a server to find out if it was too late to tell the chef "no parsley." Our table had placed its order ten minutes earlier.

"The chef already knows," the server assured me. "He's cooked for Ms. Parker before."

I ate with strangers who'd paid six thousand dollars at a charity auction for the three open seats at a table for four in one or another of the restaurants that I was visiting for the purpose of a review.

I ate with dates. I was almost always seeing someone, because my determination to have an active romantic life trumped pickiness, and I still got too excited when someone for whom I felt even the barest flicker of interest was interested in me. I seldom saw any of these people for very long. We'd turn out to be incompatible in ways that could have been predicted at the outset, had I in fact been less eager, more skeptical and more alert.

But as I traveled further and further from my loneliest years and as dating came to seem less remarkable, I did get wiser and more cautious. The frequency of my casual encounters diminished. They weren't really what I wanted. What I wanted was someone steady, something intimate, a relationship like the one I'd had with Louis. But that wasn't easily found.

I ate in the service of contrived journalistic experiments. During one week I stayed in a different Manhattan hotel every night so that I could assess room service dinners and breakfasts. On a three-day trip to gastronomically advancing Atlantic City, I hit seven relatively new restaurants, fitting in that many by having two dinners on Thursday, another two on Friday and three in a row on Saturday.

I ate at some of the most revered temples of refined cooking, including elBulli, on the northeastern Spanish coast. To get a reservation I had to use my *Times* credential—permissible in this situation, because I was far from New York and reporting on the restaurant rather than reviewing it—and I wound up getting a meal more elaborate than any other diner's that night. It comprised about thirty courses: all the dishes that were being served to everyone in the restaurant, plus another dozen that the chef and owner, Ferran Adrià, made specifically for me, so I could sample what he considered his greatest hits.

I also ate at places of less lofty repute. I checked out Hooters one night because I'd heard the chicken wings there were excellent—that turned out to be an exaggeration—and I thought that a post about the meal in the newspaper's dining blog might be fun. I repeatedly visited the steakhouse in the Penthouse (as in magazine) Executive Club because I'd heard the aged beef there was exceptional—that turned out to be no exaggeration at all—and I thought an actual review of the restaurant might be entertaining and worthwhile.

For the first of those visits, I happened to arrive before my companions and was alone in the lounge when one of the many barely clad women who sidled through the place—and sometimes stepped up onto a stage to dance—slipped into the chair beside me.

She introduced herself. I wasn't sure I'd heard her name correctly.

"Mahogany?" I asked, checking.

"Yes," she purred.

"Mahogany," I asked, "do you know where you're going to?"

She didn't miss a beat, moving on to another of Diana Ross's hits. "I'm coming out!" she sang, waving her arms, wiggling her hips.

She said she was running low on cabernet. I took the cue and asked if I could buy her a fresh glass.

"Yes," she said. "And you can pour it on my toes."

On a subsequent visit to the steakhouse, officially named Robert's, a woman who identified herself as Foxy approached my table to hawk neck and shoulder massages at twenty dollars apiece.

"Foxy," I began, then stopped myself, wondering if I was being too familiar. "Are you and I on a first-name basis, or should I address you as Ms. Foxy?"

"You can call me Dr. Foxy," she said.

"Is that an MD or a PhD?"

"Yes," she answered, as if that settled it, and went back to rubbing lotion on the shoulders of one of my dining partners. I had told him I'd expense the massage, which was integral, after all, to an appraisal of this particular dining experience.

My point is that I ate out almost as often as a person could, seven nights on many weeks and more than once a night on some occasions. And most of these meals weren't anything like a typical diner's, because a typical diner didn't get every possible course at every restaurant while also sampling the bread basket—the bread, after all, might be worthy of special praise or derision—and partaking of the petits fours, should the restaurant be the kind in which they were served. A typical diner could, and usually did, pick and choose his pleasures, focusing on starches if he liked to carbo-load, meats if he was on a carnivorous tear.

I had to sample it all.

And in order to work my way through a restaurant's entire menu over the span of several visits and to try at least a few dishes twice, I sometimes ordered even more than the three or four courses that the place normally served. I might ask for two kinds of the wood-oven pizza, which most other diners selected as an appetizer or entrée, as preappetizer snacks for the foursome in which I was eating. I might then ask for a fifth communal appetizer in addition to the four individual ones we'd ordered, and I might later ask for a fifth communal dessert.

None of these meals could be constructed in a way that reflected health or weight concerns. If the restaurant took pride in its twenty-ounce rib eye, I took the measure of that steak. If fettucine with a heavy cream sauce and a blizzard of pancetta was on the menu, it would also be on my table during one of my visits. Fruit sorbet wasn't a tenable alternative to molten chocolate cake. It was more like a cop-out, even a dereliction of duty, because the sorbet, unlike the cake, was probably prepared elsewhere and merely purchased by the restaurant, and thus not a test of the kitchen's skill.

So my only real option for keeping at least some cap on the calories I ingested was the most time-tested, most widely advocated and least flashy method of all, the one on which the truly enduring diet organizations were founded, the one too unimaginative and incremental in its impact to ever foster the kinds of short-lived cults that developed around the cabbage soup diet, the grapefruit diet and their ilk. It was the method I adhered to during my single most gut-endangering foray as restaurant critic: a cross-country drive, from sea to greasy sea, devoted to sampling familiar and unfamiliar fast foods.

I wanted a real digression from my usual high-end dining, so I traveled from New York to Los Angeles with a changing cast of companions on a trip that was part roving binge and part warped road movie: "Transfatamerica," we dubbed it. Instead of three-hour meals at beautifully set tables, I ate three-minute meals in the driver's or passenger's seat, the dashboard doubling as a buffet, an automotive altar across which Quarter Pounders and bean and cheese burritos were arrayed. Until I hit an In-N-Out Burger in Torrance, California, on the eighth day, all of my fast food was consumed, as fast food often is, in the car, which smelled worse and worse as the trip went on. Like an obtuse houseguest or a Supreme Court justice, the scent of a White Castle slider lingers.

My odyssey ultimately spanned nine days, fifteen states, 3,650 miles and forty-two visits to thirty-five restaurants (I hit some more than once), for an average of nearly five fast-food restaurant visits a day. And for each of those visits, I wouldn't get just a burger or other sandwich apiece for my companion and me. Determined to try as much as was reasonably possible of whatever was on offer at Wendy's, KFC, Culver's (a Wisconsin-based burger chain in the Midwest and Texas), the Varsity (an onion ring institution in downtown Atlanta), Yocco's (hot dogs in Pennsylvania), Raising Cane's (chicken fingers in Louisiana) or Taco Cabana (Mexican delights in central Texas), I'd get enough food for four or five people.

But I'd never finish all of it, or even close to all of it.

"Have you tried the fries?" I'd ask Alessandra, my McPartner from Atlanta to Dallas, who had replaced Kerry (New York to Atlanta) and would later be replaced by Barbara (Dallas to L.A.), the friend who had helped me with my *Ambling* photograph.

"Fries: check!" Alessandra would say, and I'd transfer the paper sleeve from the dashboard to a bag we were using for garbage, even though most of the fries were still in it.

"The super-duper double-trouble whatever burger?" I'd ask after about a quarter of it was gone.

She'd nod again, and the burger would go into the garbage, too.

A third of the way into the chicken sandwich, we'd throw that away. And then we'd toss the basic unadorned cheeseburger, a sandwich small enough that fully half of it was gone, each of us having eaten a whole quarter.

"Taste and trash," I'd remind Alessandra, restating our method for managing all of this food without having to loosen our clothing.

"Taste and trash," she'd repeat, then glance longingly at the frozen custard dessert with crumbled Oreo cookies that she was holding. She wouldn't want to stop at the three spoonfuls she'd had, just as I hadn't wanted to stop at the four I'd permitted myself. But there was no justification for more than that. She'd sigh and dispose of it as well.

Soon the dashboard would be clear and the garbage bag full and we'd pull out of our parking space in the restaurant's lot, swing by the nearest trash can or Dumpster and be on our way.

It was an extreme example of my job survival mechanism, of what I did to a lesser extent at elBulli and in Atlantic City and on most nights in New York. I'd abandon the double-cut pork chop after two bites from its edge, where the meat had a band of fat attached to it, and three bites from its center, which was the best gauge of whether the meat was over- or undercooked. That was all the pork chop I needed, and afterward just a half of one of the three large profiteroles would do. By the end of a given evening I'd have eaten a full meal—really, a fuller than full meal—but I hadn't staged the kind of bacchanal a less frequent diner often does in a serious restaurant on a big night out.

I approached the most wildly caloric days and potentially ruinous meals as dares, challenges, my task to get a fair sense of everything without pushing the ultimate tally of calories—which I couldn't, and didn't, actually count—any higher than I had to. It wasn't exactly easy, but it wasn't all that hard, because I knew that another big meal, probably a good one, maybe even a great one, would come along the next day and again the day after that. I didn't experience the old panic: *eat all of this before someone else does, before you lose the chance, before you consign yourself to a fast or a juice cleanse or swear off carbohydrates or banish all fat.* Forced to eat a certain amount, I developed an ability not to eat too much more than that.

I now had something other than massive volumes of food to reward and satisfy the eating-obsessed part of me. I had an incredible variety of food. I had that Italian pleasure of lingering at the table, of dining at length, nibbling on this, sipping that. And I had the challenge and diversion of coming to conclusions about everything I tried.

"I love the caramelized surface of these scallops, but they're undercooked inside," I'd say to my friend Charles, who would note that the kitchen had been sloppy with his foie gras, stippled with tough, ropy veins. I'd try it and concur, then move on to the gnocchi, and wonder if they'd been doused with too much butter.

I'd pause almost as soon as I thought that and I'd marvel: *Too much butter?* Had there ever been such a thing as too much butter for me in the past? Now there was.

This mulling over the nuances of what I ate helped keep the weight off, at least according to the yardstick I'd long used in lieu of scales: my pants. When I'd returned from Italy, I wore a mix of 36s and generously cut 34s. After a year in New York, I wore only 34s. After another year, I actually found a few 33s I could squeeze into. The 36s were deep in the back of the closet.

But making my eating life about quality instead of quantity was only part of the answer. An equal part was rolling like a ball, crawling like Spider-Man and going through all the other paces to which I let Aaron and the trainers after him subject me.

On my own I wasn't so shabby about exercise, and often pushed myself harder than I'd been able to in the past. In Dallas, midway through the fast-food odyssey, I took a long morning off, drove about fifteen minutes from my hotel downtown to White Rock Lake and ran—slowly, and with a sad little limp toward the end—the entire trail of more than nine miles around it. In Barcelona, on the day before elBulli, I spent ninety minutes in a gym, using the treadmill and the elliptical and lifting some weights.

And at home in New York, I exercised an average of two out of every three days, and I usually exercised hard: a solid eighty minutes. Half of that time would be spent running on a treadmill at the Reebok club or on the trails in Central Park. The other half would be devoted to some mix of weights, mat exercises and stretching.

But my feeling about exercise was that if I wanted to keep at it with the intensity and steadiness that I had to, given how much I wound up eating even when monitoring my portions, I should outsource some of the responsibility and get others to fill any gaps in my motivation and help make working out as interesting as possible. I should schedule firm appointments. I should pony up the money for trainers.

My success with Aaron had persuaded me of that, but Aaron himself couldn't last. About four months after I started making my Wednesday train trips to D.C., I stopped, the commute becoming too monotonous and costly. While I was lucky enough to be able to afford private training, its expense offset largely (and poetically) by my low food bills as a professional eater, I couldn't keep up with both the training *and* the train tickets. So at Reebok I connected with Cathy, a Pilates instructor.

Pilates, according to Cathy, would give me actual abdominal muscles, as opposed to whatever lay dormant beneath the pudding of pink flesh that was my stomach, even now. Cathy said that in time I'd be able, from an outstretched position on my back, to hinge all the way upward from my waist, my upper body and my stiffened legs becoming two halves of a V that would narrow and narrow until I was staring at my shins. She called this maneuver a "teaser." Teaser, I guessed, because it was an unattainable goal, and I and most anyone else who hadn't medaled in the pommel horse or uneven parallel bars would never quite accomplish it.

Pilates was a brimming dictionary of loopy terms that cunningly cast exercise as something else, something more like charades. In addition to the teaser there was the "elephant" and the "saw" and the "monkey" and the "tower": each a different elongation or contortion of the body, none of them all that accurately evoked by its nickname, the sum of them designed to give me a solid "core," which I now understood to be not just a spiritual asset but also a physical one. With a solid core, Cathy assured me, everything else fell into place. She made it sound like a trust fund, or like Prozac, without the narcolepsy and the sexual frustration.

It was during our fifty-five-minute Pilates sessions that she told me to bring my knees to my chest, hug them with my arms, bend my head forward and "roll like a ball," an activity supposedly helpful in hollowing my stomach.

When Cathy wasn't telling me to roll like a ball, she was telling me to "clap like a seal," which was basically rolling like a ball but with my legs pretzeled around my forearms—or were my forearms pretzeled around my legs?—so I could bang the soles of my feet together as if they were flippers.

These were exercises done on a mat. When I was exercising on the "universal reformer" or the "Cadillac"—contraptions with pulleys and harnesses and little leather ankle cuffs that seemed designed for something more salacious than a solid core—Cathy would insist that I "leave room for the ladybugs," which meant I should keep my tailbone and lower back flat but not *too* flat against the surface of the machine.

"You're killing the ladybugs!" she'd protest if I pressed my back too hard against it. Could she really hear herself? I hoped not, because all of this semantic nonsense succeeded in distracting me somewhat from the pain in my overworked, underdeveloped midsection and in making the fifty-five minutes go by faster.

But Pilates seemed to be almost exclusively about that midsection—er, *core*. What about my outlying regions? Amid all this monkeying and towering and seal-like flipper-clapping, shouldn't I do some exercises that just tested and developed my arms and legs? Like squat thrusts or bench presses?

I found Ari, and added a weekly session with him to my weekly session with Cathy. He worked out of a Spartan two-room exercise studio downtown. While Cathy was a font of the chirp and chatter on which dental hygienists once maintained a monopoly, Ari was a wellspring of

In the Pilates studio, trying to keep it all together.

the imperturbable calm associated with Buddhist monks. When I cursed him the way I had always cursed Aaron, he didn't shout back at me. He just shook his head slowly, radiating regret over the negativity that coursed through me, over how it separated me from the nirvana I might otherwise know.

He talked incessantly about the value of a good deep breath and told me to feel things in the backs of my eyes. Sometimes he made me do exercises while keeping a mouthful of water that I was forbidden to swallow. It was a way to prevent me from panting—from wasting all of that precious breath.

But I was there for more than a respiration tutorial, and Ari obliged.

He made me pretend that I was Spider-Man and that the wood floor was the side of a skyscraper. I had to make my way across it on all fours, moving sideways and fleetly, my knees never dropping, my upper arms and thighs tensed, my butt held high. This supposedly tackled some half dozen major muscle groups at once.

He made me pretend I was a frog, crouched but not *too* crouched, leaping in a forward direction for the length of two rooms. This supposedly worked wonders on the "glutes." I wasn't entirely sure what or where "glutes" were, but I trusted that mine could use significant improvement.

For Ari I jumped rope, about two hundred times per session. At first I could accomplish this only in 50-jump segments, but I eventually worked my way up to 125 jumps in a row on a good day. I'd be winded at the end, and sometimes even dizzy. I relished dizzy. Dizzy, I figured, was worth three to four ounces more of a lamb shank than I really had to eat. Dizzy was my get-out-of-love-handles-free card.

For Ari I also did push-ups: on a big soft ball; on a small hard ball; with each hand wrapped around one of two handles placed three feet apart; with my feet elevated on a short stepping stool; with my feet elevated on a taller stepping stool.

Sometimes I even smiled while I did them, or laughed.

"That's not the usual reaction," Ari said to me once.

I guessed not. But was the usual person as stunned as I was that I could get through twenty push-ups and be ready for another twenty just a minute and a half later? That I had made it to this point?

A whole wall of one of the rooms in which Ari and I did our workouts was mirrored. I couldn't avoid myself. But that was okay, because I didn't really recognize myself, either. The man staring back at me wore a light gray tank top, which left his shoulders and upper arms exposed, and it didn't look ridiculous or pointless on him, because his triceps and biceps had some minor definition. The tank top was perhaps clingier than wisdom would dictate. It did nothing to hide the way his midsection quivered when he jumped rope. But his cheeks and his chin—they didn't quiver, not even when he whipped the rope around and pushed off the floor as fast as he could.

I put Ari in charge of the *Men's Vogue* photo shoot. I knew a few of the top editors at that now-defunct magazine, and to my amusement they had asked me to write about staying fit while eating for a living. They had also asked if, to illustrate the article, they could photograph me while I exercised. They promised to obscure my face or crop it out of the picture, so that I wasn't giving chefs and restaurateurs an easily accessed up-to-date picture of me.

Ari and I prepped for the shoot, devoting a half hour of one of our weekly sessions to figuring out which of the many exercises we routinely did would give me as streamlined a silhouette and as seemingly winnowed a waistline as possible.

"What about the one where I put my feet on the ball, my hands on the bench, and make a bridge of my body?" I asked Ari.

"If you can finally get your body into a straight line, that'd be good," he said.

There was a twinge in my memory. All of this reminded me of something, but what?

Ah, yes: the fretting over, and plotting of, my *Ambling* author photograph.

This fretting and plotting felt entirely different.

For the shoot, *Men's Vogue* sent a coordinator, a photographer, his assistant and a stylist. The stylist was in charge of a rack of at least four dozen articles of clothing, mostly sweatpants, shorts and designer T-shirts in about six different colors. He also helped with such matters as taping the insides of the dark blue shorts I ended up wearing to my thighs, so the material didn't ride up on me as I did the bridge exercise and other ones.

Whenever I took a break, the stylist rushed at me with a blow-dryer and went to work on the darkening patches of my dark blue Calvin Klein T-shirt.

"He's sweating *a lot*," the stylist said to the photographer.

"I'm *exercising*," I pointed out.

"We may have to swap out the shirt, get a new one," the stylist announced, speaking once again as if I weren't present—as if I were just an object, a prop.

Wasn't this the way models were treated?

Excellent!

"When we're done here," I asked the stylist, "do I get to keep the T-shirt?" Sweaty or not, it fit me better than my usual nondesigner T-shirts, and it was a memento of the improved me.

The stylist rolled his eyes. "Sure."

"What about the wristwatch?" I ventured, testing my luck. Although I never wore a watch and couldn't see what a watch had to do with working out, the *Men's Vogue* crew had decided to accessorize my dark blue shorts and dark blue T-shirt with a black high-tech digital one. I got the sense that photo shoots were governed—and stylists' salaries justified—by a "when in doubt, accessorize" philosophy.

The stylist didn't respond. Maybe he hadn't heard me?

I usually managed to make my way to Harry's house outside L.A. every nine months or so, and was lucky enough to have one four-day stay coincide with a big party he was throwing. He loved to play host. More so than Mark, Adelle or me, he'd inherited the Bruni entertaining gene, the impulse to generous excess when it came to food and, in his case, wine.

For this party he rented a small outdoor tent so that, in the rare event it rained, he'd be able to cook on his gargantuan outdoor grill. And he needed the gargantuan grill because he was making paella for forty. He had bought the biggest paella pan I'd ever seen and more than one huge lobster tail per person, along with sausage, chicken legs, shrimp and more. He manned that pan for hours, stirring and watching, watching and stirring, and when the paella was finally done, he served it with Spanish reds from an actual wine cellar below the kitchen of his rambling house with views of the Pacific.

Harry was the sibling who surprised me the most—the way he'd turned out. Over time Mark had never really changed much. He'd taken on more serious responsibilities, but every stage of his life had been marked by the same talent for getting people to like him, the same unflashy competence, the same self-fulfilling confidence that everything would turn out okay. He'd never even toyed much with the scenery around him. Amherst hadn't looked all that different from Loomis, and from his freshman year at Amherst onward, he never lived anywhere but Massachusetts. He was living now in a house and a suburb almost interchangeable with those from our family's Connecticut years. In adulthood Mark had largely reconstituted his childhood, only with himself in Dad's role.

And Adelle's traits as a young working mother were pretty much those that she'd had as a little girl and then a teenager and then a college student: the wit that caught people off guard and threw them off balance; the intelligence that snuck up on them, because she veiled it in a consciously silly manner; the bawdy streak that had prompted her, back as a teenager, to pump me for sexual advice.

But Harry—Harry hadn't stood still. He'd evolved first from an introverted dreamer with a taste for gadgetry and science fiction into a high school student as social as any other, and less focused on schoolwork than my parents harangued him to be. Then, toward the end of college, he'd developed into a driven striver with his eye on a big career and income in investment banking. He'd achieved both, in part because he'd learned to be the smoothest of operators: better read and more cultured than many of his financial-wizard peers, a slick dresser, contagious in his enthusiasms. Looking at him, I'd know that Grandma's pithy adage—*Born round, you don't die square*—wasn't really right. A person *could* leave behind some or much of who he was. He could take on a new shape.

On the day before and then on the day after Harry's paella party, he and I went running together. Both times we drove to a beachfront parking lot near his house and did the same route: a stretch of hard-packed sand right on the Pacific, then a longer stretch of concrete bicycle path parallel to the shoreline, then a series of streets leading back to where we'd started. It was about a 3.5-mile run, and at the 3-mile mark, there was a choice, a fork. Veering to the left meant adding an extra mile, including a long and crazily steep hill that was debilitating just to look at. Twice I chose the hill—*made* myself choose it—while Harry, with a grunt and a wave, headed right. We met back at his car.

"Who won?" asked my niece Leslie, the oldest of Harry's four kids, when we returned from the second of these runs, as her sister Erica, two years younger and something of a hug machine, rushed to welcome me back with an embrace. As soon as Erica's fingertips made contact with the soggy back of my T-shirt, she recoiled.

"Sweaty!" she yelped. "Ewww."

"That's the hope," I said. "That's the goal."

"Daddy, too," she said, correctly, pointing to the dark, wet patches on Harry's T-shirt.

I told Leslie, "No one won. We weren't racing."

"But who was faster?" Leslie had watched many a family Oh, Hell game, and had even started playing in a few of them. She'd absorbed and adopted the family's competitive ethos.

"Your Uncle Frank was faster," Harry told her. "Your Uncle Frank *is* faster. He's better about staying in shape than your daddy is." That statement probably didn't sound odd to Leslie and Erica, the way it did to me—their memories didn't go back to my midthirties and to who I'd been then. They saw me as a different person.

My siblings, it turned out, had come to see me as a different person, too. During our annual week in Hilton Head, they no longer watched me when I assembled my plate in the rental house's kitchen. What I assembled usually wasn't much different from what anyone else did. Even if it was, nothing about how I looked suggested that I was being reckless if I decided on a big meal, that I was digging a perilously deep hole for myself.

I ate less than Harry, who was now slightly chunky, mainly because the double demands of a career and fatherhood left him limited time or energy for exercise. I still ate more than Mark, whose continued commitment to his mincing bites, even on vacation, had turned him into the only one of the four of us who remained downright svelte year after year.

And I ate more than Adelle, who had slimmed down considerably in her late twenties and thirties, even while she was having her two children. *Especially* while she was having her two children. During each of her pregnancies she had realized that she was in a situation that encouraged abandon around food, and she pushed back with more restraint and discipline than she'd usually been capable of. She gained an average of only twenty pounds and was thinner a month after childbirth than she'd been before conception.

The threat of extreme and sudden weight gain scared her skinny, or at least slimmer than before. That wasn't entirely unlike what agreeing to eat for a living seemed to be doing for me.

Twenty

This was the regimen, which wasn't a regimen at all:

Maybe I'd eat breakfast. Maybe not. It depended on hunger, not on any foreordained, inevitably doomed script. I listened to hunger and responded to it, because I knew from the past what could happen if I let myself get too famished or feel too deprived. And in the job I was doing now, going off the rails would be too costly.

But I didn't get caught up in hunger, because on any given day there was significant eating ahead. I didn't want to go into a job-related dinner worrying about how much I'd consumed already. And if there was a dish or two that I particularly liked, I wanted to be able to allow myself more than a few extra bites without having to fear that I was being reckless.

My apartment building was in the middle of the block, and on one end was a bakery with small, individual-size baguettes I adored. After a few mugs of coffee at home, I'd often head there for one of those baguettes, about eight inches long and cut lengthwise, with butter and raspberry jam spread in the crease. It was surely more than 450 calories, but I figured 450 calories I genuinely enjoyed were better than 275 that felt merely like sustenance—or, worse, like some kind of atonement—and left me hankering for a reward later on.

The impulsive eater in me lived on in the way I tended to tackle one of these baguettes. Five steps out of the bakery, I'd pull the crunchy bread from its brown paper bag and begin making my way through it in big, rapid bites. It would usually be three-quarters gone by the time I got to my front door, a trek of no more than ninety seconds. And whatever T-shirt or sweatshirt I'd thrown on would have red smudges on its front. Jam tended to seep from the baguette's crease, and I tended to slip into such a contented baguette-induced fugue state that I didn't notice the sticky red blobs dangling and then dropping onto me. I ruined some clothing that way. But I considered it a worthy sacrifice.

On the other end of my block—around the corner, actually—was a deli. Sometimes I'd go there instead. I'd get a toasted sesame bagel with a few slices of Swiss cheese and tomato: again, not diet food, but nothing out of control, and something that left me happier than a cup of yogurt with fruit would have and gave me enough fuel for exercise. It was the bagel with Swiss cheese and tomato I typically got if I was eating breakfast en route to the gym. I considered it a better package of vitamins and better mix of protein and carbohydrate than the baguette. But I didn't really get all that scientific in my thinking. My "scientific" thinking about eating hadn't served me so well in the past.

Review-related lunches were rare, but I usually ate lunch nonetheless, to keep going and keep intense hunger at bay. It might be something as incidental as a hard-boiled egg and a few chunks of cheese, or it might be a broad, tall, densely stuffed chicken-salad sandwich from the deli or the office cafeteria, though never with chips on the side or a cookie after. I usually tailored the size of lunch to whether—or how much—I was exercising that day, but I didn't get into precise measurements. That sort of fixation hadn't done much for me, either.

At dinner I not only contained my portions on most nights but also edited out what I could. The dessert list at many restaurants was only four or five items long, so I could work through the selections, with the help of dining companions, in one or two visits, and skip desserts after that.

But none of these dinners could be a truly light meal, given my reason for eating them, the responsibility attached to them and the aggregate amount of what I had to sample. And at many dinners I didn't want to hold back, because there was so much pleasure to be had: in the pâtés and terrines at Bar Boulud, which leaned harder on heavily salted, glorious animal fat than Starbucks did on coffee beans; in Convivio's handmade pastas, including fusilli—how I loved fusilli!—sauced with crumbled pork shoulder and melted *caciocavallo*, a mild, milky Italian cheese.

The certainty of my eating in the evenings dictated and set the terms for everything else: the times and sizes of the day's other meals; the week's tally of workouts (five on average, two with trainers and three on my own). My reviewing life gave me a firm, clear structure, which was precisely what diets were supposed to do. But diets had framed all eating in terms of what I couldn't or shouldn't have. They might wrap permissive-sounding verbiage around their prescriptions, but I still experienced them as exercises in prohibition. Who didn't? The structure I had now was based on indulgence, on what I *must* have, and that made all the difference. I was celebrating instead of abusing food. In so many previous chapters of my life I'd seen food as the enemy; now it was more a friend.

Every two to three weeks, though, I let myself abuse it a little again. I busted loose. Sometimes it was in a restaurant, where I went ahead and ate twice as much as any of my companions, because the urge reared itself and felt stronger and harder to ignore than on other nights, when

I could beat it back. Other times I busted loose at home, an hour after I'd returned from dinner, around eleven thirty p.m., when I'd hunker down in front of the television set with a pint of Ben & Jerry's just purchased from a nearby bodega or a whole roasted chicken, plucked from a shelf at the Fairway supermarket just before it closed. As if back in my cramped upstairs room in Georgetown, I'd eat the whole of the pint or the bird.

There had always been something in me that sparked to the sheer act of shoveling food into my mouth until my stomach was full to bursting: I got a high from it, like the rush of a drug. And my brain hadn't been rewired by the better habits I'd honed. But what had changed was my reaction to a binge. I accepted it as a quirk of that wiring—of my nature— and I recognized that one night of bingeing could do only so much harm. There wasn't a flood of guilt and shame afterward. And there wasn't an anxious vow of penance that gave way, that same night or the next, to more bingeing before the penance began.

I didn't keep much food in my apartment, which was where I did most of my daytime reporting and writing, because I knew my tendency toward rote, absentminded eating and didn't want to facilitate it. There were no pretzels or cookies in my cupboard. There was no ice cream in my freezer. A snapshot of my refrigerator on a typical day might have shown: a small jar of mayonnaise, used for a tuna sandwich weeks earlier; a half bottle of low-cal vinaigrette, used for a salad made only slightly more recently; a half dozen bottles of white wine, because a few glasses of that was what I most often permitted myself if I felt the need for a treat late at night, before bed; a pound and a half of ground coffee, which I drank black and in great quantities; and a jar of eye pads moistened with cucumber juice, because the pads supposedly reduced puffiness. I was a sucker for promises like that, and I liked the theatricality of putting the pads on and lying down on the couch for ten minutes before heading out to the restaurant of the night. Adelle wasn't the only ham in the family.

In August 2006 I joined her for a "sprint triathlon" in Princeton, not far from her house. Like me she'd become more diligent about exercising; in fact she'd done a sprint triathlon already. This one consisted of a lake swim of about a third of a mile, followed by about thirteen miles of biking and a 3.2-mile run. I finished in just under an hour and a half. The following August—more than three years since I'd taken the critic's job—we did the exact same course and I shaved five minutes off my time.

Dad came to watch, and told me afterward that even from a distance, on a far edge of the lake, he'd had no trouble figuring out which of the scores of swimmers plowing through the dark water was me. He could tell from my stroke. All these years later, he said, it was still strong, and it was still pretty much the same.

So that was that, then? Problem solved? Weight on track, with life to follow?

Not so fast.

One Sunday night I had my friend Kerry meet me for dinner at Cafeteria, an undistinguished restaurant in Chelsea that had flourished for years, its success fueled by its marriage of reasonably priced comfort food and a sleek, hip setting once used in *Sex and the City*. A few of the players behind it had just opened a successor, Delicatessen, that I planned to review. So I wanted to catch up on the original, which I'd never visited. I didn't need to conquer the menu. I just needed a taste of the place.

But as Kerry and I chatted and I drained a third glass of white wine, I lost track of my limited purpose and lost touch with my discipline. I left none of the macaroni and cheese sampler—three kinds, generously portioned—on the plate. I rapidly gobbled up more than my half of the meat loaf and more than my half of the fried chicken. I even gobbled up the soggy, tasteless waffle that came with the chicken.

"I think I better stop here and skip dessert," I told Kerry, who concurred: we'd had enough.

I used one of my fake credit cards to pay the bill, said good-bye to him on the sidewalk and hailed a cab, telling the driver, "West Seventy-fourth between Amsterdam and Columbus."

We went uptown through the West Thirties, the West Forties, the West Fifties. As the West Sixties gave way to the West Seventies, I leaned forward and told the driver, "You know what? You can just drop me at the corner of Amsterdam and Seventy-fourth." Right there was a bodega, and I'd decided, in a flash, without really weighing the pros and cons, without really deliberating much, to get the dessert I'd just denied myself.

In the bodega I had trouble choosing between a large square bar of dark chocolate with hazelnuts, a chocolate-covered ice cream cone like the kind I remembered from those boyhood Good Humor trucks, a classic ice cream sandwich and a package of six Nutter Butter cookies. So I got them all. What the hell. Hadn't I determined that the occasional binge was okay?

I woke the next morning to find the various wrappers from my midnight feast strewn across a leather ottoman that sat between a couch and the television set, functioning as a coffee table. I was disgusted: the wrappers were proof that I'd gone beyond the usual periodic, permissible pig-out. I bunched them up, stomped into the kitchen, tossed them into the wastebasket and looked at the clock on the stove. It was ten twenty-five. Okay: I'd spend an hour on the computer and then get to Reebok before the lunch rush. I'd have my pick of treadmills and plenty of mat space and there wouldn't be any wait for weight machines.

But I got absorbed in an article I was working on and in e-mail conversations with friends, colleagues and editors. Suddenly it was three p.m. and I was famished, unusually so, as if I'd stretched my stomach's boundaries the night before and now had more space to fill. With virtually nothing in the cupboards or refrigerator, I called a Chinese restaurant and ordered spare ribs and roasted chicken—enough for three people, it turned out. I finished it all, because it was good and because it was there, and I grew sleepy ten minutes later. I took a nap. By dinnertime, when I had to head out for the night, I'd never made it to the gym.

A minor case of the sniffles persuaded me to cancel on Cathy the next day. The Pilates sessions had started to bore me somewhat, and at my insistence they always included these sideways sit-ups that targeted love handles and hurt like hell, never getting much easier over time. They were harder than teasers, which I'd indeed succeeded in mastering. I just wasn't in the mood for them. How hard could a forty-three-year-old guy be expected to push himself?

I went to Reebok only twice over the next week and only once the week after that, when I also failed to restrain my restaurant eating, maybe because I was blue or because I was exhausted or because I'd hit a run of especially tempting restaurants—I didn't really know why. For the weekend I headed out to Dad's house in Scarsdale to join Mark, Lisa and their kids, who had come down from Boston for a visit. Mark and I set out at one point for a four-mile run. A mile into it, I had to ask him to slow down. I went the distance, but was breathing much harder at the end than he was.

That annoyed me, and my annoyance turned to alarm when, back in the city at the end of the weekend, I struggled to slip into a pair of size 34 jeans that I hadn't had to struggle with two weeks before. My weekly cleaning woman usually did my laundry for me: had she left the jeans in the dryer too long and shrunk them somehow? That was what I wanted to believe. It was the sort of theory I might have successfully sold to myself in the past.

But I knew it was bullshit. I'd noticed a subtle tightness in other pants and shirts in recent days, and I had to admit that I'd been off my game in terms of eating and exercising. On top of that, I'd been sensing for a few months that I was going through one of those faint metabolic slowdowns that happened every five years or so, one of the wages of aging. And it was happening at the same time that I was noticing more aches and soreness whenever I tried to run anything over four miles. This was something new and scary.

I left the too-tight jeans on as I headed out to dinner, a way of not letting myself ignore the issue. Lucky for me, I was eating sushi that night, and I made a point of eating only as much as I had to. Over the next nights I demonstrated a similar restraint. And on the days in between I went to the gym: no evasions, no excuses. I addressed the aches and soreness by replacing some of the usual treadmill running with brisk walking on a steep incline. It didn't produce as heavy a sweat, so I stayed on the treadmill longer than I usually did.

My friend Ned had been talking a lot about a new fitness program he was trying out with a trainer he'd just hired. It was an intense twenty-eight-minute workout of concentrated, high-stress weight lifting. That was a departure from what I'd been doing, and I needed a departure, a jolt. So I stopped seeing Cathy as often and started cheating on her with Jay, who left my muscles so fatigued that they hurt—and seemed to keep burning calories—for days after each session. A combination of Cathy and Jay worked better than Cathy alone. And at whatever point that ceased to be true, I promised myself, I'd figure out another combination. I'd keep mixing it up so I could keep going.

About three weeks after Mark's visit, the jeans I'd worn out for sushi weren't tight anymore. The recovery and relief came just in time, because Terry was in Manhattan for the weekend.

Terry lived in D.C. and had worked at Aaron's exercise studio when I first went there in 2002. For one of every three of my sessions back then, he took Aaron's place training me. I never got to know him well, and he had stopped working as a trainer by the time I reconnected with Aaron after Rome. But in the summer of 2008 I ran into him at a mutual friend's birthday party, and we flirted.

With my friend Maureen at a party in the summer of 2008.

"You don't look the same," he told me.

I nodded vaguely and changed the subject, because I never knew what to say to a remark like his, which at once shamed and thrilled me.

After the party we flirted some more, by e-mail, then had a long date when I later happened to be in D.C. Now, about four months since the birthday party, he was in town to see a play with some old buddies of his. We met for a drink.

We talked about his new job in the not-for-profit world, about mine in the epicurean one. He wondered aloud about my decision to take it, at first tiptoeing up to the question, then just asking flat out: Why hadn't it made me heavier?

I said I was watchful and balanced in a way that I hadn't been in the past.

"How did you manage that?" he asked. "What's the difference between then and now?"

We were in the backseat of a cab at this point. He was sitting closer to me than he had to, his left hand casually grazing my right arm. He was a good-looking guy, a *great*-looking guy, a life of serious athleticism reflected in his build, a face animated by optimism and confidence.

"I think the difference," I told him, "is how much I'd rather be like this. Once I pulled myself out of whatever it was I'd sunk into, I never wanted to go back. I was pretty miserable. I think remembering that and concentrating on how I feel now—being aware of how much better it is—that's the difference. I'm determined in a way I wasn't."

After he and I parted I kept thinking about my answer, which wasn't, I concluded, quite right or quite complete. The main difference between then and now wasn't determination. It was honesty. I didn't lie to myself the way I had in the past. I especially didn't lie to myself about food.

When I was honest with myself, I had to acknowledge that there'd never been, and would never be, a magic eating or dieting formula that overrode and erased whatever volume of food I consumed: no skeleton key to a skeletal me. I had all the proof of that that any sane person could ever demand.

I had to admit that the success or failure of every diet I'd ever attempted boiled down to the most basic equation of all: how much energy I expended versus how much fuel I took in. And no matter what I'd once tried to tell myself, I always knew, in the course of a given day, whether this equation was out of whack.

I knew whether I was doing a token amount of exercise or really pushing myself, and I knew that for me, exercise mattered, always making the difference. At some point during my first years as a restaurant critic I'd spotted an article about studies that maintained that overweight people who upped their exercise inevitably upped their eating proportionally, canceling out the benefits. For me this wasn't true, and I knew that because I knew the history of my own body. Most of us do, if we look carefully and candidly at ourselves. The care and the candor are the challenge.

I knew which of the dishes in front of me were the most fattening, how much of each was prudent versus reckless. I just had to listen to that knowledge. I had to accept and acknowledge that one botched day or even one botched week wasn't apocalyptic. It was life as most people lived it—certainly as I did. Yet I had to acknowledge as well that it was the right, small, short-term decisions, one after another, that yielded long-term results. Losing weight—or not gaining it—boiled down to putting back the second dinner roll I'd just reached for, running or walking the extra mile, getting off the uptown Number 1 train when it pulled into the Sixty-sixth Street stop, near my gym, rather than staying on until Seventy-second Street, going home and unwinding until dinner out.

And I had to understand that if I set some matinee idol's physiognomy as my goal, and wallowed in self-pity at any condition short of that, I was acting like the same self-defeating fool who'd fried his face in front of a sun lamp and bleached his hair in pursuit of a silly ideal. That was truer than ever now, after those years in my thirties of so much extra weight. I had to accept that I'd never be as taut as I'd fantasized about being.

As I honestly reflected back on all the eating I'd done—all the *overeating* I'd done—I had to recognize that I'd almost always gotten something out of it. Accomplished something with it. The hunger in me wasn't an invention or an act of will: it was there from the start, and it was bigger than most people's. But the chubby boy who ate more adventurously than his siblings caught the notice of grown-ups that way, and some of the notice was admiring.

Through my eating I probably drew a few more hugs from Grandma than Mark or Harry had. Through my eating and dieting I forged a sort of pact with Mom, and while my gluttony earned me her pity and censure as well as her delight, those were forms of attention, too. In college and in my twenties, my eating—or at least my worrying about it—gave me the cop-out I apparently wanted sometimes, an escape clause from the awkwardness and vulnerability that went along with physical intimacy. My most extreme eating during the Washington years wasn't as strategic—its costs vastly exceeded its benefits—but it was the predictable consequence of all that preceded it, the ugly flower of destructive behaviors that had taken root years before. When I was truthful, I could see all of that.

The truth: this self-awareness might well spare me any further rides on the gain-and-loss roller-coaster, might put an end to yo-yo me.

The truth: I couldn't be sure. For now I was on the straight and narrow—or narrow*ish*. But it might not stay that way. I was getting slower and creakier. But I was trying. I was making a real effort.

On December 31, 2008, we gathered at Dad's: my siblings, their spouses, my nieces and nephews. Dad was actually in Atlanta for the winter with Dottie, who had been living there when they met and had held on to her place after they married. But the rest of us packed into his Scarsdale house to welcome the arrival of 2009 together.

Adelle roasted an enormous beef tenderloin and laid out several pounds of boiled shrimp, along with cocktail sauce. Sylvia arranged about six cheeses on a large platter, and kept asking me which I'd tried and what I'd thought of them. It tickled me how everyone in the family had instantly attributed such keen epicurean discernment to me the minute I started reviewing restaurants: how they'd suddenly begun consulting me on dinner party menus and whether the rack of lamb was ready to come out of the oven. Before, I'd just been the family member who could put away more of the lamb than anyone else.

They seemed to have as much fun with my job as I did, and that made me feel so proud, especially when one of my nieces or nephews, whose ages now spanned six to twelve years old, beamingly told me that some teacher or other adult in their lives had asked if they were related to the Bruni who reviewed restaurants. They thought it was cool beyond words that some people who didn't actually know their uncle nonetheless knew who he was. And everyone in the family got a kick out of the mention of me in a question on *Jeopardy*, which asked contestants to connect my name and my large spending allowance to the right position at the *Times*.

They got a kick, too, out of this odd Web site where a person could buy T-shirts, sweatshirts, bibs and even pet apparel with the words "I Am Frank Bruni" on them. The joke behind the clothing seemed to be that its wearer would set himself or herself up for better treatment in restaurants.

"You know," I told my family members, "I often get these weird reports from people in the restaurant business about diners making reservations in my name."

"Why would they do that?" asked my nephew Harrison, tuning in to the conversation late. Like Harry in the past, he got distracted.

"Sometimes because they think it'll guarantee them a better table," I explained. "But other times, I don't know." In fact I'd recently received an e-mail from the owner of a restaurant in Arlington, Virginia, who asked: "Did you eat at our restaurant today? A gentleman ate at our counter and, after paying, identified himself as you." The gentleman was someone else, and I wondered what he thought he was accomplishing by brandishing my name on the way *out* the door.

At my dad's house that night I noticed how Leslie, nearing thirteen, had started picking at her food and controlling her portions. That seemed normal enough for a girl her age. I made a silent wish that it would stay normal. She still reminded me of Mom in terms of how headstrong she was. But she reminded me of Grandma in terms of how attuned to public appearances she could be. Both women lived on in her.

Along with the beef tenderloin there were mashed potatoes, but I passed on those, just as I'd avoided all the peanuts and almonds lying around during the cocktail hour, because I knew that I'd want seconds of the beef.

I also had seconds of a frozen peanut butter pie that Lisa made for dessert.

"The recipe says it's low-fat," she reminded me.

"That's what Mom always said about that multicolored sherbet thing of hers," I said, referring to a dessert with three kinds of sherbet, angel food cake and Cool Whip. "But when you're trafficking in that much sugar, I'm not sure the fat content really matters anymore."

The next day I didn't feel as stuffed as I had after so many Bruni Thanksgivings and other family get-togethers in the past, but I felt fuller than I'd hoped to. And so I regretted that I'd made a date for that evening with Tom, a handsome, considerate guy I'd met a month and a half earlier and been dating exclusively since. He seemed like a keeper—like the first keeper in a very long time. I wanted him to see only the best of me, and I had the sense that the tenderloin and peanut butter pie might be visible on me in an ever-so-slightly increased width of love handles, an exaggerated roundness of belly.

But honestly: Could I look *that* much different than when we'd seen each other just three days before? Could his interest in me hinge on such minor fluctuations in appearance, and if it did, was it an interest worth worrying about and working to sustain?

We went to a new Greek restaurant in my neighborhood. While we stood in the bar area drinking wine and waiting for our table, he kept his hand on my back. He mentioned a trip he'd be taking to Europe in a few months and said I should consider going with him.

So he was already looking that far ahead? Apparently the steak and the peanut butter pie weren't such spoilers.

For dinner that night we had a chickpea spread, a fish roe spread, a dish of plump and tender meatballs, a slab of swordfish smothered in capers and some honey-drizzled pastry for dessert.

"Hey, hey," he said as he dug further into the dessert, "don't you want some more of this? You better take some more of this before I finish it."

He was working his way through it quickly, the same way, I now realized, that he'd worked his way through the rest of the meal. I hadn't noticed any restraint in him, any self-consciousness. A part of me envied that, a part resented that, another part was just a little scared. I couldn't let myself be like him. When and how should I tell him why? And what would he make of it?

I took another bite of the dessert, just so I didn't seem to be avoiding it. But I stopped there. Somehow, I'd learned to do that. At least for now.

Acknowledgments

Without the permission and patience of so many family members who gave generously of their time and recollections, I wouldn't have been able to lend the detail I did to the anecdotes in this book. I'm hugely grateful to all of them: my father, Frank Sr.; my siblings and siblings-in-law, Mark, Lisa, Harry, Sylvia and especially Adelle, who combed her memory longest and hardest; and my wonderful, wonderful uncles Jim and Mario and aunts Vicki and Carolyn. Thanks, too, to Lisa's mom, Betty Valek, for helping me get the time line of a pivotal Thanksgiving right.

Thanks to my nieces and nephews, Leslie, Frank, Erica, Sarah, Harrison, Mark, Gavin, Christina and Bella, for forgiving me when I cut visits short or stole away with my laptop instead of hanging out with them.

I got crucial, concrete input for, and help with, this project from Alessandra Stanley, Maureen Dowd, Ned Martel, Kerry Lauerman, Barbara Laing, Soo-Jeong Kang and in particular Tom de Kay. I thank them so very, very much.

It would be impossible to mention all the additional friends and colleagues who listened to me prattle about this book, assisted me with a specific aspect of it or just made me feel calmer while I chiseled away at it. So this is woefully incomplete, but:

Jennifer Steinhauer, Marysue Rucci, Elinor Burkett, Anne Kornblut, Campbell Brown, Jeremy Peters, Rick Berke, Jill Abramson, Renee Murawski, Julia Moskin, Kim Severson, Ginia Bellafante, Vivian Toy, Jason Horowitz and Gary Simko—you're awesome.

And both I and this book would be in considerably worse shape without the support I've received over the last few years from Melissa Clark, Kate Krader, Alice Feiring, Elizabeth Minchilli, Bill and Emma Keller, Bill Schmidt, Sam Sifton, Dwight Garner, Kit Seelye, Barbara Graustark, Trish Hall, Pete Wells, Nick Fox, Kathleen McElroy, Charles Isherwood, Frank Rich, Alex Witchel, Don Van Natta, Lizette Alvarez, Seth Gilmore, Christian Cervegnano, Stuart Emmrich, John Haskins, Rusty O'Kelley, Gerry Marzorati, Sarah Lyall, Ed Wyatt, Michael Kimmelman, Ashley Parker, Florence Fabricant, Zahra Sethna, Marian Burros, Esther Fein, John Barrett, John Berman, Kerry Voss, Adam Nagourney, Danielle Mattoon, John Geddes, Ariel Kaminer, Eric Asimov, Biff Grimes and Helene Cooper.

Thanks to Lisa Bankoff for embracing this project and finding it the right home, and to Jane Fleming, Ann Godoff, Tracy Locke, Liz Calamari, Lindsay Whalen and the folks at Penguin Press for taking such very good care of it when it got there.

Thanks to Tom Nickolas for making the home stretch a happy time and me a much happier person.

And thanks above all to two loving, dynamic, difficult, complicated women who are still with me every day, so long after they left: Adelina Mazzone Bruni and Leslie Frier Bruni. Somewhere, somehow, we'll eat again.